PENGUIN BOOKS

Full Steam Ahead, Felix

Praise from readers of *Felix the Railway Cat*

'A lovely book that makes you happy and warm, whether
you are a cat lover or not'

'This book made me laugh, and it made me cry – what
more could you want from a book?'

'A little ray of sunshine in a bleak world'

'I have just finished reading this delightful story,
written with great warmth and humour by Kate Moore,
who has captured the essence of this fantastic feline
and her warm-hearted friends'

'A lovely story about a world-famous, floofy cat'

'A heart-warming tale, demonstrating, without a doubt,
the amazing intelligence and empathy of cats'

'A sweet and gentle read. Cat lovers will thoroughly enjoy it'

Felix lives at Huddersfield train station in west Yorkshire alongside her colleagues and 5 million customers. Born to a loving family in 2011, she was originally thought to be a boy and named Felix – before a trip to the vet proved otherwise. She began her independent working life aged just eight weeks old and was promoted to Senior Pest Controller in 2016. Her interests include chasing pigeons, napping on the job and tummy tickles.

Bolt was welcomed on to the team with open arms in September 2018 at eight weeks old. Confined to the office for his first few months, he's already made a big impression on the team.

His time is mainly spent having naps, cuddles and teasing his superior, Felix.

You can find out more about the duo's exploits at
www.facebook.com/FelixHuddersfieldStationCat

Full Steam Ahead, Felix

*Adventures of a Famous Station Cat
and Her Kitten Apprentice*

KATE MOORE

PENGUIN BOOKS

PENGUIN BOOKS

UK | USA | Canada | Ireland | Australia
India | New Zealand | South Africa

Penguin Books is part of the Penguin Random House group of companies
whose addresses can be found at global.penguinrandomhouse.com

Penguin
Random House
UK

First published by Michael Joseph 2019
Published in Penguin Books 2019
001

Text copyright © First TransPennine Express Limited, 2019
Written by Kate Moore www.kate-moore.com

The moral right of the author has been asserted

Set in 12.69/15.24 pt Garamond MT Std
Typeset by Jouve (UK), Milton Keynes
Printed and bound in Great Britain by Clays Ltd, Elcograf S.p.A.

A CIP catalogue record for this book is available from the British Library

The royalties from the sale of this book will be donated equally between Action for Children
and Huddersfield Samaritans (registered charity numbers 1097940 and 219432 respectively).

ISBN: 978–1–405–94230–0

www.greenpenguin.co.uk

For all the team at Huddersfield station

Contents

1. Rise and Shine

At precisely 5 a.m. the first shafts of sunlight spilled across St George's Square. A summer's day was dawning in Huddersfield, Yorkshire, in July 2016.

The light was muted at that early hour, gently illuminating the bronze statue that stood in the square's centre and the figures who topped the surrounding buildings: the trident-wielding Lady Britannia and the curly-maned big cat who stalked on the rooftop of the Lion Building. That striking structure was Grade II-listed, but that wasn't unusual in this historic town: Huddersfield was home to over 200 listed buildings – the most in Yorkshire – and each of them was bathed in ever-increasing brightness as the sun began to climb higher in the sky.

The town was still and almost silent at that time of day. Here and there sparked the first signs of life: a delivery driver parking up, his hazard lights flashing, to drop off his goods; a still-the-worse-for-wear group of lads meandering down the street, their unsteady zigzag walk revealing that they were still sobering up from the night before, having not yet gone to bed. A pigeon squawked and fluttered on its corrugated-iron perch. A big black crow became airborne. And a fluffy black-and-white tail flicked steadily back and forth as a diligent animal patrolled her patch.

The rising sun's strengthening beams also picked out a

handful of solitary figures who were hurrying across the pedestrianised square in the early-morning light. There was a middle-aged man in a dark suit with a briefcase, a fresh-faced lass in pink-and-black workout gear, and a pregnant woman in a summer dress who was dragging a holiday suitcase behind her. From all walks of life, they were all drawn like magnets to perhaps the grandest listed building of them all: Huddersfield railway station. It stood at the top of St George's Square, directly opposite Leo the Lion, and seemed to face the coming day with a dependability born of its centuries of service.

Never had a station looked so welcoming – or so grand. Completed in 1850, the magnificent building had a spectacular classical portico with imposing Corinthian columns, the latter of which stretched all the way along the station's 416-feet façade. Its sandstone walls gleamed in the sunshine, looking just as inviting as its newly opened blue front door. As steadfast as the sunrise, Huddersfield station opened its doors promptly at 5 a.m. every morning, and today was running as smoothly as the clockwork in its railway clocks.

And so the passengers scurried onwards, up the steps and into the station, each of them bleary-eyed or bushy-tailed, and all intent on reaching their final destinations. As one chap crossed the threshold, a yawn took hold of him and he stretched his jaws wide, wearily smoothing down his black beard afterwards. There were not many upsides to being up at that hour . . . but these passengers were about to discover one.

There were a few clues, had they cared to look around. A brightly coloured packet of Dreamies that was poking out of the pocket of the TransPennine Express (TPE) team member manning the gateline that morning . . . A fish-shaped squishy toy covered in yellow-and-red polka dots that lay abandoned on the concourse floor . . . And what was that in the corner? That thing with a black-and-white cartoon image on it, and five purple letters arched over its window? Was that . . . a cat flap? In a *station*?

Those in the know kept their eyes peeled as they journeyed through the station, crossing the gateline with a twist of disappointment that they had not yet caught sight of the vision that they sought. She was there to greet passengers at the door most mornings, but she was not there today. Often, she took up residence at one of the five serving windows in the booking office, just to the left of the main entrance, but the office was not due to open until 5.45 a.m., so she was not on duty there yet. Blind white shutters covered those windows, their blankness only serving to emphasise that she was not present.

You could almost tell who was in on the poorly kept secret and who was not. Those who streamed through the barriers, their eyes focused only on the display boards overhead, were not part of the privileged few. It was those who moved slowly, eyes darting this way and that, who knew what they were looking for. Those same people tended to turn left once they made it through the gateline, where they walked along the concrete catwalk that was platform number one.

They saw the sign almost as soon as they had passed the Coffee Xpress concession, where the tempting aroma of freshly ground coffee beans was already scenting the station air. The sign jutted from the sandstone walls with prominent importance. 'Customer Information and Assistance' it read. Below it an open door invited customers into a small lobby with a thin grey carpet and a single serving hatch. As you approached from the main station entrance, it was impossible to see round the corner to the hatch. You almost had to be facing the door square on before you could see if she was there.

And, this morning, she was. Chest puffed up and proud, she sat with a regal air atop the desk, waiting to assist in whatever way she could. Her snow-capped front paws were pressed neatly together, as though she felt that when on duty she should be professionally turned out: no slouching or spread-eagled limbs here. Her white bib shone brightly in the dawn light, making for a vivid contrast to the ebony fur that gleamed elsewhere on her ever-so-fluffy little black body. Americans describe such colourings as 'tuxedo' and it did indeed seem that she had slipped on her most expensive designer black tie to come to work. Nothing but the best for her customers.

Her long white whiskers twitched as she took in the morning scents. A pair of exquisite emerald eyes blinked lazily as customer after customer came to say hello. Their own eyes sparkled as they met her, but not enough to outshine the glitzy twinkle of her glittery purple collar, nor the gilded glow of the circular gold tag that hung round her neck. They gently stroked her silky-soft fur and excitedly cooed greetings and impassioned well wishes into her white-tufted ears. They exclaimed and oohed and ahhed and sighed deeply with contented satisfaction, thrilled that their treasure hunt, this time, had ended with a pawprint that marked the spot. Such customers came away feeling lucky and lighter, and that this was going to be a very good day indeed.

And how could it not be? For they were some of the chosen few. They had just been granted an audience with none other than Felix, the Huddersfield station cat.

Frankly, did life get any better than that?

After a while that morning, Felix decided it was time to move on. She was a busy cat, in demand across the station, and she could not spend all day in one spot. Each day, she set her own rota, and she clearly felt she had fulfilled her responsibilities on the customer-information point for the time being. Soon, the announcer with whom she shared the serving hatch would report for his shift; she could tag-team with her colleague to ensure the point was well looked after. So, with a single sporty leap, she jumped down and padded out on to the platform.

As she emerged, her appearance was unmistakeably noted. Surreptitiously, from a short distance away, a middle-aged lady in a forest-green anorak and sensible brown brogues – who had been painstakingly tapping out a text message, one letter at a time – somewhat awkwardly angled her phone anew and snapped a sneaky picture of the station cat. Felix didn't even flinch. Since July 2015 she had had her own Facebook page, and over the past year it had grown to attract a massive 80,000 followers online. Her popularity had been particularly boosted in January 2016, when she'd been promoted to senior pest controller by her employer, TransPennine

Express, and thousands upon thousands of fans world-wide had wished her congratulations. Social-media stardom had brought a fair few of those fans to the station, and so this famous Facebook cat had long become used to the clicking sounds and camera flashes that her presence seemed to inspire.

Undaunted, Felix lowered her head to the ground and sniffed at the platform. No crumbs here. Shame. She raised her head to squint at the pigeons who lived in the corrugated-iron roof above the station. They had probably hoovered up any leftovers; it was just the kind of thing those pesky pigeons did. Somewhat disgruntled, she gave herself a good shake and several loose strands of her fluffy fur escaped her pelt; they danced in the air like confetti around a blushing bride, making her velvety nose give a sudden sharp sneeze. Then she padded on, stretching out her tippy-toes to show off the little black patches that adorned them, as though she was a ballerina on stage at the Royal Opera House and knew all eyes were on her twinkling toes.

Felix reached the edge of the platform. Though she had long been able to cross the tracks safely (and had her own Personal Track Safety card to assert her authority to do so), on this occasion she stopped sensibly at the yellow line that marked the platform's border and sat down. Her enormous eyes drank in the sights of the slowly waking station. She glanced north, towards platform two and the looming black mouths of the railway tunnels. The Head of Steam pub was located in that direction, but at this hour it was quiet and no kegs of beer were being rolled around with a musical clinking sound, as sometimes

6

happened. She looked in the opposite direction, to where a forty-five-arch viaduct stretched far away into the distance, so that even Felix's powerful cat vision couldn't see to the other side. Things were a little busier this way as the rush-hour commuters started to arrive, flooding through the gateline like an oceanic wave, ready to catch their regular services. It all seemed too busy for Felix that morning, so she faced away from the arriving passengers and instead blinked thoughtfully across the tracks to platform four, as though considering her options.

One of them was to visit the railway garden, which flourished opposite her on platform four, right in the middle of the station. The garden was the handiwork and legacy of a much-loved and -missed former colleague, Billy Bolt, who had died back in 2015. Felix and he had been firm friends and she often liked to hide among the garden's long grasses or to roll in its catmint leaves – but not today, she decided. Getting smoothly to her feet, she turned her back on the garden and retreated to perhaps her favourite spot of all: the silver bike racks just beside the customer-information point. It was a location she had loved ever since she was a kitten.

Felix had lived at Huddersfield station since she was eight weeks old. She had grown up here, slowly learning to become used to the roar of the train engines and the ebb and flow of the people passing through. She was not a stray or an adopted moggy: she had been headhunted for the role as a baby and parachuted in as a pest controller from the very start, her job officially green-lit by HQ. However, while she did have an official name badge to describe her role – 'Felix, Senior Pest Controller' it read, with the smart, purple-and-blue TPE logo in the corner – in truth, she was just as much a pet. Having given five years of service to date, she was a beloved member of the team. In fact, she was everyone's favourite.

Her name always needed a little explanation. When Felix had first started work at Huddersfield, her new colleagues had believed her to be a boy. Soon after her arrival, all those folk who worked on the railway network, along with the TPE team, had been invited to submit name suggestions for the new male kitten, with the chosen one being drawn at random. Felix was the chosen name – and only after she had been christened was her female gender discovered. But, by then, the name had stuck. Luckily, it rather suited her.

That summer's morning, Felix wound her way between the bike racks' metallic bars and sat with a sigh among them, her black back pressed to the yellow-brick wall. At that hour the racks were largely empty, just the odd D-lock reserving a spot, like a towel thrown on a sunbed at a holiday resort. Soon, however, Felix knew they would fill up as the commuters who cycled to the station left their bikes behind as they boarded their trains. That was how she liked it best, for being hidden among the bicycles gave her the perfect vantage point to observe the comings and goings of the station – of her home.

She watched now as those colleagues of hers who were on the early turn arrived for work. Given her concealed location – she had chosen to hide behind the one bike in the rack – it looked rather as though she was conducting a spot check on whether they were late for work, carefully noting down any infractions. Her emerald eyes missed nothing, sometimes shining as the rising sun glinted off the green. Here came a train driver with a cold bald head, clutching his lunchtime sandwiches tightly. Despite Felix's attempt to disguise her presence, he soon spotted her sitting there and called out a cheery, 'Eh up, lass,' as he walked by. Another worker, dressed in all-over orange hi-vis, merely eyeballed her as he passed. An unspoken, somewhat cursory acknowledgement passed between them: a gruff greeting on this summer's day. As she took in the morning traffic, Felix's head turned left and right like that of an avid tennis watcher. She listened hard, too. She could hear the clink of keys in people's pockets, the thrum of the engines as the formerly sleeping trains now came to life, and the rhythmic beat of footsteps as people passed along the platform.

But still she didn't hear the sound that she was waiting for.

Voices carried easily at the station. She could hear the conductors riding on the trains calling out to the platform staff and vice versa, and the occasional burst of laughter of friends travelling together. Her twitching ears processed each and every sound. So, when Felix suddenly heard a woman's voice, flavoured with a Yorkshire burr, call out to her in a jolly tone, 'Morning, gorgeous!' she was more than ready. As if responding to a cue, Felix jauntily poked her head up from between the bikes. Then she sprang from her hiding place, as though released from starting blocks, and rushed to greet one of her favourite people on the planet: team leader Angie Hunte.

Angie had been central in bringing Felix to the station and had mothered her ever since with love and care. Even though the cat was now five years old and fully grown, Angie still called Felix her 'baby girl'. A big-hearted, fun-loving woman of Barbadian heritage, Angie had worked at Huddersfield station for more than two decades and was very much its undisputed reigning matriarch (second only to Queen Felix, of course, to whom everyone took second billing). Felix's special greeting for her made her morning every day, and Angie chattered away happily to her as Felix bounded up to her feet. Instantly, the fluffy black-and-white cat weaved affectionately in and out of Angie's legs. She made her presence felt with a series of insistent demands for Angie's attention *now*.

'Come on then,' said Angie cheerily, as she gave in and scratched the cat firmly behind her ears. Felix's tail flicked back and forth in appreciation. 'Are you coming with me, then?' Angie continued.

Felix didn't need asking twice. As Angie headed to the customer-information point and entered the back offices through the door in the little lobby, the cat followed in her footsteps. Angie held the door open for her and Felix shot inside, before looking back over her shoulder anxiously to ensure that Angie was following, not wanting them to be separated. The two girls companionably entered the team leaders' office, which the six team leaders shared on rotation, as each took responsibility for the running of the station on their shift.

Angie was immediately hard at work, printing off passenger lists and preparing for her handover with the team leader who had preceded her on duty. Somewhat uncharacteristically, Felix watched everything patiently from the floor, her eyes following Angie's every move and her ears attuned to every word cast her way, as Angie chatted to her as she went about her work. In the end, Felix's patience was rewarded.

'Come on then,' Angie said to the little cat at last. 'I have to go out in a minute for the security checks. Now's your chance.'

That was all the instruction Felix needed. In an instant she was up on the desk, not wanting to miss her opportunity for a cuddle before her mum went out on to the platforms again.

'Gizza hug,' Angie said affectionately, with a cheeky smile. She sat behind the desk, her chair pulled in, and jutted out her chin. Felix, knowing this dance of old, stepped forward on the desk to join Angie, her snow-capped paws treading confidently. The cat got very, very close to Angie's face, until her big green eyes were only millimetres away from Angie's brown ones. Then the two leaned forward, so that their foreheads gently touched. Felix pressed lovingly with hers, rubbing her head against Angie's over and over again. The purr that began motoring inside that cat was loud enough for all to hear. It came from deep within Felix like a heartbeat, happy and contented and full of pleasure.

Unfortunately for Felix, all too soon Angie had to break away. Well, she *did* have other duties, despite what Felix might have thought. She wasn't actually employed to be at the cat's beck and call *all* day. Angie pulled on her smart navy jacket and her yellow hi-vis vest, and turned to the cat, now ready to head outside. Very often, Felix would join her, but today the cat had stretched out across the desk like a supersized queen on a golden throne, taking up all the space. It was just as well Angie didn't need to use the computer!

'Someone's looking relaxed!' the team leader quipped. She bent down and looked into Felix's eyes somewhat jealously. 'Shall we swap?'

But the station cat, for the time being, had had enough of work. Huddersfield station is staffed 24/7, and Felix had kept up her usual routine of manning the night shift the previous evening. Though Angie was heading out on security checks, Felix's rota told her that it was time to take a catnap. The sun might have been rising and shining outside but inside the office Felix's eyes were beginning to shut. Giving her a final stroke, Angie let her be and bade her a tender farewell, gently closing the door behind her.

Left alone in the office, Felix's ears twitched every now and then, as she listened sleepily to the distant sounds of her colleagues clocking on or to the rumble of the cars starting up in the taxi rank outside. Every now and again, as regular as clockwork, a station announcement could be heard, proclaiming the coming or going of yet another train service. The station was going about its business, unstoppable as the sunrise that had so recently blessed the day, but for the time being the station had to cope without its cat. She had much more important things to do. As the regular announcements acted as a lullaby, Felix the cat fell fast asleep.

Which was just the way she liked it.

2. A Rosemary by Any Other Name

Felix's head jerked sharply to the right. Something had caught her attention: something very, very interesting indeed. Out on the platforms, she leant forward, her head and neck outstretched, her eyes fixed and unblinking, the better to see. She inched further forward and peered in the direction of the King's Head pub at the southern end of platform one. Then she was suddenly up on her feet and trotting fast on a mission of discovery.

Rumble, rumble, rumble! went the sound that had caught her attention. *Rumble, rumble, rumble!* As she neared the source of the sound, she was excited to see that it was being caused by some people dressed in yellow hi-vis jackets – the costume that her beloved TPE colleagues always wore when they were out on the platforms. With increasing enthusiasm, she bounded up to them and cast her eyes skywards, expecting to see one of her favourites looking back. When, instead, a young man with strawberry-blond hair greeted her expectant eyes, she stopped running abruptly – and with rather cutting disappointment. *Oh,* her sudden halt seemed to say, *you're not the one I want.*

The young man was called Adam Taylor. Just as Felix had identified in her clever little way, he was not a member of the TPE team. In fact, Adam was a volunteer with the Friends of Huddersfield Station, a volunteer group who staffed the local information desk on the concourse and who also took responsibility for maintaining the many plants that were dotted about the platforms in blue pots. Adam and his fellow volunteers had to don the yellow jackets whenever they gardened on the platforms – thus accounting for the very confused look that now crossed the little cat's face.

Despite Felix's evident disappointment, however, she certainly hadn't lost her curiosity in what Adam was up to. As he turned and walked away from her, that intriguing *rumble rumble rumble* sound started up again. Felix prowled after him enquiringly, her head on one side, assessing the situation.

Aha! She had it. Adam and his fellow volunteers were dragging a large blue-and-white water butt with them as they trudged round the pots to water them, and its black wheels – which could pull up to 80 litres of water – were making a right racket on the concrete platforms. Every now and then, Adam would bend down to the bottom of it, where a little tap projected, and fill up his bright red watering can.

He was very new to gardening on the station, having only volunteered for that aspect of the job in May 2016, but he'd been volunteering with the Friends since the year before, starting in March. It had literally been a lifeline for him. About eight years prior, at the age of nineteen, he had been diagnosed with multiple sclerosis (MS). A daunting diagnosis for such a young man, it had left him with paralysing depression and anxiety. Fearing for the future, struck low by the physical impairments that limited his hopes, he found he soon retreated from the world, sitting at home for days on end with the lights off and the curtains drawn. His condition left him unable to work, but also seemingly unable to communicate with others. He shut down, barely speaking to anyone unless it was an online interaction on a computer. Yet he found that the longer he stayed at home, the more and more depressed he became – even suicidally so on a few occasions. But it was thanks to Pathways, a mental-health team based in Mirfield, that he started to get his life back.

He was assigned a really caring gentleman as a mentor, who slowly reintroduced Adam to the idea of leaving the flat for more than just necessity and who helped him to rebuild his confidence. After nearly a year of working with him, Adam began looking for jobs, although he knew that his condition meant his options were restricted as he was unable to work full-time or to do roles that were physically taxing. But the Job Centre, upon learning that he loved transport, had soon put him in contact with the Friends, who were always looking for more volunteers to help care for the station. Adam had signed up immediately and simply turning up to the station every Friday morning, helping others and being part of something, had really helped him feel that he *did* have some worth in the greater world, after all.

Recently, one of the long-term volunteers had announced that she'd like to step back from gardening duties, as it was beginning to get difficult for her to kneel down to do the pots. Adam had debated long and hard about whether he should step up. His MS meant he couldn't walk long distances without extreme levels of pain, and the platforms on the station, when walked from end to end, are, in fact, a surprisingly long distance. The MS also affected his sense of touch; he almost had to work out anew each morning how much pressure to apply when using his hands and feet. Was gardening something that would help or handicap him further?

But Adam had loved his time volunteering at the station so far and he'd wanted to do more. He had a bit of a green finger with plants at home – perhaps that would translate to the larger canvas of the platform pots? His doctors had also told him that he had to be very careful that his muscles didn't waste away, and Adam hoped the gardening might help to strengthen them. Apprehensively, he put himself forward and joined the small team who maintained the station's plants.

It was tough to begin with. The plants were watered every week. At first, Adam struggled, but in time it became less effort and he found, if he took some specially prescribed medication beforehand, that he could do it all without too much pain. And, of course, having the companionship of a little black-and-white cat, as he sometimes did, also made the hours fly by.

Adam had first met Felix the year before, when she was wandering around on the concourse and he was manning the local information stand. She had come straight up to him and he had given her a few pets.

He soon found that her approach was not a one-off. When Adam had first started volunteering, his mental-health problems were still a powerful influence and, even though he was enjoying his time at the station, self-doubt and anxiety gnawed away at him. Sometimes he would take himself away to sit quietly on a bench at the station, unwelcome thoughts whirring every which way in his head.

Felix used to come up to him and nuzzle him. It was in no way a demand for attention, such as she would insist on, diva-like, with Angie Hunte. Instead, she was there for Adam, and he found that, as he stroked along her black back, he suddenly felt happy again. Cats had always had that effect on him. His grandmother – with whom he'd lived for many years – had two, Jet and Mitty, who were black and tortoiseshell moggies respectively. Playful and full of life, they had always lifted his spirits – and he now found Felix was intent on doing the same.

The more time he spent at the station, the more he realised that it wasn't just him that Felix was helping. As he observed her going about her business, he noticed that Felix often sat next to the person on the platform who looked as though they needed cheering up the most. One morning, he observed her with a middle-aged man. The gentleman was looking very downcast, just staring at the floor, so caught up in his dark thoughts that he had completely failed to notice the fluffy black-and-white cat who was watching him so intently. Felix had definitely noticed *him*. Gently, she went up to him and nuzzled his knees, before leaping on to the metal bench beside him and settling down for a cuddle. The chap instantly perked up.

People wrote to tell the station staff how Felix had helped them on difficult journeys – on their way to say goodbye to a terminally ill relative, for example, or when they had to go to work the morning after that relative had died. 'It was very difficult going to work this morning,' confided John Rooney in one such letter. 'My grandad had died in the early hours. I was waiting on the platform

17

and Felix came up to me and rubbed her head on my knee and let me stroke her. She made me feel so much better and it was as if she could sense my grief. Please give her a Dreamie or two from me.'

With Felix being such a special cat with such very special skills, Adam felt lucky indeed that, on this summer's day in 2016, Felix had chosen to accompany him on his watering duties. Together, they trotted along the platform and Adam carefully attended to each plant. Thanks to Felix's friendship with Billy Bolt, and the hours she had spent beside him as he planted the station garden, the cat perhaps felt she was something of an expert gardener. At the least, she surely had the feline arrogance that she always knew best – so she probably wasn't expecting to learn anything from this little outing with Adam.

Oh, how wrong she was.

When she was 'helping' with the watering, Felix tended to stand by the side of the pots, like an independent inspector. She would look from the plants to the purple-shirted volunteers, occasionally cracking out a right scowl if she felt their work was not up to scratch. As the resident station cat, she seemed to feel a protective responsibility for the platform plants. 'These are mine – don't damage them,' her flashing eyes seemed to signal dangerously.

On one or two of the pots, however – the larger size with more generous rims – Felix had sometimes made it a habit to jump up on to the edge. There she would balance nimbly, casting a closer eye on proceedings and occasionally having an enthusiastic nosy through the begonias.

On this particular day, Felix made just such a leap. Whether she mistimed it or *intended* to experience the soft landing of the soil, Adam did not know and Felix wasn't telling, but she ended up sprawled in a patch of rosemary – and her disturbance of the plant released its distinctive smell.

Well, it was distinctive to Adam, who knew exactly what it was, but Felix seemed not to know quite what had hit her. Her green eyes went very wide, as if it was a shocking new scent. She blinked in confusion, seeming to have no idea where it was coming from. Curious now, she continued to rustle the green-spiked plant, causing its leaves to release yet more fragrance. Well, at that stage she looked round rather fiercely, as though the smell had offended her, and ducked her head once more beneath its stems while twitching her nose furiously.

As she had beaten Adam to the pot, he had not yet attended to it, so the plant was untrimmed, with several dangling branches waggling about, which now teased Felix further still. With increasing urgency, she batted at those low-hanging branches, as a detective might do when hunting through the undergrowth for clues. The smell was really rather powerful – Adam was six foot tall and even he could smell it as it wafted out all across the station!

Felix appeared utterly transfixed by it, pulling some incredibly perplexed expressions on her bewhiskered face that were truly funny to observe. What *was* this maddening smell? Eventually, she figured out where it was coming from – but only after she had interrogated that rosemary plant as only she knew how: by batting it, swiping it, and rolling around as close as she could to it without falling out of the pot! It became pretty precarious, but she seemed to prioritise wrangling with the rosemary over any sense of decorum.

Once she had successfully identified the smell's source, however, it soon became clear that she was *not* a fan. Curiosity may not have killed the cat, but it had certainly left her with an unpleasant tingle in her nostrils. With a final haughty shake of her regal head, she leapt down as quickly as she could and stalked off down the platform, without a backward glance at Adam or the plant that had so offended her.

Despite Felix's rejection of it, the rosemary remained at the station. Every now and again, Felix would pass it on her patrols, but Adam never once saw her jump on to that plant again. It seemed she had decided that particular adventure was not one she cared to repeat.

Ah well, Felix — better luck next thyme.

3. The Pest Controller in Action

With a careless coo in his irritating voice, the pigeon pecked his way along the platform, chirruping to his mates about all the tasty treats he was finding. With narrowed eyes, Felix watched him from afar.

Felix and the pigeons were at war. It was not – as yet – a bloody war, but it was nevertheless a long-running enmity that showed no sign of ceasefire. The pigeons had been at Huddersfield long before the pest controller had first reported for duty. No matter what Felix tried to do about their invasions on what she saw as 'her' territory, they were not giving ground to the station cat.

That didn't mean that Felix didn't do her best to hunt them down and see them off, however. If she saw a pigeon on the platform, she would delicately rise to her feet and lower her belly to the ground, as though she was a commando creeping through a battlefield. Before she took a single step, she would wiggle her behind, building up momentum, getting her hips and legs and paws all limbered up, ready to strike. Watching her, the TPE team thought it looked as though she was giving herself a pep talk. 'I'm gonna get this one. This one's mine . . .' But every time she launched an attack, the pigeon would easily see her coming – a blur of black and white – and it was far too easy for it to flap its grey wings and fly casually away, leaving Felix denied once more.

It was ever so frustrating – not least because Felix had more than earned that promotion to senior pest controller. After a slow start on the pest-controlling front – it had taken her a while as a kitten to find her four feet – she now excelled at mouse-catching, regularly leaving little 'gifts' for Angie Hunte. ('That's lovely, Felix,' Angie would say in a pantomimed voice. Then she'd holler with feeling, 'Help!' She loved Felix dearly, but not those grim gifts.)

Others were more respectful of Felix's achievements in her chosen field. She had impressed Dale Woodward, who worked with her on the platforms, when they had shared a night shift one evening. Dale was a fellow in his fifties with a balding head and prominent features, who'd worked at the station for more than a decade. That night they had both been out on platform one when Dale had suddenly spotted Felix assuming her hunting pose, her back haunches tense and tight and her eyes fixed firmly on the far rail, next to the wall of platform four. Dale had followed her line of sight and squinted hard. *I can't see nowt*, he'd thought in confusion. But within thirty seconds, Felix had run from her position, dived down on to the tracks and across that rail, and returned with a dead mouse in her mouth, having completed her mission with laser-like accuracy. Pleased as punch, she had then trotted along the platform to the customer-information point, where she deposited her handiwork with ill-disguised pride. She always left her offerings there; sometimes, the early-turn staff would arrive to find two or three dead mice laid out on the mat – something that was guaranteed to turn their stomachs at that particular hour of the day.

Felix hunted mice all over the station. On the platforms. On the tracks. But perhaps her favourite haunt for hunting was Billy's garden. It was not quite as well maintained as it had been in Billy's day – though Adam and the other volunteers tended it from time to time, their focus was on the floral displays in the plant pots, which often proved such an all-consuming task that it was difficult to keep on top of the garden too. But the lack of maintenance was certainly not a problem for Felix: in fact, she found that she liked the overgrown plants and the tall sheaves of grass even better than she had before – for they provided perfect camouflage for her hunting. It was not uncommon for the TPE team to be looking about for her, wondering where on earth she'd got to now, when they'd suddenly see a fluffy black-and-white head pop up from where she'd been hiding among the tall grasses, as she prepared to pounce on yet another unsuspecting subject.

But despite her mouse-catching prowess, the pigeons continued to elude Felix. It was such an embarrassing disappointment for the senior pest controller. After all, it was not as though her failure wasn't apparent. While her team members said proudly that, thanks to her hard work, they never now saw live mice at the station, the pigeons still boldly strutted about the platforms as though they owned the place.

Nor were they the only birds with whom Felix had to contend. Huddersfield station was also home to a small contingent of big black crows, who chose to roost alongside the pigeons on the steel girders that criss-crossed beneath the station's corrugated-iron roof. They had terrorised Felix when she was a kitten, but by now she had called a truce. Though they still tried to taunt her, swooping down from their perches in packs of two or three, Felix would not take the bait. Whenever this murder of crows would congregate beside her, cawing out derisively, Felix merely looked at them levelly with her big green eyes, knowing that, for all their bluster, they did not dare attack. The crows no longer had any power over her: after all, they came in numbers for protection, while she was a superior, solitary queen.

But her failure to catch the pigeons *did* bother Felix. Time and time again she would try to stalk one to success; time and time again she failed. She must have felt as though she would never, ever achieve her ambition.

Summers in Huddersfield were always busy times on the station. Children were on holiday from school, families were going on vacation, and there were days when the platforms were so packed to the rafters with holiday-makers, each with their own bulky suitcase, that there was an awful lot of clutter about. On one such day, Felix was hard at work on platform one, greeting passengers. She was midway through expertly weaving in and out of all the new obstacles with aplomb, as though they had been placed there simply for her entertainment, when she came across a very chilled-out family who were waiting for their train to the airport. They were already so much into their holiday vibe, dreaming of sunlit islands and sangria, that they did not notice the determined black-and-white cat prowling among their bags.

Someone else didn't notice her either: one Percy Pigeon, who was gaily grabbing what crumbs he could as he paraded in front of those self-same suitcases . . .

Felix spotted him and froze. Even as she watched, Percy let out a contented coo as he gobbled down some tasty morsel. Felix's green eyes narrowed, and tension slowly spread through her limbs.

To her back was the Coffee Xpress concession. This concentrated the boundaries of her stalking field, as though she was in a bunker or a foxhole, with only the enemy ahead.

An enemy who could not see her.

The cases provided the perfect cover. As the family excitedly chattered away above her head about their upcoming holiday, Felix took a single, slow step forward, being very careful to remain behind the shield of their suitcases. The family had unwittingly parked them up in an ideal configuration, allowing her to plot her attack and make her advance, while still keeping eyes on the pigeon.

'Coo, coo!' called Percy happily.

Behind the suitcases, Felix took another step forward.

'Coo, coo!' he called again, with no sense of the terrible danger he was in.

Like the calm before the storm, Felix paused for a pregnant moment, gauging strike distances and speed and space. Her brain whirring, in a few short seconds she had completed the complex calculations that she hoped would see her succeed. Never before had she had such an opportunity. She knew, all too well, that she might never get such a one again.

There was a slim gap between the cases ahead. Felix eyed it with interest and intent. She knew she had one chance to get this right; she had to dart through that gap, before which the pigeon pranced, and at just the right moment pin him down with a swipe of her perilous paw.

'Coo, coo!' called Percy, as though encouraging her. Bring it on. Felix was ready to answer.

She gathered her legs beneath her till her muscles quivered. She was right beside that all-important gap, her velvety black nose almost poking out from her lair, trying as hard as she could to keep her whiskers still so that she did not give away her position. If Percy looked her way right this minute, he would see her: game over.

But Percy was far more interested in pecking at the crumbs on the platform. He did not turn his head.

In her mind, though she did not know the numbers, Felix must surely have been counting down, choosing the right moment to strike. But little did she know: time was running out. For, above her head, the orange digits of the station display board moved on. The Manchester Airport train would soon be here. Which would make its move first: the locomotive or the lion-like cat who was even now hunting her very own Huddersfield 'gazelle'?

Three, two, one . . .

A scream tore through the station.

4. Famous Felix

Felix pounced. *She succeeded.* Her claws latched on to the pigeon's back and a flurry of feathers burst into the air as though a pigeon-down pillow had exploded on the platform. The holidaying family, having known nothing of Felix's plot, screamed loudly in alarm, completely terrified, as feathers puffed fulsomely into the air. There was little immediate sign of where they had come from or what on earth had caused this peculiar phenomenon; utterly startled by the explosion, the family scattered, leaving their luggage unattended, and all eyes turned as one to the commotion.

Then, as though echoing their cries, there was a heroic squawk from the pigeon. Amid the flurry of feathers, Percy was still alive and he was flapping, flapping, flapping to try to tear himself free! With an almighty screech and a muscular ripple of his wondrous wings, he somehow managed to pull away from Felix's clutches, even though her claws had most definitely snagged him. He may have left half his feathers behind, but – to the railway cat's frustration – he had somehow lived to fly another day. He retreated to the iron girders above to lick his wounds while Felix looked up in absolute disbelief, sitting in a sea of feathers and abandoned cases.

As the feathers slowly drifted back to earth, the family returned to their luggage, their hands to their mouths.

No longer scared, now that they realised what had happened, they found themselves laughing instead, giggles escaping them as they took in the unusual scene. Poor old Felix! Denied again!

'Not to worry, my girl,' said Angie Hunte later that day, as she watched the whole episode back on the black-and-white CCTV, having been alerted to it by a colleague who'd been present. 'I love you just the way you are.'

And Angie Hunte was not alone in that. As the summer of 2016 drew on, Felix's popularity continued to soar as her Facebook friends followed her adventures online. They loved to log in and find out what the railway cat had been up to each day. As only a handful of fans actually made it to the station in person, the man behind the page found he had his work cut out for him to keep the online followers fulfilled. Always there was a hunger for new posts, new pictures and new videos. But he was more than happy to deliver.

His name was Mark Allan, and he was a mild-mannered commuter in his fifties who worked in Manchester five days a week. He commuted through Huddersfield station, catching the 6.40 service each weekday morning. He and Felix had become friends in spring 2015 and he had set up Felix's page for her shortly thereafter – mostly as something of a creative outlet, given his job in finance was a very serious one. Her subsequent online success had come as a wonderful surprise. Now, with 87,000 Facebook fans (and counting) hanging on the railway cat's every post, he was rather enjoying the challenge of coming up with new ideas. He found he was always thinking about what he and Felix could do next, and he would mull ideas over even when he wasn't at the station – just as he did one August day that summer, as he was clearing out a wardrobe in his Huddersfield home.

'What's this?' he muttered, as he reached into the back of the cupboard and pulled out a sorry-looking mess of multicoloured plastic. 'I remember this . . .'

It was a blow-up globe – something he'd bought for his children years before to show them the locations of all the countries of the world. He pressed his lips to the toggle and with a series of determined puffs fully inflated the globe. *Oh yes*, he thought, *I can have some fun with this* . . . Given Felix's fans came from all across the world, from America to Hong Kong and everywhere in between, the globe seemed a particularly apt prop for this global superstar to play with.

The following morning, on 22 August 2016, Mark got to the station around 6.30 a.m. As usual, despite the early hour, there were still a fair few commuters already on the platform, rustling newspapers as they caught up on current affairs and nursing cups of takeaway coffee. It was a rather windy morning and people glared crossly in the direction of the railway tunnels, which were causing the wind to whistle down the platforms towards the King's Head. Though it was allegedly the height of summer, that bitter wind was a hint that, in Yorkshire, winter is never far away.

Ignoring the weather, Mark walked with increasing excitement towards the customer-information point, already anticipating Felix's reaction to the blow-up globe. It seemed she was excited too: as she did most days, she was already waiting for him on 'their' bench, close to the

Head of Steam pub, eager to see what treats he had brought for her today. The pub staff had got there early that morning as well – already, they had their advertising A-frame hoardings out on the platform, promoting the jazz night they were holding in two days' time.

'Good morning, Felix,' Mark said to his little friend, bending down to stroke her as she arched her head into his now familiar hand. Then, without further ado, he whipped out the blow-up globe and proceeded to inflate it with a series of short puffs, attracting a few bemused looks from his fellow commuters. Once the globe was inflated, he popped it down on to the platform, soon followed by a Dreamie to encourage Felix to investigate further. Mark chuckled to himself as he set the scene he hoped to photograph. He could just imagine it: Felix checking out her world domination, looking for the locations of all her many fans. He had already come up with the caption: 'My global appeal is growing.' He hoped it would go down a treat.

But, that morning, Felix's treat was not going down at all. Without wanting to gossip, it is fair to say that she has a reputation as a rather greedy cat, yet this morning even the temptation of a treat had not brought her to the globe's side, as Mark had hoped. She looked at the scene with caution, none too sure about this latest prop that Mark had brought to their daily meeting. In the business world the mantra is 'no idea is a bad idea' – but it seemed that Felix did not subscribe to that particular ethos.

Mark was standing back, his phone ready to take the picture, while he encouraged Felix to come. Usually, she 'obeyed' promptly (as much as any cat ever 'obeys' a human), eager for snacks and photo shoots. But today she merely narrowed her eyes and looked suspiciously at the globe. Untethered, the beachball-like sphere was gently rocking in the breeze and its independent movement was clearly freaking Felix out. What was this brightly coloured creature, which wasn't a mouse or a pigeon or a crow? What was she to *do* with it?

Mark could see pretty quickly that she was not going to come, so he reworked his vision. Instead of snapping Felix next to the globe, he would try to capture it in the foreground with Felix in the background (where she was keeping her distance from this unfamiliar foe). He took a few steps back to line up the shot.

Whoosh! A particularly blowy gust of wind whistled along the platform – and took the inflatable globe with it!

Well, Felix might have conquered her fear of crows, but she was not yet ready to tackle this strange new bird! She legged it – leaving Mark alone on the platform with a runaway globe.

He grabbed for it; it danced out of his reach. He stretched out his other hand; it rolled just that little bit further away. Then the wind gusted once more and the globe flew even further along the platform in the direction of the King's Head.

Mark started sweating. He had visions of it changing direction and blowing on to the tracks, where it could potentially cause many hours of expensive delays (something that Felix's employers – and the passengers – would be none too pleased about). Consequently, Mark threw caution to the wind and flung himself after it at top speed, his eyes fixed only on the prize.

Bang! In his focused quest he ran headlong into one of the Head of Steam's A-frame hoardings. With a cacophonous clatter, the metal advert fell to the ground and all heads swivelled to the commuter. Teetering, he just about managed to retain his balance, if not his dignity, and somehow styled it out. Best of all, he managed to capture the globe. All in a day's work for Felix's Facebook manager!

What had been particularly striking for Mark, even in the relatively short time that Felix had become famous, was how very much she meant to her fans. Earlier that summer, there had been a dramatic incident at the station where an armed man had run into the train tunnels. Huddersfield station had been put in lockdown while the police resolved the dangerous stand-off. Felix, sensibly, had tucked herself away during the entire saga and was never involved, but her thousands of fans did not know that. As soon as news of the ongoing drama hit the headlines in the *Huddersfield Examiner,* her fans were on Facebook clamouring for an update from Felix to let them know she was OK. Mark – who had known nothing of the incident until his account was suddenly flooded with messages – was very happy to let them know that was the case.

Perhaps it was that incident that started more people coming to the station, needing to know she was OK – to see with their own eyes that the station cat was the same confident diva she had always been. There had been a rush of visitors when Felix had first been promoted, but this had tailed off in the intervening months. Nevertheless, that summer Huddersfield station had played host to Felix fans from Switzerland, New Zealand,

Kazakhstan and Canada. There was even someone from the Isle of Wight! The team also remembered meeting a blushing bride who had come all the way from Australia to marry in England, and as she'd had a few days spare after the wedding she had chosen to use those first few days of married life to come to Huddersfield to meet the cat. Meeting Felix was, you might say, the icing on the wedding cake.

Felix wasn't always ready to meet her public. She could be grumpy if she was disturbed from a catnap, and it wasn't unknown for her to lash out if she was in a testy mood. At other times, she was simply AWOL, off on a patrol, and her colleagues had no idea where she was. However, on other occasions it was neither her mood nor her absence that was at issue. Passenger Stuart Gelder remembered walking through the ticket barriers one day and spotting Felix on the platform . . . enthusiastically licking a bin bag (one of her not-so-secret guilty pleasures). It was hardly her most glamorous moment. Yet Stuart added affectionately, 'Even though she wasn't at her most majestic, I was still ecstatic to have finally seen her.'

Many visitors wanted to see Felix dressed up in her famous yellow hi-vis jacket. Oh yes – she had one too, just like every member of the TPE team. She had worn the jacket when receiving her promotion and the adorable pictures of her in her 'uniform' had gone viral. But, not too long afterwards, Felix had thrown a diva strop about wearing the jacket – perhaps feeling, somewhat justifiably, that her pretty black fluff was already perfection . . . and how could anyone improve on that? Unlike the mere mortal human employees of the railway company, she felt the uniform was beneath her. She had chosen her moment carefully, and then, while dressed up in it one day, she had cleverly run off to one of her favourite hidey-holes: the disused train carriage on platform two. Here she had wiggled her way beneath the carriage, and then wriggled and jiggled until she'd managed to lose the coat. Ever since then, she'd insisted that her birthday suit was all the decoration she needed to meet her public.

It often fell to Angela Dunn, who worked in the lost-property office, to try to help the visitors meet their idol. Angela was a lovely lady with short grey hair and wire glasses. She had been a firm friend of Felix ever since the start. On one of Felix's very first days at the station, Angela had found the kitten a soft brown bear from the lost toys she cared for, a friend to keep the kitten company in her new home. Felix and the bear had been inseparable for many years, but the bear was no longer on the scene. No one seemed to know what had happened to it, but Felix did not seem to mourn its loss: perhaps another sign that the little cat was all grown up these days. Felix always remembered Angela's kindness, however. She was a very frequent visitor to Angela's office.

Although, truth be told, Angela was never quite sure if it was *her* the cat had come to see – or the collection of snuggly coats and jumpers that made the perfect place for a catnap.

One day, Angela received a message from Mark Allan to say that the mother of an autistic boy had contacted him to ask if they could visit Felix. The team were always careful to emphasise that nobody could guarantee when

Felix would be at home. With mice to catch and places to explore and nice long naps to enjoy, Felix simply could not be available 24/7. It wouldn't have been fair to expect her to be. Nonetheless, Angela promised to do what she could to help the visit go smoothly.

When the day arrived, she discovered that Felix was indeed available and ready to meet her public. Perhaps the cat had taken inspiration from the bronze Harold Wilson statue that stood in St George's Square outside the station, which the moggy passed day after day. The statue was engraved with one of Wilson's quotations: 'The leader of the party, and no less the prime minister, has a duty to meet the people.' Perhaps Felix had taken his words to heart.

Angela knew which train the mother and son were arriving on and she decided that she wanted to give them a royal welcome from Queen Felix. So she scooped up the cat – Felix, for once, allowing herself to be carried – and headed out to platform one to await their arrival.

Though Angela had never met the family before, she instantly knew – even before they'd left the train – exactly who they were. The beaming smile on the mother's face told her everything she needed to know. She watched from the platform as the mum guided her son, who was about fourteen, off the train. He wore a bright-blue T-shirt and comfortable Adidas sweatpants and seemed oblivious to the world around him, locked as he was in the world created by the big fat headphones placed over his ears. Yet, as they stepped off the train, his mother touched his arm to command his attention and pointed out the cat, who was now waiting patiently on the platform for him.

The boy turned his head slowly. Once his eyes alighted on Felix, a broad grin spread across his face. He walked over to her and plonked himself down on the platform beside her. And, having homed in on her, she became his world. He simply sat there with her happily, occasionally stroking her or tickling her behind her tufty ears. Somehow, she seemed to be able to tell that she was needed for the long haul, so she lay right down on the platform with him, stretching out on her side and relaxing her snowy-white paws. For the next fifteen minutes, she was completely his. Angela Dunn, watching closely, could tell that the whole experience was pure pleasure for the lad.

Though the boy remained silent, his mum seemed to feel the need to speak. 'He just loves Felix,' she confided to Angela. 'He read about her and he saw her on TV, and I knew it would make his day to come and visit her. And will you look at that?' she whispered, her voice catching as she watched her boy with the cat he loved. 'Will you just look at that . . .?'

Truth be told, the mother wasn't the only one with a tear of happiness in her eye.

Perhaps a week or so later, Angela happened to be passing by when another family with an autistic child asked to see Felix. This time, the family asked another member of staff, who was not as familiar with Felix's movements as the lost-property lady. Politely, he had said, 'Sorry, she is not available' – but without actually checking for Felix in her favourite hidey-holes.

Well, the little lad was absolutely crushed. There were tears and tantrums and a wailing voice that caught at your soul: 'But I *really* wanted to see Felix!'

Angela stopped where she stood, deliberating. The family were already walking away, their shoulders slumped. She hesitated for only a second longer, and then ran after them.

'Excuse me!' she called out.

They turned round, the boy still hiccoughing with hurt.

'I hear you'd like to see madam?' Angela said brightly, using her personal nickname for Queen Felix. The family nodded, hope darting back into their eyes as they looked at the kindly woman. 'I can't make any promises,' she told them, 'but let me see if she's free.'

She found her fluffy colleague dozing in the back office, and on this occasion Felix did not object to being woken. So that little boy got to meet the station cat, just as he had dreamed.

For Angela Dunn, it was a watershed moment. For while she always put Felix's welfare first, she felt that if Felix could make somebody's dream come true in such a simple way, it was really important to try to make it happen. After that, she became the main contact for visitors at the station who had come to see Felix (along with the ladies in the booking office, if Angela wasn't on shift). It didn't happen all that often, but it soon became a fairly regular occurrence for Angela to assist people who wanted an audience with Her Majesty. She would usher them in to meet the queen and talk them through the etiquette of interacting with such a feisty cat.

That summer, Angela was fifty-three. She had never expected to change career at her age. But it seemed that it was never too late to become a lady-in-waiting – at least, not when it came to Queen Felix.

5. Cat Burglar

As the autumn of 2016 unfolded, Angela found her services were in demand – but not always needed. Lucky customers sometimes had to look no further for Felix than the serving counters at which they bought their tickets.

Felix liked to hang out in the booking office. When open, it was always staffed, so it was the perfect place to chill out if she wanted company. She could often be found sharing a shift at a serving window, sitting proudly up on the counter. She had even been known to inspect customers' discount railcards for validity, her green eyes going over every detail.

Another favourite perch was the top of the printer where the tickets came out. Here her fluffy tail would frequently get in the way of the output of those cream-and-orange train tickets. Funnily enough, no one ever seemed to mind.

There was much to explore in the ticket office. Sometimes Felix simply wandered about the place, sniffing out what was new. That year, a life-size model of the railway cat was one such – perhaps surprising – new addition. Back in the summer, Felix had completed a 5k charity 'fun run' (via a GPS tracker on her collar) for the children's charity Fairy Bricks – which donates Lego sets to children's hospices and hospitals, brightening the lives of sick children – and in gratitude for the £5,200 she raised, the charity arranged for a life-size model of Felix, made from Lego, to be built and given to the station. It had immediately taken pride of place in the booking office. And as Felix's popularity had continued to grow throughout the autumn, it now formed the centrepiece of a sort of 'Felix gallery', in which ceramic cats and children's sketches of Felix joined the big Lego model.

Goodness only knew what Felix thought of it all as she investigated each new addition with a sniff of her velvety nose. What did she see as she stared into the life-size model's plastic eyes? What did she make of all these 'other' cats – who were actually only representations of her own spectacular beauty? Felix's reaction was not completely out of character; after a full study, she tended to turn her back, curl up and go to sleep.

The booking office was a favourite location for a snooze. Here she slept on top of the Delay Repay forms, or among the lever-arch files on the metal shelves, or even on the black-plastic photocopier, which could get nice and toasty after it had been used. A super spot was the shelf right above the electric fire. She would curl up there contentedly, near the kooky sign that read: 'A very spoiled cat lives here'.

There was perhaps no one who spoiled Felix more than TPE's maintenance man, Dave Chin. Not when it came to cuddles, at least. Dave – a weather-beaten chap who had big rough hands and an easy smile – was not based at Huddersfield but roamed all over the railway network, wherever his services were required. If anything went wrong, a cry would go up for Dave, and Dave would come, practical and handy in his orange hi-vis suit. He had once spent a fair amount of time at Huddersfield, as he used to do all his paperwork in the station buffet on platform four, but with a lot of the records now going digital, he came to the station far less frequently.

But, when Felix had been a kitten, he'd spent a lot of time at the station getting to know the railway cat. So close had they become that Dave had become known as the Felix-whisperer. Felix had quite the reputation when she wanted to throw a strop – and plenty of staff members had the scars to prove it. Never did Felix want to throw a strop more than when she had to travel in her carry case. (The irony of a railway cat who hated travelling was not lost on anyone.) She would fight every journey with all she had. Due to their closeness, for a long time it was only Dave who could get the reluctant cat into her carry case. There was something about the maintenance man that made Felix putty in his hands. Even at the great age of five and a half, Felix would allow him to cradle her like a baby: on her back in his arms with her belly exposed and a silly-sausage expression stuck to her sweet fluffy face. If Dave had been willing, she'd have let him walk round with her all day like that.

So imagine her delight that autumn when her long-time partner in crime called by to see her one afternoon. Dave found her in the booking office and before too long Felix was blissfully luxuriating in a lovely long cuddle in his arms. As Dave tickled her toes and stroked her belly, she flung her head back in feline ecstasy. Jean Randall, a dark-haired old-timer who was working in the office that day, rolled her eyes indulgently at Felix's flagrant surrender.

Well, who should come to the desk that day but Mark Allan, Felix's Facebook manager? He knew all about Dave and his cat-whispering skills, of course, having documented them for Felix's followers. The cat's loyalty to the maintenance man was legendary up and down not only the railway but also the social network.

I wonder . . . Mark thought mischievously that afternoon. *I wonder how far her loyalty* really *goes?*

Though he and Felix were close, Mark knew that he was no match for Dave in Felix's affections. But Dave versus Dreamies? Now, *there* was a challenge.

As had become habit by now, Mark happened to have a packet of cat treats in his pocket. Like a Boy Scout, he thought it always best to 'be prepared' when it came to Felix. You never knew when she might do something fabulously funny so Mark liked to keep the tools of his trade about him just in case. Now, looking at Felix behind the counter in the booking office, stretched out in Dave's arms and seemingly lost to the world, he felt it was time to put those pocket treats to use.

Ever so slowly, keeping his eyes fixed on Felix, Mark dug his hand into his coat pocket, where the cat treats lay within their plastic pouch. Deliberately, he twiddled his fingers gently against the packet and a barely audible rustling sound resulted.

Barely audible to him – but *not* to Felix.

How will she react? he wondered, as he noticed her ears pricking up at once.

Well, he barely had time to compose that thought – before Felix had leapt from Dave's arms with unseemly haste. Then she flung herself on to the counter at a million miles an hour, rudely pushing her way past Jean, who was attempting to serve Mark. She stood eagerly at the edge of the desk, as close to that tantalising sound as she could possibly get. Once in position, she glared insistently at Mark, demanding that he now come up with the goods she *knew* he had.

Seeing her flagrant abandonment of Dave for the far superior temptation of a treat, all three humans roared with laughter. Mark did as he was silently told, stepping forward and pulling the packet from his pocket, before placing a treat down on the counter. Felix watched his hands closely, all thoughts of Dave long gone, before she bent her head to the counter and gobbled up the treat with lip-smacking satisfaction, her little pink tongue gathering up every last crumb.

Jean smiled and tutted at Felix. That cat . . . She would do anything for food!

That, in fact, was a universal truth that was widely acknowledged. And Felix's love for food was so evident that it soon became one of the first things new joiners to the station learned.

That autumn, Felix gained two new colleagues. First up, arriving at the station in October 2016, was a new team leader called Jacqui. A petite woman with curly brown hair, she had previously been an announcer at Manchester Piccadilly. Over time, she and Angie Hunte became very good friends, bonding over their shared love of cats and cruises. As she was to many others, Angie became a mentor to Jacqui, expertly steering her through the station's ways with a steady hand. Jacqui took to calling her

'Mrs H', which was something of a bittersweet moniker for Angie – for Billy Bolt had used to call her that too. Yet Angie found she rather liked it; hearing the pet name again as she went about her work was almost a way of bringing Billy back.

As it was the team leaders who took responsibility for feeding Felix, Jacqui swiftly became an important person in Felix's life too. She also quickly learned of the mischievous cat's duplicitous ways. Jacqui would feed her promptly, and she *knew* she'd fed her, but not five minutes later Felix would come begging for more, trying hard to convince her that she'd not had anything to eat for *weeks* on end. She'd turn her green eyes molten with persuasive pleading and mew plaintively, her cries so tragic it was almost like an opera where everybody dies.

But Jacqui wasn't having any of it. She had three cats of her own – Deanie, Smudgie and Pickle – and she knew all the tricks in the book. 'You've had your food,' she would say firmly to Felix. 'I've not forgotten, you know!'

Joining Felix and Jacqui at the station that autumn was another new recruit, Karl, who worked out on the platforms as an RSA (Railway Supervisor, Grade A). He was a really good lad: the type of bloke who you'd ask to do two jobs and he'd actually do three, just to help you out. Karl couldn't believe his luck to land a job on the railway, for it had been his dream vocation ever since he'd been a lad. He knew lots of the folk at Huddersfield station already, because his previous job had been working with the rail-replacement buses. In that role, he'd become used to a bit of banter on nights with Dale and the others, so when he joined the station properly he slotted right in, immediately becoming a much-loved member of the team. Karl was everybody's friend.

He was short and stocky, aged twenty-eight, with close-cropped blondish hair and bright brown eyes. He had kindness stitched right through him. Very quickly, he became bezzie mates with Sara, an attractive blonde-haired young woman who worked in the booking office. Karl was the type of bloke who, on meeting him for the first time, you could talk to as though you'd known him for years. He and Sara soon developed a sort of big brother/little sister relationship: forever friends who could laugh and cry and work and drink together and who would be there for each other through wind, rain or snow. Which was just as well, given the weather Huddersfield was getting that winter.

Karl was a fan of the little black-and-white cat too and Felix was very accepting of him. Karl soon joined the other 'minions' at the station catering to her every whim. In line with most cats, Queen Felix expected her human colleagues to bow before her. If she needed a door opening, Karl soon learned that he had to do it, even if she then changed her mind. If she was sprawled in the corridor, taking up half its width and lying right in the way of everybody coming and going, he had to step over her, even if he almost split his trousers taking such an enormous stride. 'She has the upper hand of all of us, that cat,' commented his new colleague Liz on the gate-line, with not a little admiration.

Yet Felix was finding that her minions were not *quite* as malleable as they once had been . . .

Perhaps unsurprisingly, given her penchant for stuffing

44

her face, Felix had recently been given a couple of verbal warnings from the vet about watching her weight. An announcement even went out on Facebook, asking visitors not to feed her treats, yet simultaneously warning them that, without them, Felix might not now look so kindly on entertaining. It wasn't exactly that the stardom had gone to her head, but increasingly Felix had insisted on a 'rider'; she could be lured out, but only if she knew she'd get a treat at the end of it. But with the vet's warnings ringing in their ears, the team at the station had to put a stop to all that – at least for now.

To Felix's frustration, the gravy train of treats was cancelled. And there was no Delay Repay form for *that* kind of complaint. But Felix was a clever little kitty – and with five years' experience on the station, she knew exactly what she had to do to set this 'injustice' straight. There was food for the taking out there – you just had to know where to look.

One evening, Dale Woodward watched her as she pottered around on platform one. It was about teatime and a young lad soon came sauntering along the platform with his takeaway tea in a brown paper bag. He took a seat on a metal bench while he waited for his train. He happened to be close to Felix.

Felix, in fact, had spotted him the very moment he'd appeared on the platform. Now that he'd chosen his spot to sit, she crept closer and closer to him. She'd been around the block enough times by now to know what was in that brown paper bag: McDonald's. Felix was a fan of McDonald's. So she watched him with an unblinking stare. She licked her lips and inched even closer to the unsuspecting lad.

Focused on his tea and his grumbling belly, the man opened up the carton that he'd taken from within the bag. It held a sweet-smelling burger. Cheese oozed out of its side, its juicy meat patty squished into a fluffy burger bun. Oh, it smelled good. It looked good. Jaws stretching wide, he chomped down on the burger and savoured his first bite. As he chewed, he used his other hand to start scrolling through his phone. His attention was soon fixed on his social media, while the burger hovered in his free hand, his fingers only loosely securing it.

As though the burger was a pigeon in her sights, Felix dropped low to the ground on her belly and started crawling towards it, commando-style. Once she had slunk surreptitiously up to the bench, she risked a jump up on to it, landing silently on her padded paws. The hungry lad was so engrossed in his phone, he did not even notice her presence. For such a charismatic cat, Felix could be surprisingly stealthy when she wanted to be.

She was now a paw's stretch away from that sweet-smelling burger. Without missing a beat, without a single hesitation, she swiped it right out of the man's hand.

'What on earth . . .?' he exclaimed in dismay, as his tea tumbled to the ground. The look on his face was priceless. Felix was already down on the ground, where the chap's dinner had exploded on to the concrete in a modern artwork of burger, lettuce and bun. Felix was already doing her very best to remove any evidence of the cat burglary.

In fact, Felix was making quite the reputation for

herself, as that wasn't the cat's only food-related crime. One evening, Angela Dunn came out of the toilet, where she'd been changing for a night out, to find Felix rifling through her locker, which – without thinking – she had left open while she'd nipped into the loo inside the ladies' locker room for privacy. She had only been absent for four or five minutes. But, in that time, Felix had hopped into the locker, retrieved an unopened bag of Dreamies and completely annihilated the packet in her bid to get the goodies inside. Having clawed all the way along the top of it with her super-sharp nails, she had succeeded in tearing it open and then helped herself. By the time Angela returned, Felix was unashamedly pawing at the packet and expertly scooping out yet more treats.

'Felix!' Angela admonished. 'That's naughty!'

But Felix's only response was to purr just that little bit louder, even though she was already at top volume. Her gluttony pushed her volume right up to eleven, as a deep, throaty and very satisfied purr echoed around the locker room.

When Angela took the bag off her, Felix still had the temerity to look unashamed. She sat down on her bottom and looked up expectantly. 'OK,' her happy green eyes seemed to say, 'you can feed them *to* me now. Good idea! That's *much* better than me having to do it for myself.'

Angela posted about that particular incident on Felix's Facebook page, along with a short video of the cat caught in the act. 'Angela, just accept it,' she captioned it. 'This is what happens when you leave your locker open!' Ooh, she was a monkey.

The staff doubled down on their efforts to restrict her

diet – but they found that Felix outwitted them time and time again. The station was a busy place and there was always food about. People dropped things and unhelpfully left them where they fell. One evening, Dale came across a good chunk of chips that had been carelessly dumped by the front door of the station. It was evidently a trip hazard so he hurried quickly away and asked the cleaners to come and brush them up.

'It's just this way,' he said, as he ushered his colleague back to the spot.

The cleaner looked at him quizzically. He had his brush and pan in hand, ready to sweep up the chips, but instead of bending to his task he simply looked at Dale, as though worried he'd gone mad. As he glanced down at the empty stretch of station floor, Dale could see why: there was nothing *to* clear up. Felix had eaten the lot. She sat there licking her lips, looking pleased as punch. 'What?' she seemed to be saying as Dale tutted and shook his head at her. 'I was only helping!'

Frustratingly, this wasn't the only occasion that the greedy Felix was aided and abetted by passengers. During a security check one morning, Angie Hunte stumbled upon a tin of tuna that had been left out on the floor by the station steps. It had clearly not just dropped from somebody's shopping bag: the ring pull had been deliberately removed. A very tempting treat indeed for any station cat who happened to be passing . . . Angie caught that particular 'gift' in time, but on other occasions she was too late. Felix was once spotted sat beside an empty Greggs bag licking her lips, which was evidence enough that she had wolfed down whatever had been left inside.

On another occasion, the team found a woman feeding her bright orange Wotsits. Wotsits! To a cat! They were gobsmacked.

To Felix, it was all a bit of a game, but the team were worried. Though Felix wasn't too overweight – and her daily patrols up and down the platforms meant she got a fair amount of exercise – if this continued, they were worried she might get sick. For who knew what she might potentially eat next? In addition, human food is well known to be no good for cats – a cat eating just 25g of cheese is the equivalent of a human eating 3.5 hamburgers. A single Wotsit, meanwhile, is the equivalent of half a chocolate bar. Once again, the team appealed to people to be sensible about feeding Felix . . .

They could only hope that, this time, they would listen.

6. Christmas Wishes

''Tis the season to be jolly! Fa-la-la-la-la-la-la-la-la!'

The harmonies of the TPE choir soared right up to the high ceiling of the concourse of Huddersfield station. Dressed in their smart navy-and-purple uniforms, about a dozen of the TPE team – from all over the network – got together each December to go carol singing around all the stations. It was a railway tradition that always told the team at Huddersfield that Christmas was just round the corner.

And what a year it had been for Felix the railway cat. She had started 2016 as a hard-working but relatively unknown station moggy. Now, twelve months later, not only did she have the promotion she had always dreamed of, she was also a global Facebook phenomenon. Whoever was doing her end-of-year appraisal surely had to give her top marks!

It certainly seemed that Felix's accomplishments had not gone unnoticed – and not just by TPE. As the year came to a close, a few attempts were made to headhunt the station cat for a whole new career.

'Training up the new British Transport Police recruit!' was the caption on one Facebook photograph, of friendly Felix beside a uniformed BTP copper. 'Detective Felix at your service!' Given her criminal career as a cat burglar, however, it perhaps wasn't the wisest move . . .

On another occasion, Stephen Hack from Reading, who was a railwayman himself at Basingstoke, tried to coax Felix away to tackle their pigeon problem. (Little did he know about Felix's 'pigeon issues', but she did excel at banishing them from the platforms at the very least.) Basingstoke station was home to so many pigeons that on one occasion more than thirty of them had lined up along a road bridge at the end of the platform, as though they were posing for an end-of-term class photo. Yet Stephen's attempt to bribe the station cat with a lifetime's supply of Dreamies was doomed to failure; Felix wouldn't leave the wonderful family she had at Huddersfield. And that family now turned their attention to one of the loveliest activities of the live-long year: putting up the station's Christmas tree on the concourse.

Ever since she was a kitten, it was one of Felix's favourite days. The moment she saw Dave Chin ambling along the platform with his arms full of Christmas tree, or Chrissie from the booking office gathering up her box of festive decorations, excitement began to build in her belly. TPE always chose a gloriously tall tree and for Felix it meant a tip-top playground.

For years, Felix had made it a habit to climb all the way to the top of the tree. There, she would cling to the tallest branch like a lookout on a pirate ship, watching below for trouble or treasure. Allegedly, the gold cardboard angel who shared the uppermost branch with her was the climactic ornament in Chrissie's multicoloured display, but Felix knew the truth. *She* was the bestest, fluffiest bauble of them all.

With great excitement, Felix skidded into the lobby

and surveyed the playing field. Chrissie had already completed her decorations, so Felix enjoyed a bat-and-forth session with the glinting spheres, as they spun and sparkled on the ends of the quivering, pine-scented branches. Soon enough, however, she turned her attention to the big climb.

Felix arched her neck backwards as she looked up at it. It seemed a very, *very* tall tree this year. Did she *really* use to go *all* the way to the top? Felix gave a harrumph and sat with a sigh on her ever-increasing bottom. It seemed an awfully long way up this year . . . Nevertheless, undeterred, she flexed the sharpened claws of her paws and went for it, scurrying up the tree trunk with nimble efficiency.

Unusually, this year she abruptly stopped halfway up. Then, like a high-wire artist edging out from the rooftop of a New York skyscraper, she tiptoed out on to a sturdy midway branch. Feeling it was more than strong enough to take her weight, she then settled down with her back against the wooden trunk.

Well, what a cosy spot! Green pine branches attractively fringed her viewpoint as Felix curled up in the scented grotto of her elevated lair. With branches all around her, it was a snug in every sense of the word. In fact, in some ways this was even better than the top of the tree, for the overhead branches partly concealed her from view. Felix, a cat who was so often on display, seemed to enjoy carrying out covert ops for once.

She gazed below her at the concourse. There were Karl and Sara, talking nineteen to the dozen as usual; Sara let out a huge guffaw at some joke that Karl had cracked. She could see, too, the purple-shirted Friends of Huddersfield Station, as they guided visitors to Huddersfield's hidden gems. The station also regularly played host to local companies who sold homemade cheese, bread or pies right by the gateline, and her nose twitched wistfully as she watched shoppers being handed their tasty treats.

There was another attraction in the lobby too: a portrait of Felix herself. And not a simple child's drawing or a rough sketch – this was a top-notch, bona fide professional painting, such as might hang in the corridors of power in a stately home. Its magnificent vision suited Queen Felix down to the ground.

The portrait had, in fact, had its grand unveiling just a few days before, and the guest of honour at the dedication ceremony had been the town's deputy mayor. Displayed in a dramatic, bespoke and rather gaudy golden frame – which included a diamanté tag declaring its subject as 'Felix' – the portrait was now unmissable in the lobby, hung prominently on the white wall beside the gateline. It had been painted by the professional artist Rob Martin, who regularly travelled from the station as he went about his work. Earlier that year, the team had mentioned to him about doing a painting of their senior pest controller and the idea had become reality.

It was an incredibly striking piece of art. You perhaps noticed first – as you did with the real cat – Felix's gorgeous big green eyes, which were wide and reflective. Rob had captured her fluff and her whiskers, her tufty ears and her white-tipped tail with genuine skill – all the more impressive when you learned that he had not asked

Felix to pose for him (as fun as it might be to picture Felix in modelling mayhem . . .) but had instead worked from a photograph. Controversially, however, Rob had decided that, in light of her oft-confused gender and her Yorkshire roots, he wanted to paint her wearing a dress – a green-with-red-bow dress, which was actually modelled upon one worn by the famous Yorkshire novelist Charlotte Brontë, whose bicentenary of birth was celebrated in 2016.

Well, from the moment it had been unveiled by the deputy mayor, the picture had certainly provided a talking point! Straight away, people wanted selfies taken with it; and if Felix's fans ever failed to find their flesh-and-blood idol while on a visit, they at least now had her portrait to gaze upon instead. It wasn't unusual to see people stopping in their tracks on their way into or out of the station, doing a double take as they first caught sight of the artwork and then paused to drink it in. Folk gazed up at it thoughtfully, much as art aficionados muse upon the work of an old master. Rob's desire to paint a *proper* portrait of Felix had real impact; it would not have looked out of place on the walls of the National Portrait Gallery, hanging alongside esteemed portraits of the kings and queens of England. For Queen Felix, of course, that was perfectly apt.

From her perch amid the Christmas tree, Felix couldn't actually see her portrait – but she could see the queue of customers at the busy booking office. Maybe she watched with some amusement – certainly, superiority – as they unwittingly passed her by. Little did they know that the famous station cat was lurking overhead, sitting partway up in the fairy-lit tree. Only those with their eyes peeled like Christmas Day spuds spotted that amid the twinkling lights was a pair of emerald eyes shining brightly alongside them.

But, once she *was* spotted, the secret was soon shared among the passengers queuing to buy tickets below.

'Look! She's in the Christmas tree!' someone might gasp in delight, as they suddenly caught sight of the secretive spy cat.

Those same words would echo down the line, like a festive feline version of Chinese whispers.

'She's in the tree . . .'

'She's hiding, look.'

'Oh, look, how sweet is she?'

The answer, of course, was *very*. So much so that in December – in light of Felix's stellar achievements and rising fame – TPE decided to release a limited-edition Felix-focused calendar. Featuring twelve adorable pictures of the station cat, it included images of Felix as a kitten, on patrol and playing in a cardboard box. It even included the snapshot that had launched her to global fame: Felix in her yellow hi-vis vest with her senior pest controller badge proudly on display. December's image, of course, was Felix in a Santa hat – even if, due to her diva demands, she wasn't so much wearing it as momentarily consenting to have it draped upon her. The company planned to sell the calendars online, with all proceeds going to the Huddersfield Samaritans.

Felix's calendar was released for sale on 7 December 2016 – and very quickly caused chaos, much as the cat herself could do when left alone with a packet of Dreamies.

Though TPE, sensibly, had chosen to retail the calendars on a bespoke website (and not the one they sold their train tickets through), not five minutes after the calendars had gone on sale, the website crashed. Thousands of people were clamouring for a calendar! They wanted a little bit of Felix magic every day of the coming year and this was the perfect way to secure it.

Jack Kempf, who worked in communications at head office, had taken responsibility for the calendars. He somehow managed to get the website back up – only for the first thousand calendars he had printed to sell out instantly. He organised a second printing, but again the website crashed – and, in the end, TPE had to get a whole new server just to manage the demand! Within eighteen hours, every single calendar had gone.

In less than a day, Felix had raised a staggering £18,000 for the Samaritans. It made a huge difference to the charity. The Huddersfield Samaritans office was located down a dark, quiet street. With the counselling service being run 24/7, volunteers sometimes felt unsafe arriving or leaving in the middle of the night. Thanks to Felix, they were able to add new lighting and CCTV to help with security, so that the people giving up their time to help others could feel protected.

There was also enough money to change the signage on the building, which had previously been so old that it hadn't even had the phone number on it – quite an important thing for the Samaritans to promote. Finally, Felix's fans had given so generously that the charity was also able to refurbish its waiting room. It meant that people who came to them in person had a warm, safe and clean space to wait until a counsellor became available. It made a real difference to people's lives. And it was all thanks to Felix. What a special cat she was.

One little girl in particular was about to discover that for herself. Towards the tail end of 2016, just before Christmas, Eva came through the station one day with her mum, Helen. Eva had blonde hair with a curl to it and enormous big blue eyes, which were framed by huge pink glasses. She was dressed in a deep-blue coat that was covered in stars. Judging by the irrepressible energy she had, which bubbled within her like the burble of a brook in a summer meadow, she was something of a star herself.

'Look, Mummy, look!' she called as she and Helen entered the station to catch a train. They came through Huddersfield station regularly – once or twice a week – on their way to visit Helen's parents in Shepley. But on all their previous visits, three-year-old Eva had never before noticed the exciting thing she was now pointing at.

Helen's eyes followed her little girl's finger . . . and then she started giggling too. Eva had spotted the station's cat flap, with its friendly-looking cartoon cat and those five letters spelling out 'Felix'.

'Who's Felix, Mummy?' Eva asked eagerly, once Helen had told her what the letters said.

'Felix is the station's cat,' Helen explained. She had heard that Huddersfield had one, though she had never seen her.

Eva's little mouth circled to an 'o' of wonder. The idea that there was a railway cat was so marvellous that she was momentarily struck dumb – but it lasted only a beat before she started excitedly asking questions. 'How come the station has a cat, Mummy? Does she go on the trains like us? Do you think she goes exploring? How *brilliant* is it that she's got her own way through to get on the trains, Mummy? Do you think she is having an adventure *right now*?'

Eva's questions lasted all the way through the gateline, on to the train to Shepley and all the way to Grandma's house. Helen, quickly researching online to find the answers to her little girl's barrage of questions, soon found Felix's Facebook page. She excitedly showed it to Eva. After that, every day, they looked online to see what Felix was up to. Doing so soon became the highlight of their day.

Eva was a very imaginative little girl. In her mind, Felix had more adventures than even the Facebook page showed. She had a fairy tale in her head that the station cat went on escapades all across the country, every day leaping on to a different train and going off to see the world. (In fact, since arriving at Huddersfield as a kitten on the Penistone line, Felix had never once stepped foot on a service.) Eva's passion was art and it wasn't long before she was regularly drawing pictures of a fluffy black-and-white cat called Felix. She would stick her artworks up on the fridge when she was done and then chatter away to her brand-new friend.

Helen encouraged her to paint Felix as much as she could. It was good for Eva – but not only because it's good for all children to be artistic and express themselves. It was good for Eva in particular because Eva needed all the help she could get to try to improve her poor eyesight. When she drew or painted or crafted, as she loved to, she had to use her failing vision, and Helen hoped that her sketching might just strengthen it, as the doctors said it might.

It had been the year before, when Eva was only two, that they'd first identified a problem. It was Helen's dad, Grandad Peter, who had realised that their beloved girl's left eye was slowly turning inwards. They'd taken her to the opticians, who'd quickly realised her vision was poor in both eyes, and glasses had been prescribed. The first time Eva put them on, she'd exclaimed in delight, 'Mummy! Wow! *I can see!*' It broke Helen's heart to think about how Eva must have struggled before then.

But the glasses were failing to rectify the sight in her very bad, turning-in left eye. Recently, the eye specialists at the hospital had said that Eva must now wear an eye-patch for four hours a day at home, over her good eye, to try to strengthen the sight in the bad. Helen and Eva had picked out a pretty fabric patch – pink with white hearts – which went over her head and glasses. Now, when Eva sat at the kitchen table at home and drew her pictures of Felix, she always did it with her patch on, try-ing to focus through her bad eye as she brought her vision of Felix to the page.

'Mummy, do you think we can meet Felix one day?' Eva asked breathlessly the December they'd first discov-ered her.

'Well, we can try,' Helen told her brightly.

So they had gone to the station, but there had been no sign of Felix. When they asked the platform staff for help, they were simply told that she wasn't about.

Eva's shoulders had slumped with sadness.

'We can try again,' Helen told her.

But, dejected, Eva had gone home disappointed. And perhaps she looked at the night sky that winter, that sky that matched her starry coat, and sent a wish to meet Felix winding upwards. Perhaps it soared to the sky and lodged in a cloud . . . but there it stayed.

It wasn't yet time for that Christmas wish to come true.

7. Clever Cat

'Here we are, sweetheart,' said Jean Randall to Felix on Christmas Eve 2016. 'Welcome back! Welcome *home*.'

Felix gingerly stepped out of the carry case into Jean's kitchen and had a good old sniff at the strange air of a domestic setting. Huddersfield station is staffed 24/7 – but only 363 days of the year; it always shuts on Christmas Day and Boxing Day. Of course, the beloved railway cat was never going to be left alone in the dark and cold of the deserted station. So, when the festivities rolled around each year, Felix got to go on her holidays too, staying with a member of the team who had volunteered to take her home. Jean, who worked in the booking office, was this year lucky to be welcoming Felix for the third time.

The cat certainly seemed pretty comfortable as she had a good nosy about the downstairs of Jean's cosy cottage, which had been built in 1802. There were two rooms on the ground floor for the holiday-happy cat to prowl about: a long kitchen-diner and the living room, which had shiny wooden floorboards and a striking stone fireplace. Two years before, Felix had caused chaos when she'd tried to get up the chimney – Jean had nearly had a heart attack, having to grab the cat's hind legs to prevent her from getting away – but this year Jean was steps ahead. Forewarned is forearmed and all that! Even before bringing Felix home, she had made sure to stuff the chimney with an old pillow wrapped in a black cotton blouse, wedging it in tightly to make sure there were no gaps.

Felix, however, seemed to remember where she was — for as soon as she was let out of her box, she swiftly left the kitchen and headed straight for the living room, the scene of her erstwhile escape act. She proceeded to sit slap bang in front of the fireplace, looking up thoughtfully.

'Ha!' cried Jean triumphantly. 'I've got you this time, Felix. You've no chance.'

At her words, Felix cast a considered look back over her fluffy black shoulder. After a beat, during which her green eyes seemed to flash somewhat mischievously, she turned back to the fireplace and stood up decisively. As Jean watched, Felix tentatively put her paw on the hearth . . .

Yet she soon seemed to realise, from the distinct lack of a draught coming down the chimney, that her adventures in that direction had been strictly curtailed this time.

'We are not going through all that again!' Jean announced firmly. And, after that, Felix paid the fireplace no further attention.

She was far more interested in the French windows in the living room, which looked out on to Jean's garden. She prowled over to them and looked out curiously. Jean didn't have any cats of her own, which is why she could host Felix, but her garden was a beloved location for the local cats to wander through. Sure enough, only a few seconds after Felix had taken up her position by the window, a confident tabby cat wandered into view.

Felix's head swivelled to see him. She leaned forward eagerly, eyes fixed firmly upon this newcomer. The tabby looked straight back somewhat cockily. He was a chubby thing, his weight and handsomely groomed pelt showcasing that somebody somewhere *really* loved him, and he gazed at Felix with all the arrogance of a cat who knows his own worth, and is free to roam wherever he likes outside. (The latter was a luxury that Felix was prohibited from enjoying while staying at Jean's – the railway worker daren't risk losing the famous Felix!)

This was not the first time Felix had encountered her own kind. She'd even had a (celibate) romance once, going off regularly with a feral stray who'd hung about the station waiting for her, courting her with mice he'd killed. (Angie Hunte had not approved of the love affair; she'd thought he was too 'rough' for her baby.) But the feral black cat had not been seen for a good few years now.

More recently, Angie had seen Felix interacting with a sleek white cat, who would wait for her by the disused train carriage on platform two. Unlike her more brazen former boyfriend, who used to come right up to the office door to court Felix, the short-haired pale cat seemed to have better manners and never imposed himself in such a way. He was a clean, well-groomed pussy who seemed rather reserved. Angie had never seen Felix go off with him as such, but every now and then the two cats would both sit by the disused carriage and gaze at one another coolly, like two teenagers early on in the night at a school disco who are both too scared to cross the dancefloor and confess their love. Perhaps a romance would blossom between them one day, but it was a little too early to tell.

Romance was definitely not on the cards that Christmas Eve at Jean's house, as Felix glared at the fat tabby cat through the French windows. It was more of a stand-off. The tabby, however, ultimately had the upper paw, being free to come and go as he pleased, while Felix was trapped behind glass. In the end, it was the tabby who triumphantly declared the stand-off over. He sauntered smugly on, the sassy wiggle of his ample backside seeming to sneer at Felix as he went.

He returned a few times before it got dark that day, appearing to enjoy taunting her. Nor was he the only visitor to the garden. Felix watched them all come. It was almost as though she had set up a post there by the windows: a diligent lookout set to defend Jean's home. She observed not only the returning tabby, but another three cats as well: an all-black moggy, a piebald short-haired and a lean tortoiseshell, who seemed to show off by demonstrating her skills for catching birds. Felix gazed impassively at them all, unable to join in the fun.

Watching her, Jean couldn't help but feel pity. She went off to set up a little display for Felix on her dining-room table: all the presents she would get to open the following day.

Well, 'little' may not be an accurate description, as Felix's fans had been incredibly generous; the cat had been sent enough gifts to fill a huge Christmas gift bag. In fact, there had been even more presents – but there were only so many toys and treats that Felix could play with or eat in one lifetime. Therefore Felix's lady-in-waiting, Angela Dunn, had arranged for the extra presents to be passed along to a local cats' charity, so that cats less fortunate than Felix would also receive a gift that Christmas.

Hearing the intriguing rustling sound of gift-wrapped

packages, Felix soon came trotting over to investigate. She leapt up on to the bare wood table to have a nosy round. The gift bag was a close-up illustration of Father Christmas's belly – of the buttons and the belt round his middle, which were straining from his girth. Jean allowed Felix to have a happy little sniff at the tantalising scents emanating from the gift bag – much as an indulgent mother might let an excited child shake the boxes under the tree – but eventually she encouraged the cat to move on.

'Now, now,' she scolded lightly. 'No more of that. You're not allowed to have them till tomorrow.'

Jean was really looking forward to a nice, chilled Christmas with Felix: just the two of them hanging out together on the festive day. Jean was an avid reader, currently right in the middle of devouring *How Green Was My Valley* by Richard Llewellyn, and she was anticipating cosying up on the settee with Felix for hours on end as she turned the pages and listened to the cat's contented purring.

Before they settled in for the night that Christmas Eve, Jean outlined to Felix one last house rule. She was about to go upstairs to get changed – and she didn't want Felix to follow her. As she tried to sneak out of the living room, Felix came charging towards her, wanting to come too.

'No, Felix,' Jean said, apologetically.

Jean kept a tall glass vase on her stairs and had a bright white duvet in her bedroom, and neither seemed likely to survive long with a black-haired station cat on the loose. Gently, she eased out of the room, managing to shut the glass-paned door with Felix on the other side of it. The glass in the door was clear, so she could still see Felix, who looked back at her with a mournful expression.

'Stay here,' Jean said. 'I'll be right back, I promise.'

When she returned a short while later, Felix was still sat waiting for her behind the glass, like a convict in prison on visiting day. Jean felt bad, but she knew it was for the best. She carefully opened the door and crept inside. Felix seemed not to have any hard feelings though, for as she took out her book and sat down on her sofa, Felix leapt up on to her knee and climbed over her shoulder to the back of the settee. There, she spread herself out, all along the back of it, looking like a discarded stole in a film starlet's dressing room. Calm and content, it was a wonderful way to spend Christmas Eve night. And tomorrow, Jean knew, would be more of the same.

Ding-dong!

Jean and Felix looked at each other in surprise. Though some of Jean's family were due to pop by later, it was 9 a.m. on Christmas morning and she wasn't expecting any guests yet.

'Who's that at this time?' she asked Felix in confusion, as she went to answer the door.

'Hiya!' exclaimed an old friend cheerily on the doorstep. 'We just thought we'd pop by to say hello!'

She stepped swiftly inside, ushering her grown-up daughter with her, whom Jean hadn't seen for many years. Once inside, the two of them looked around curiously, her friend immediately clocking that the living-room door was shut, which was unusual. It meant only one thing, much as it does when the Queen of England's Royal Standard flag is flown at Buckingham Palace: Queen Felix was in residence.

'Oh!' her friend said mock-innocently, as though only just remembering. 'You've got Felix this Christmas, haven't you?'

'I have,' said Jean with wry amusement. She was under no illusion that they had come to see her – the station cat was clearly the main attraction. 'Would you like to meet her?'

'Oh yes please!' both women chorused happily, clapping their hands together with joy. So Jean introduced them. They had their cuddle and then – after only another five minutes of chatting – they swiftly took their leave.

Not half an hour after their departure, the doorbell rang again. Once more, Jean heaved herself off the sofa and went to answer the door.

'Happy Christmas!' cried a young man on the doorstep. 'I haven't seen you for ages, Jean!' There was a beat. The railway worker waited patiently, knowing all too well what was coming. 'Am I right in remembering that you have Felix this year . . .?'

'I do,' said Jean, opening the door wide and shaking her head with resigned acceptance of her lowly position in her own household. 'Come on in, you.'

So he too entered and had a Christmas selfie with the station cat before making his way off for lunch with his family.

Not half an hour later, the doorbell rang once more.

'Surprise!' chorused some old family friends. 'We were just driving past and we thought we'd dash in to see you . . .'

Jean replied drily, 'She's in the living room.'

Nor was that the last of them. All morning, Jean was up and down like a yo-yo. She'd never had so many guests on Christmas Day. So much for her quiet Christmas! She took to calling out, 'Felix, come here! Somebody has come to see you,' as each visitor arrived. Though the guests were genuine friends, very often they'd be followed by someone that Jean had never met before. 'I've brought so-and-so with me,' her friend would say, rather breezily. 'She's such a huge Felix fan. I hope you don't mind . . .?'

And Jean didn't – for she knew first-hand what a very special cat Felix was.

Felix seemed to relish the attention. It was helpful that the guests had unknowingly staggered their arrival, for Felix sometimes struggled to meet big groups all at once, but, as first one friend and then another stopped by, Felix was quite happy to meet these individuals one-on-one. In fact, she had a whale of a time. She looked much more like a star at a red-carpet film premiere than a cat at Christmastime, as the cameras snapped and her fans fawned dreamily over her.

Sometimes, however, Felix looked at her visitors lazily, choosing not to comprehend their requests for a more dynamic shot. In such instances, Jean would intervene.

'Let me try this,' she'd say brightly. She picked up one of the toys from Felix's Christmas gifts – a long wooden stick with a hot-pink feather on the end – and energetically waved it in front of Felix's black-velvet nose.

Well, *that* always got the railway cat moving, like a train pulling swiftly out of the station.

Swipe! Felix's paw stretched out and reached for it.

Pounce! She was up on her feet and dancing like a boxer in the ring.

Grab! It will be mine!

Jean could entertain her for hours with it, as her friends (and *their* friends) snapped away with their smartphones, taking lots of shots of the station cat in action.

By lunchtime, there was a lull in visitors – enough for Felix finally to be formally given her gift bag of presents. Jean knew what a clever cat Felix was, and that she didn't need any help opening them. Felix was five – she'd been given plenty of gifts over the years, so she knew all about how to unwrap them. Jean fetched the gift bag from the dining-room table and placed it on the floor for Felix.

Wiggle wiggle wiggle went the cat's whiskers, as she investigated the gift bag thoroughly. *Sniff sniff sniff* went her nose. She could smell that there were Christmas treats in there . . . And, with a cat like Felix, once she had identified that a treat was in the vicinity, there was literally no stopping her. Not thirty seconds after Jean had put the bag on the floor, Felix had dived upon it to make it tumble to its side; and not thirty seconds after *that*, she was head-first inside Santa's big belly. She was in her element then, pulling out package after package, tearing off the wrapping paper with her sharp white teeth and revealing just what a good kitty cat she'd been all year. As well as the treats, there were catnip pillows and mechanical mice, and yet more sticks with feathers on the end. Though the treats, understandably, garnered most of her attention at the beginning, later on she singled out a yellow felt mouse that she happily played with all afternoon.

Eventually, darkness fell beyond the French windows. 'We can chill out now, Felix,' Jean announced. 'Surely nobody else is going to come round now!'

In fact, they did have one more visitor after sunset, the final fan in a very busy day, but after they had left Jean felt it was safe to batten down the hatches and truly relax in her favourite pink dressing gown. Wanting to wash away the day first, she went upstairs to have a quick shower before changing. She went on to autopilot as she climbed the stairs, her brain already turning back to Llewellyn's classic book and the convoluted lives of its characters. *What is going to happen next?* she wondered. *Who will live and who will die? What secrets might be revealed next?*

Not until she started to descend the stairs, wrapped up in her cosy pink dressing gown and with herself rather pink from the hot shower too, did Jean suddenly remember that she hadn't closed the door. *Oh no*, she thought, her heart beginning to pound. *Just what mischief will that cat have got up to now . . .?*

First one step, then the next; slowly, she walked down her stairs. She imagined all manner of chaos – the glass vase knocked over, stolen food . . . Or might Felix have even hidden herself away upstairs somewhere, so that Jean would have to spend the rest of the night hunting for her? Felix was known to be a fan of hide-and-seek at the station and was really rather good at it. *Oh dear God*, Jean thought with increasing panic, *what if I can't find her . . .?*

But as Jean rounded the corner of the stairs she saw there was no need to worry at all. Though the glass-paned door was wide open – just as she had left it – Felix sat in the exact same spot she would have done if it had been closed. It was as if there was an invisible line marked on the threshold of the living room and Felix had not crossed it. Knowing the rules – knowing that

Jean had said she could not come upstairs – Felix had listened and obeyed.

Well, *that* was a turn-up for the books! Jean felt her heart melt to see her sitting there so obedient and mature. The rampaging kitten she had once nurtured – and chastised – at the station was long gone. It was almost as if Felix had sat and passed a test; in her knowledge of the rules and decision to abide by them, it really showed that she was out of her kitten phase and undeniably an adult.

There was something a little sad in that moment for Jean, to know that Felix's childhood – even her adolescence – was now well and truly over. But mostly she just felt proud. 'You clever cat, Felix,' she told her warmly. 'What a very good girl you are.'

There was a final twist in the tale. After an evening spent reading on the sofa, Jean gave a yawn and decided to retire to bed. She went round turning off the lights and locking up the house, ready to head upstairs and slip beneath her snow-white duvet.

She was very nearly done in her preparations; all she had left to do was to shut Felix in. At the living-room door, she paused for a second, looking down at the lovely little black-and-white cat. Felix had been following her around like a shadow, but as they'd reached the threshold she'd stopped patiently in the doorway, knowing that she could not pass.

Felix looked at Jean. She blinked those big green eyes and Jean felt something dislodge inside her. 'I was *so* good earlier,' those eyes seemed to say, so *very* persuasively. 'Don't you think I deserve a reward . . .?'

Jean wavered only one moment more. 'Oh, come on then,' she said indulgently. 'Come on upstairs with me, Felix.'

The cat didn't need telling twice. Formally given the green light, she shot up those stairs faster than Usain Bolt. And the station cat went to sleep that night not in a cat basket or on a cat blanket downstairs, but curled up with Jean in her cosy bed . . . atop the finest white linen money could buy.

She really was a *very* clever cat.

8. All Change

Come the new year, Felix the railway cat was back to work with a vengeance. On New Year's Day 2017, she trotted along the platforms with an easy stride, knowing the station and its rhythms like the back of her paw. Here came the passenger services roaring into the station, making not a few hungover patrons clutch their heads and wince with pain. Here came the tum-tee-tum trundling noise of suitcases, as festive revellers retraced their steps and found themselves homeward bound after their Christmas holidays visiting far-flung family. Here came the customer-information point, with the lost-property office just across the way, where Felix was expecting to put in a shared shift with Angela Dunn.

But here Felix came unstuck. Although it was mid-morning, time enough for both serving hatches to be open, instead there was a blue blind pulled down across the customer-information point, while the stable door of the lost-property office was firmly shut. Deterred, Felix sat back on her haunches, her furrowed fluffy eyebrows indicating that she was pretty perplexed.

Unbeknownst to Felix, a wave of modernisation had swept across Huddersfield station that new year, just as the wintry weather was sweeping through the Yorkshire countryside beyond, and these familiar landmarks, some of Felix's favourites, had been caught up in a raft of changes. Recently, it had been decided that a fully auto-mated announcing system would be used at the station from 1 January 2017, so the announcer's office – which had been attached to the customer-information point – was now closed. With no one working in the room beyond the window any more, the serving hatch imme-diately became redundant too because there was no one there to staff it. In time, the white sign that had once guided passengers into the lobby was taken down to avoid confusing people. Instead, a simple sign declaring 'Bicycle Park' pointed to the silver racks that at least, from Felix's perspective, had not changed at all.

In lost property, too, the old system was discarded, and Angela went to work in the booking office. Physic-ally, the lost items were now kept in the Hub, the array of offices above the station concourse, which meant they were behind a security-coded door and up two flights of stairs. For Felix and Angela, it was the end of an era.

That new year, Angela Dunn trudged into work with a very heavy heart. She had loved working full-time in the lost-property office, reuniting worried passengers with their treasured possessions. It was a shock to the system to be returning to shift work in the booking office and she was apprehensive about it.

Nor had it been a particularly happy festive season in the Dunn household. Back in 2015, Angela and her husband of thirty-one years had decided to call it a day, and Angela was still figuring out the brave and sometimes blighted world of being single and divorced in her fifties, after more than three decades as part of a pair. Though it had been a rea-sonably amicable split – she and her husband had not even argued once – it was nevertheless tough getting used to being on her own, especially at Christmas. This year, she hadn't even bothered putting up any decorations. And whereas once upon a time she had catered for twelve for Christmas dinner, year in and year out, this year she'd served herself beans on toast. There just didn't seem any point in it all, not when you were on your own.

The first week of 2017 – the first week of her new routine – was really hard-going for Angela, and for Felix too. But they found they helped each other through the changes. Almost as if Felix knew that Angela needed her, she would hang out on the platform or by the bike racks – even, sometimes, in the car park itself – waiting for her beloved colleague to arrive for work. It meant that Felix was the first colleague Angela saw every morning and it made her day. Felix would come over to say hello the moment she appeared, purring softly with pleasure. And then the two of them would walk together into the back office, where Angela would put her things in the ladies' locker room, now ready to face a day of serving customers. Despite the hardness of her life changing, and the sometimes awful feeling of having to get up at 4 a.m. for her new shifts, she found she felt much brighter about it all than she'd ever hoped she might – and it was all due to Felix's considerate attentions.

It certainly was all change at the station that January. As well as the modifications to the announcer's office and lost property, Felix found that Sara from the booking office was now out working on the platforms with her best friend Karl.

Sara was a long-time friend of Felix, having worked at the station since December 2014. In fact, they were almost relatives, as Sara's uncle was Chris Briscoe, whose cats Lexi and Gizmo were Felix's parents. The railway was something of a family business, as Sara's mum, step-dad, aunt and uncle all worked in the industry. Following a couple of years after school of working for a printing company, Sara had followed her family into the business too. Now twenty-three, she found she loved it, for every day was different.

Of course, having regular cuddles with Felix was an additional perk. Sara found that if she took a seat on the single chair in the ladies' locker room for five minutes before her shift started, Felix would often come and sit up on her knee. When she was in the mood, Felix could have a right good cuddle. Sara really liked that; she really liked Felix. The diva's temperament wasn't to everyone's taste, but Sara admired her independent spirit.

Now, as Sara took up her new role out on the platforms, she found that she and Karl grew even closer, as they were paired up on shifts most of the time. Karl was a really funny bloke, which made their shifts together fly by. He could tell instantly if ever she was sad and would cheer her up straight away with a big brotherly hug, teasing her affectionately about being a 'unicorn princess'. He had a southern accent, whereas Sara had a thick Barnsley burr, and they would tease each other mercilessly about the difference between their voices. Karl had a lovely girlfriend he was head over heels in love with, and Sara loved to hear him talk about her. She was currently single, but hoped one day to find the right man; Karl was always on the lookout for a bloke who was good enough for his best friend.

While they waited for him to appear, Karl and Sara and lots of the other 'young 'uns' at the station regularly enjoyed nights out together. With the railway feeling like a family, it was only natural that many of the younger staff socialised. They all got on really well and it was easy as anything for one of them to suggest a drink after work . . . then before they knew it one drink had turned into five and they'd ended up at Maverick's in town, dancing to cheesy eighties music until 4 a.m.

Among the 'young 'uns' on these nights out was Chris Bamford, a black-bearded lad, who was another Felix favourite. He had become particularly close to the cat in the past year as he'd helped Felix adjust to her rise to fame, often volunteering to assist with her media appearances. She used to follow him around the station, sometimes even into the car park for an inspection, and as she did so she upped the entertainment value of the outing by swatting playfully at the laces on his steel-capped boots. Brazen as anything, she would bat constantly at them with her paw as they bounced along in time with Chris's strong and steady footsteps.

'Felix, be careful!' he would admonish her, fearful that he might just step on the station cat by accident as she dangerously darted in between his feet, her eyes fixed firmly on the teasing spectacle of those bouncing laces.

She would merely look up at him happily, her tail wagging back and forth like an eager puppy's.

Another 'young 'un' was Dan, who'd started at the

station just before Christmas as a new team leader. He was a good-humoured guy, aged twenty-seven, with a reddish-brown beard and dark eyes. Like many of the team at Huddersfield, he'd always wanted to work on the railway and had achieved his dream when he'd moved from a high-pressured job managing car parks at Manchester Airport to the team leader role at the station.

As a team leader, one of Dan's first priorities was meeting Felix, whose role at Huddersfield he had learned all about while doing research before his interview. He was a cat person himself and thought the idea of working at a place that had its own cat was pretty darn cool. But while he was excited about the idea of working with Felix, he worried whether the feeling would be mutual . . .

To Dan's relief, very quickly it became apparent that it was. From the moment he started working there, it was noticeable that Felix was not at all shy around the person who was now sat in the team leaders' chair. She came and lay in the way of Dan's work just as she did with all the others, and would harangue him for love and attention (and food) as she did with everyone else. It wasn't long before Dan became a favourite of Felix. He was more than happy to give her some love and this affectionate attitude towards her soon had Felix following him around and running head over paws to greet him. Sara, arriving for work one day, witnessed Felix darting in the direction of Dan with unbelievable keenness as soon as she heard him coming.

'That's right, your boyfriend's here now,' Sara teased the cat – not missing the irony that Felix seemed to be doing better in love than she was. *Sigh.*

Felix was not the only team member with whom Dan instantly hit it off. The Manchester-based man had been quite apprehensive about starting work at Huddersfield – especially in a management role when he'd never worked on the railway before – but he found that Karl in particular was an immediate friend who made him feel welcome. He soon made friends with Sara too; the two of them found they had a huge amount in common and an identical sense of humour. Soon, Dan found that there wasn't a day that went by when he wasn't sharing a good laugh with her. The three of them – Dan, Sara and Karl – made a close-knit trio who brought a new, youthful energy to the team.

As for Felix, she found that the new year brought yet more fans to her Facebook page – and on 8 January 2017 she reached a very special milestone. Felix the Huddersfield station cat now had 100,000 followers.

It was fitting, for Felix's fame and fortune were about to get bigger than ever before. For the past year, she had dominated the 'new' medium of social media. Yet Felix was about to prove that she was no flash-in-the-pan new-media star. Felix was on the cusp of bringing that same six-figure success to the oldest media of them all.

For Felix was about to become a literary superstar. Are you sitting comfortably? Then she'll begin . . .

9. Read All About It

Penguin Books. It is perhaps the most famous publisher in the world; its logo of a black-and-white bird on an orange oval background instantly equated with literary quality. Since launching in 1935, the publisher's authors have included such heavyweights as George Orwell, D. H. Lawrence and even the Brontë sisters themselves. In February 2017, the latest author to join its stable of world-class writers became none other than Felix the railway cat.

The news that Felix was to publish her life story (so far) was met with equal parts amusement, surprise and satisfaction among the team at Huddersfield station. She had become such a successful social-media celebrity that in many ways it seemed a natural next step; for Angie Hunte, for example, it was nothing less than Felix deserved. For others, however, the idea that a whole book could be written about a single cat — and that people might want to read it — was mind-boggling. Team leader Geoff, a dry-humoured, straight-talking chap who found the cat's celebrity astonishing, found that his eyes rolled so far back in his head that it was touch-and-go whether they might ever return.

Yet in her five short years on the planet, Felix had certainly had an awful lot of adventures. Her biography charted her journey from confused kitten to senior pest controller, describing how the little cat had learned her trade and learned to love life on the railway. At first rather scared of the trains and the far-flung platforms, she gradually built up her courage until the entire station became her playground. More than anything, the book revealed how this very special cat had captured people's hearts as she rose to international acclaim.

Angie and the team – who all contributed to the book by telling their stories of Felix – were delighted with the end result, believing it captured life at the station with plenty of Felix flair. But although the team enthusiastically embraced the idea of their pest controller becoming a published author, there was no guarantee that her fans would feel the same. Clicking 'like' for free on Facebook and checking Felix's posts was one thing, but to dedicate money and time to buying and reading her life story? Well, it was a different kind of commitment to the station cat.

Regardless of the end result, the team at TPE wanted to celebrate the extraordinary achievement of their colleague. On the eve of publication, not yet knowing how the book would go down, an intimate launch party was held in the first-class lounge at the station. It was a bit of a thank you for everyone who had been involved in Felix's rise to fame. The platform teams had never signed up to being Felix's personal secretaries but, since she had become famous, communicating with her fans had become all in a day's work. TPE wanted to say thank you for making all this possible.

Mark Allan, Felix's Facebook manager, was one of those who came along, mingling with new team leader Dan, station manager Andy Croughan, Jack Kempf from the communications team and Andrew McClements, a former team leader at Huddersfield and the person who had promoted Felix in the first place, launching her to worldwide fame. He now worked at TPE's head office, but he had never forgotten the cat who had helped to get him there.

Finger food from the Head of Steam was served to all the guests, along with flutes of paw-secco so that everyone could toast Felix's new book. In keeping with all literary launch parties, copies of the book were there too, with Felix looking terribly regal and smart on the cover. There were also speeches – many speeches – to celebrate the station cat. Perhaps the most significant of these came from Leo Goodwin, TPE's top dog, its illustrious managing director. (Felix, for once shying away from the spotlight, modestly made no comment on her own success that night.) Leo recorded a video for the team for this very special event.

'Hello everyone, I'm sorry I can't be with you all this evening,' he began on film, as though the mini-movie was the acceptance speech of an absent Oscar winner. (In truth, of course, an invite to the launch party was nearly as hot a ticket as that Hollywood ceremony.) 'I just wanted to say a few words and to thank you all for your hard work. No one expected Felix's rise to fame and I know it hasn't always been easy. Whether you've contributed to the book or press stories, posted for Felix on social media, or introduced Felix to one of her thousands of fans, you've all taken the time, often your own time, to help keep her story going.

'I think all of us have at times laughed off Felix's new

celebrity status, but she has become a very important part of TPE and we've been able to use the publicity to help a lot of people. She's now raised thousands of pounds for charity, and will continue to raise even more through this book for Prostate Cancer UK [all royalties from the book were being donated to this worthy cause].

'The social-media accounts also truly brighten people's days,' Leo went on, 'and hopefully by being our senior pest controller at Huddersfield she brightens yours, too. I hope you all enjoy this evening and thank you again for everything you have done to make this possible.'

The team were eagerly letting their hair down now that their shifts were over, so after a hearty round of applause it was bottoms up on the champagne flutes as they toasted Felix.

As any author soon discovers, writing a book and launching it is only the first step of the publication journey. The next day, Felix learned that lesson first-hand, as she was booked for a very important commitment. At 7.35 a.m., she was due to appear on *live* national TV (something she had never done before) as she kicked off the publicity campaign.

The whole idea of a live interview rather set the cat among the pigeons, so to speak, as Huddersfield was a busy working station. Its automated announcements broadcast regularly on its tannoy; its train services rolled in unstoppable as tides. The idea of Felix – feisty Felix! – participating in a live TV interview while all this hustle and bustle was going on was enough to give her PR team multiple migraines. And it wasn't as if they were starting with a low-profile programme to ease themselves into the campaign.

Oh no. Felix would be making her live TV debut on ITV's flagship breakfast programme, *Good Morning Britain*, which broadcast to a million viewers each morning.

The media appearance, therefore, was weeks in the planning. The studio in London was constantly on the phone. It had been decided that Andrew McClements – who had, after all, been responsible for Felix's rise to fame – would appear alongside Felix on national telly to help her promote her book, and he was given some top tips by the TV execs on their dos and don'ts for live interviews (these included: don't look at the camera directly and – whatever you do – *do not swear* . . .). The interview had to be scheduled promptly and the programme makers knew that they *had* to stick to that schedule, despite the likely disruptions of live TV, as a minute or two either side might see Felix's big moment rudely interrupted by a loud locomotive barrelling down the tracks. As for the unknown impact of the dozens of commuters who'd be out and about at that hour – and no doubt interested to see what was going on – well, everyone would just have to hope for the best . . .

Of course, at the centre of it all was Felix. The night before, as he checked on her in the back office, Andrew McClements apologised to her. For there would be no night shift for the station cat that evening, as was her usual routine: she had to be kept in overnight to ensure that she was ready to purr-mote her book to the nation the next day. Felix did not seem too impressed by the change in schedule, but in the end she gave in to the temptation of an indoor snooze.

On 24 February 2017, Felix woke to find that the

station was bustling with even more activity than it usually was on a busy working day. There were a few unfamiliar black-shirted workers scurrying about with boxes of books; these were staff from the local Huddersfield Waterstones, who had come in to sell books. There was also a large film crew lugging huge, heavy cameras and a funny-looking fluffy grey microphone, plus the suited TV presenter who'd be conducting the interview. Andrew was also there, but as he no longer worked at Huddersfield even his presence was now out of the ordinary. Felix blinked around her with her big green eyes, as if to suss out why there was such a commotion.

Andrew soon picked her up for her starring role on-screen. Though he and Felix didn't see each other much any more, his new job at HQ still required him to come to the Hub at Huddersfield fairly frequently and he always made a point of seeking Felix out for a friendly chat. Consequently, Felix had not forgotten him and now allowed him to lift her up without a squeak of protest. She soon settled down in his arms, lying horizontally in them and facing front out, so that the cameras would have a great shot of her. Though Andrew felt pretty petrified about the task that lay ahead, Felix seemed to take it all in her stride.

Walking out on to platform one, however, Felix started to tense up. Things were very different out there and the pest controller, used to patrolling her patch, sniffed warily. In front of her beloved bike racks was now a long table covered over with a cloth, on which the Waterstones team had stacked up several piles of books – all ready for a 'signing session' after the interview. Alongside it, colourful star-shaped helium balloons in red, gold and blue danced busily in the early-morning breeze, attracting many commuters, who came over to see what on earth was going on.

Also out on the platform, and waiting for them, was the brown-haired presenter with his fluffy grey mic. Andrew and Felix walked over for a quick chat before the show went live. He explained that he needed to film some establishing shots with them before the live interview – such as Andrew and Felix walking together down the platform – and that he also wanted to have a quick rehearsal of the interview before the cameras rolled for real. Andrew nodded, nerves growing.

Felix, on the other hand, lay comfortably in Andrew's arms, her tail flicking thoughtfully and her keen green eyes drinking everything in. In particular, she was fascinated by the fluffy mic that the presenter held tightly. In some ways, given its luscious thick grey pelt, it looked rather like a moggy itself – albeit, disturbingly, one without any features. This meant it couldn't stare back at Felix, and the station cat was intrigued by that. It seemed to give her the upper paw. She watched it with the same undivided attention that she had once given to the fat tabby cat at Jean's – and she was determined not to be outwitted again.

Andrew and the presenter continued to conduct their last-minute checks, having a 'dry run' of the interview before the real thing. Consequently, the fluffy microphone was soon thrust towards Andrew and Felix as the cameras recorded, but did not broadcast the exchange.

The presenter asked a question and Andrew opened his mouth to answer, his eyes fixed on the interviewer.

Felix, however, was not listening to her former colleague. Instead, she narrowed her eyes as the cat-like mic came swiftly towards her. It was an attack, in Felix's mind, an invasion of her space, and with a triumphant, gloating purr from the very back of her throat, she grabbed at it. As Andrew looked on in horror, she batted it briskly, first with one paw and then with the other, until she had pinned that expensive mic between her claws with determined efficiency. Even afterwards, she continued to crow about her catch with joyful pride – and the microphone, naturally, recorded every exultant purr. As the professional piece of kit had the same audio clarity that one might expect in a top-notch recording studio, she sounded rather as though she was an expert jazz crooner, singing sultrily about the one who *didn't* get away.

And that microphone truly didn't get away. Once he had got over the immediate shock, Andrew – and the presenter – chuckled heartily, but they quickly realised that Felix wasn't joking. As the presenter tried to pull his microphone away from Felix, she pulled back with all her might, digging in deeper with her super-strong claws. He pulled and she pulled, and she pulled and he pulled, in a terrific tug-of-war that Felix was absolutely determined to win. And she did . . . She held on so tightly that, in the end, she disconnected that microphone from its amp! The presenter was left holding the disconnected wire, while Felix took home the main prize of her fluffy foe. She looked as proud as punch.

Well, what a to-do! And although, eventually, Andrew successfully persuaded Felix and the mic to part ways, the incident couldn't help but pile on the pressure for the live broadcast. For what if Felix cut the sound when they were live to the nation? What would happen then?

Andrew's mouth felt dry as dust. Encased in his smart navy suit jacket, his shoulders tensed up, even as he held the cat. He cuddled Felix as tightly as he dared, stroking her to calm himself as much as her. It wasn't really helping . . .

The presenter turned towards him with focused intent, as the orange digits on the platform display boards moved inexorably onwards, bringing them ever closer to the appointed hour.

'We'll be live in just a moment,' he said.

Then the cameraman spoke up too, already putting his hand out behind the camera, his fingers silently counting down the seconds. 'Going live in five, four . . .' His fingers continued the countdown, even as Andrew heard the digits in his head. *I hope this works*, he thought desperately. *I really hope Felix behaves . . .*

Three, two, one.

A glowing red light on the camera switched ON.

10. A Sprinkling of Stardust

'Felix has become an internet sensation after starting work at Huddersfield train station!' Kate Garraway announced on the sofa in London. 'Nick Dixon got to meet her . . .'

And with that short and sweet introduction, they were suddenly live on air from Huddersfield station to the nation.

'Andrew, what's the appeal of Felix?' the presenter pressed him.

Andrew began to answer, speaking as clearly as he could. 'I just think she is a working cat . . . She keeps everyone at Huddersfield happy – the staff, the colleagues, everyone at TransPennine Express . . .'

As he spoke, he felt Felix begin to dig her claws into his arm, as though she was reminding him that he had to present her in the best possible light. *Ouch!* thought Andrew – but he couldn't let the pain show. He remembered all too well the mantra that the TV execs had drilled into him beforehand: *whatever you do, do not swear . . .* It was advice not easily followed when Felix chose to make her move!

The pressure of her sharp claws made him want to grimace, but he somehow followed Felix's not-so-subtle instructions, concluding, through his gritted teeth, 'She just brings a smile to everyone's face!'

With that, Andrew's part in the proceedings was

over. He and Felix stayed onscreen as Nick spoke next to a representative from Prostate Cancer UK. Andrew kept on stroking the station cat, but Felix did nothing to pull focus from the lady, who said what a difference she hoped the money raised would make. All royalties from the book would be going to support those men and their families who had been affected by this terrible disease, she said.

Throughout the entire segment, which was about four minutes long, Felix was as good as gold, sitting professionally in Andrew's arms until the broadcast had safely returned to London and the presenter told them that was a wrap. It was almost as if she knew how important this was and she waited patiently for the cameras to stop rolling, not even wriggling once to try to get away. After all the nerves and preparation, everything had run like clockwork.

It was the same with all the publicity Felix had to do — and she did *lots*. The glamourpuss graced the covers of *The Lady* magazine and *Big Issue North*, the latter to resounding success when 'her' edition of the magazine sold so well that it was reprinted no less than three times to keep up with demand. *Big Issue North* was launched in response to growing numbers of homeless people in the north of England; it still works today to give a helping hand to those in poverty, with its sellers earning fifty per cent of the cover price of every magazine they sell. So it was particularly special that Felix could help the homeless and poverty-stricken in this way, not least because homelessness often affects the railway network in particular, stations being one of the places the homeless can migrate towards as they provide a temporary shelter when all other avenues have closed. Mark Allan estimated that through that charity drive alone, Felix helped to raise around £12,500.

There was also lots of Felix publicity on TV and radio, the recordings of which Jack Kempf kept, as an official TPE record of everything Felix had done. By the end of her PR campaign, he had dozens of files in his special Felix folder.

It was brilliant for Felix to have secured so much PR – but the bane of the TPE IT manager's life! Jack kept getting emails from the IT department, which pleaded with ever-increasing desperation, '*Please* delete space in your drive!'

But while Felix's media files may have been clogging up Jack's computer, her hard work was getting the message out there about her book – and *how*.

The weekend after her book's first full week on sale, Mark Allan was flicking through the Sunday newspaper. His wife joined him happily, pleased that for once he wasn't glued to his phone updating Felix's Facebook page (she was fond of saying wryly, 'You spend more time with that cat than you do me!').

But it turned out not to be a Felix-free day, after all. For as Mark turned the pages of the 'Culture' section of *The Sunday Times*, he came across the national book bestseller lists, which chart the top-selling titles of the previous week.

Felix the Railway Cat was sitting pretty at number three. The senior pest controller was not only an author, but a bestselling one at that.

Mark's wife's jaw nearly hit the floor and she looked at her husband with pink-cheeked pride. 'Look, darling!' she exclaimed happily. 'It's in the *Sunday Times* bestsellers!'

She saw his efforts for Felix rather differently after that.

Many of Felix's fans were not content merely to read her book. They wanted an autographed copy. Andrew and Jack scratched their heads about how best they could help Felix to supply such a thing. She simply wasn't a paperwork kind of puss so it really needed some thought. Then Andrew hit upon a brilliant idea: perhaps they could get a mould of her paw and create an autograph stamp from that! Full of enthusiasm, he ordered the bespoke kit, which required Felix to press her paw on to a special piece of paper to create the mould, and headed straight to Huddersfield to secure her paw-tograph.

Well, it *was* a brilliant idea . . . but it turned out that Felix was more reclusive than Harper Lee. Though Andrew tried to persuade her to let him hold her front leg so he could press it to the paper, Felix gave him short shrift. He came away with a few new scratches . . . but no mould. Back to the drawing board.

In the end, Jack managed to order a special pawprint stamp for all the paw-tographs. Mark Allan had a few chuckles when he saw it, as it was super-sized, about as big as his palm. 'It was more like a lion was signing it than a cat!' he exclaimed, chuckling heartily. But, in fact, its size made it nice and clear for everyone to see it, and no one seemed to mind. Orders soon flooded in for copies that were 'signed by the author' and Felix found herself on the bestseller list for weeks. Waterstones in Huddersfield was soon bombarded with calls and emails from around the world as people clamoured to purchase one of their exclusive paw-printed editions. One unconfirmed rumour even had it that the book was the store's bestselling title since Harry Potter! Certainly, the book seemed to have a magical effect on Felix's fans – and that was something the team at Huddersfield station noticed straight away.

Prior to publication, there had been regular visitors to Huddersfield to meet Felix, but it was only one or two every now and again, perhaps a couple of times a week. Now Angela Dunn found that she was called to her lady-in-waiting duties two or three times *per shift*. The book had reached a whole new audience: people who had never even heard of Facebook, but who loved to read. The glorious image of Felix on the front of the book had captivated a new generation of hearts and minds; children fell in love with Felix through the book and only afterwards discovered that their parents could show them her social media too. Elderly ladies, meanwhile, spotted the book in their mail-order catalogues or at their local library and snapped it up, being big cat fans. The revelation to all that the book was non-fiction – that the cat was real and *could be visited in person* – soon brought swathes of visitors in a volume the team had never seen before. Felix had been famous before, but this was on another level.

And the team found that there was another difference: people were excited to meet *them* after reading all about them in the book. The team didn't even have to be at the station for it to happen. One day, not long after the book came out, Angie Hunte nipped into Tesco after work while still wearing her TPE uniform. As the checkout lady scanned her items, she greeted her cheerily and in a familiar manner. 'Hiya, Angie!'

'Oh, hello!' Angie replied, surprised; she was not sure why she was receiving such a personal greeting.

'I've read all about you!' the checkout lady enthused, giving her a wide, warm smile, eyes twinkling like stars.

Then strangers started stopping Angie in the street to chat about the cat.

'How's Felix, Angie?'

'She's grand, thanks,' Angie would reply – always friendly, no matter who it was who had waylaid her.

'My girlfriend's absolutely crazy on that book,' a fella might say. 'She'd love to meet the cat.'

'Well, come up and see her, then!' Angie would encourage him.

'Can we?'

'Of course!'

Angie felt as though Felix had cast a spell over them all, as though the station cat had somehow waved a magic wand with a flick of her padded paws – and in so doing covered Angie and the others with a little of her special stardust.

For Angie, though it was peculiar to be recognised so frequently, the real benefit was that Felix had encouraged people to see the softer side of the railway team. It was important because sadly it wasn't uncommon for railway staff to bear the brunt of customers' frustration if their journey was delayed; team members had been verbally abused, spat at and even assaulted. Felix's book reminded readers that the team were individuals too:

good people who were simply trying to do their best, and who were coping with their own struggles even as they helped customers.

One of Angie's struggles that had been mentioned in Felix's book was her grief when Billy Bolt had died. Angie found, however, that many readers now shared with her that they too had felt his loss when he'd passed on in the book; some of them had even cried. Though his absence was still mourned at the station, it was nice to know that he lived on through the book in a way. Angie always made a point of showing those visitors where Billy's memorial bench stood proudly on platform four, and they would all go over and read the gold plaque that honoured his memory, standing respectfully for a few minutes beside it, clearly thinking of him. It made Angie smile to think what Billy might have made of it all – of all these strangers mourning his death anew.

'Give over!' he would have said, she thought; and his gruff, no-nonsense voice rang as loudly in her head as if he had really been there. 'I don't understand what all the fuss is about!'

As for Felix, she found that the fuss over her was really quite extraordinary. If she was out on a patrol and a fan spotted her, all hell would break loose. That fan would run to her, exclaiming with glee, taking pictures and stroking her. And their excitement would cause all the other commuters on the platform to look around wildly.

'What's going on?' they would say, curiously.

Then *they'd* spot the cat, and her celebrity would precede her, making her immediately recognisable. In an instant their cameras would be in their hands and they'd all be calling to her.

As the news spread that the station cat was out and about, it was as though the sun was slowly emerging from behind a grey Yorkshire cloud, lighting up the faces of all those present. People's expressions literally changed from shadow to smile as they rushed to record their meeting with Queen Felix. Some curtseyed to her as they met; others became really chatty. A four-year-old girl in a purple padded coat and hot-pink trousers plonked herself happily next to Felix on the floor one afternoon and proceeded to tell her *all* about her brand-new shoes, which were pink and turquoise and covered with images of smiling cartoon cats. Others burst into tears upon meeting her, because she had grown to mean so much to them and they couldn't believe they were finally getting to stroke and cuddle this very special cat.

Though it must have been intimidating, Felix held court as though the dedicated attention and heartfelt emotion were nothing less than her due. Her tail would be straight up, proud and perfect, its little white tip acting like a tour guide's clipboard, held aloft to indicate that people should follow. She caused a commotion wherever she went: a saunter through the concourse via the booking office, for example, would see all the people in the queue sigh dreamily. So intent would they be on photographing Felix that they'd unwittingly lose their place in the queue and have to start their wait all over again. Yet any half-hearted complaint would soon fade to silence as they scrolled through their smartphone and caught sight again of their fluffy friend, now caught forever on film.

Out on the platforms, meanwhile, people would literally follow Felix as she strolled along the platform, snapping away. At such moments, she prowled along as though the platform was a catwalk at a fashion show and she had been headhunted to model the latest trends. From left to right, her bottom would wiggle gaily, while her white-capped paws padded with perfect timing so that those watching could capture the glory of her glamourpuss saunter. She was a proper little poser, in fact – holding still with professional poise as a man with purple headphones angled his phone to take her portrait, and moving again only once his work was complete.

As though conscious of the commotion she caused, however, Felix's favourite spot for a meet-and-greet remained the former customer-information point, which was tucked out of the way so she didn't hold up the station's business. It was Felix's happy place. From here, she could hear what was going on in the back office – the slam of doors, laughing voices and even the occasional decisive stamp of a stapler – yet also keep an eye and ear on the proceedings out on the platform. She liked to face into the wind, which would at times bend her white whiskers, enjoying the breeze blowing through her fur. It acted almost as a natural hairdryer, styling her for her next celebrity appearance.

But Felix wasn't always ready to meet her fans. So many came these days that it was inevitable that Felix, eventually, would run out of patience, something her fans didn't always understand. She might have willingly spent time posing, but after a while she would stalk off, her independent feline spirit summoning her away. Some fans, however, followed her, bent double as they walked, so that they could keep on stroking her. Others walked along backwards, snapping her like a pack of paparazzi.

One afternoon, a big group of excited lads surrounded her. They had loud voices that echoed around the station as they struggled to pull their posh camera kits out of their bags to snap the station cat. At their boisterous cries, Felix's green eyes widened in alarm.

Luckily, just at that moment, one of her colleagues happened to come along. He opened the door leading to the back office as he went through it and Felix, seizing her chance, darted swiftly after him. The door closed firmly behind them both.

'Bollocks,' brayed a young man harshly, as the cat disappeared from view.

For Angie Hunte, Angela Dunn and all the other team members, Felix's welfare had to come first. That was more important than ever, now that so many people were coming to meet her. They soon learned to 'read' Felix, and began to know whether she was in the mood for meeting fans or not. If she was having a doze in the ladies' locker room and some fans came calling – 'Is Felix playing out?' one little girl once asked – Angie Hunte would respectfully knock on the door before entering to see if Felix was free. Felix was still Angie's little girl, so she treated her with the same care and kindness that she would any child of hers who was being woken from a nap.

'Felix,' she would call softly, tapping gently on the door and opening it slowly so as not to cause alarm. 'There's somebody here to see you . . .'

Sometimes Felix was more than willing to make her fans' dreams come true and would happily come out to say hello. At other times, it was all too much, especially if she'd already been in demand that day. On such occasions, she would fix Angie with a strong, non-negotiable look in her green eyes that clearly said, 'You just try disturbing me, missus.' At such a time, even a single step towards her would provoke a guttural growl and Angie would know to back away and go out to break the bad news. The broken looks of disappointment were hard to bear, especially if they were children or had travelled a long way, but the team had to put Felix first.

Angie learned to interpret Felix's moods when she was out and about, too. If the cat had chosen to sit on one of the metal benches that were spaced along the platforms, she very much *wanted* attention and eagerly sought out strokes with insistent prods of her fluffy black head. If she was sat up at the erstwhile customer-information desk or curled up on the lobby's grey striped carpet, meanwhile, she was in an easy-come-easy-go mood, and would be pretty laid-back if anyone approached her. When she chose to sit at the bike racks, she normally wanted to be left alone. That was 'her' space and 'her' time, and she did not always look kindly on having it disturbed.

All manner of people came to see her at the station: men and women, old and young, locals and people on their travels. For team leader David Jackson, however, there was one visitor – or should I say four? – that he would never forget.

It happened on one of those early spring days, when you can feel the promise of warmer weather on its way.

David was out on the platforms that afternoon when he was approached rather officiously by a lady in a short-sleeved shirt. She carried two cotton tote bags, one over each shoulder, and had a manic energy to her, as though excitement was buzzing through her veins.

'I've come to see Felix!' she announced, straight to the point.

As with all the other members of the Huddersfield team, this was a statement that David had already heard several times this shift. He already knew that Felix was off on a patrol somewhere, so he apologetically broke the news. 'I'm sorry, but Felix is out and about and we don't know where she is.'

'But . . .' the woman began, as though she couldn't process that response. 'But I've brought my cats to see her!'

At this extraordinary statement, David looked closer at the two bags that were resting upon her shoulders. Sure enough, they were moving, as though each held a couple of animals . . .

'Er, how many cats do you have?' David asked, uncertainly.

'Four!' she said enthusiastically. 'Look, this little one looks just like Felix, so I had to bring him down!'

She thrust one of the bags towards David and, somewhat apprehensively, he peered inside. And there in the tote bag sat a little black-and-white cat, who did indeed bear a strong resemblance to Felix. His limbs were entwined with his neighbour's as they fought for space inside the bag; the second cat was white with tabby markings.

To David's astonishment, neither seemed at all perturbed to be travelling around in this fashion. They merely blinked lazily at him when he peered inside; this was clearly not their first adventure of being taken outside in such a way. Though he did not see inside the second bag, it was evident from the way it was moving that the other two cats must be entwined within it. They had travelled all the way to the station on the bus, the lady said.

'I really am very sorry,' David said again, once he'd recovered his equilibrium. 'But cats or no cats, Felix isn't here.'

Goodness only knew what she would have made of those particular feline fans!

11. Fun and Games

On 17 May 2017, Angela Dunn walked into work with a lovely lightness in her heart. Today was a very special day. Today was Felix's sixth birthday.

For days beforehand, gifts and cards had been arriving for the station cat from her many admirers. Angela's first job that day, as Felix's lady-in-waiting, was to gather all those gifts and open them up. If anyone had enclosed an SAE with a request for a response, it would be Angela who would 'help' Felix to 'write' a reply, just as the Queen of England's personal secretaries do. Angela planned to put up all the birthday cards in the booking office, where passengers would be able to see them.

After a lovely greeting with Felix, who had decided that her sixth birthday merited a day-long snooze, Angela turned her attention to the gifts. *Goodness me*, she thought, as she surveyed all the presents and unopened envelopes. *What a popular puss she is!* Undeterred, she gathered up a precarious armful of gifts and cards, and made her way along the back-office corridor towards the booking office, where she planned to open them all.

Just then, Geoff, the team leader, unexpectedly stepped out of the team leaders' room. Angela, her arms piled high with presents, only just managed to stop herself from running into him.

'I'm so sorry, Geoff!' she cried. 'I didn't see you there with all this stuff in my arms.'

'What *is* all that?' he enquired in his gruff voice.

'Well, Geoff, it's all Felix's birthday cards!' Angela exclaimed proudly. 'Will you just look at all these presents, Geoff? Isn't it nice for Felix to . . .?'

But Angela suddenly found her voice trailing off. Because although Geoff was known for being taciturn, the dark look that crossed his face at her words was quite something to behold.

'I am fed up,' he said crossly, 'of being upstaged by that bloody cat.'

Angela's brow creased in confusion. 'What on earth do you mean?' she asked. She couldn't think why he could be so cross. Geoff and Felix had a well-known love-hate relationship: Geoff would dramatically ban Felix from the office when he was on shift, for example, shouting at her to 'Get out!' But at his command, Felix would scamper away in delight, her movements playful, for this was a game she had played with Geoff of old. The cat seemed to enjoy the back-and-forth banter between them: he would shout and she would scamper. But she always came back for more. There was seemingly no banter in Geoff's complaints today, though.

'It's my birthday too!' he suddenly exclaimed, unexpectedly. 'That cat has stolen my birthday!'

Angela's lips formed a silent 'o'. Although the team at Huddersfield celebrated big staff birthdays – when team members turned thirty, or forty, or fifty, or any number with a zero at the end – Geoff had not had such a birthday since he'd started working there, and so the team had not known when it was.

'I had it first!' he went on, grumbling – and he was only half joking. 'Whose idea was it to make her birthday today? That's what I want to know! I want proof. I think it's rubbish, personally. I think they made up that bloody date. She has stolen my birthday: end of. That bloody cat . . .'

And with that Geoff banged out of the back-office door, still grumbling.

Oh dear, thought Angela. She felt terribly bad – even more so when she opened card after card for Felix and saw that there were none for Geoff. For all his words, too, Felix's birthday date was set in stone, because Chris Briscoe, her 'grandfather', knew exactly when his beloved cat Lexi had given birth to Felix. Geoff may have had it first, but he was going to have to learn to share . . .

Felix did not have a birthday party – but the younger contingent of the Huddersfield team were determined that fun and games were nonetheless on the agenda. That, to their minds, was one of the best things about having a station cat: the games you could play with her when you were on duty.

In true diva form, she was very selective about what she would deign to play. Team leader Dan had been a bit disappointed to discover that she wasn't a cat who was interested in *all* toys. She had discerning tastes. After he'd started working there, he had tried on occasion to throw a ball down the long back-office corridor to see if she might chase it, but it was very, very rare that she would.

She would usually look blankly at the moving ball as though it was utterly underwhelming, before looking wearily back at Dan as if to say, with cutting derision, 'What was *that*? What do you think I am, Dan, a *dog*?'

However much Felix might try to style it out, she hadn't always been that way. As a kitten, she had loved to chase her favourite brown bear up and down the corridor when it was thrown for her — but as Felix had matured, so too had her love of games. She was over the 'kid stuff' now. Dan and the others would have to mix it up if they really wanted to retain her attention.

And so they did. That spring, Dan schooled her in perhaps the nation's favourite game of all: football. Well, not football per se; in truth, it was more like goal-keeping training . . .

Dan discovered her talent between the posts entirely by accident. On a night shift one evening, he and Felix had both been on the concourse: Dan standing by the computer on the gateline, near the booking office, while Felix was at the opposite end, about thirty feet away, close to her cat flap. As had happened with Mark Allan and others before him, Dan found that he happened to have a packet of cat treats in his pocket (Felix had a funny way of making this a common feature of her favourites . . .). Though the team asked Felix's fans not to feed her, the staff were still allowed to hand out snacks every now and then. Having discovered the cat treats in his pocket, Dan thought he'd throw one for her.

'Felix!' he called, to get her attention.

Her head snapped round at once, eager to know what her friend wanted.

The moment she laid eyes on him, Dan released the treat towards Felix, sliding it across the tiled concourse floor at speed. Felix ran for it instantly, her eyes trained on the 'ball'. With a scattering of paws on the shiny surface, she scrabbled towards the flying treat, her paws outstretched heroically in a spectacular skid. And she nailed it: nothing was getting past her posts.

Oh, it *was* a sight to see! She could have been a goalkeeper for England, if the ball was made of Dreamies. Dan tried it again soon after; impressively, Felix still kept a clean sheet. They could never have played this game during the day – Felix would have ended up sliding under some businessman's briefcase and tripping him up – but when Dan worked the night shift he would occasionally put Felix through her paces, staging a penalty shootout session that she always, always won.

Nor were her tricks limited to just football that spring. One cloudy afternoon, Sara called out on the platform, 'Felix! Felix, catch!' The railway worker's long blonde hair cascaded over her shoulder as she looked down at the station cat.

In response, Felix balanced carefully on her hind legs and sat up to attention, like a begging dog at a circus show. She may not have been willing to chase balls down the corridor for Dan, but when treats – such as the one in Sara's outstretched hand – were involved, Felix was *always* game.

The cat kept her green eyes fixed firmly on the treat, as Sara continued to instruct her to catch. Milliseconds after Sara released the cat biscuit, Felix caught it nimbly between her two front paws, stopping the treat in its tracks as it descended. It seemed she had a future career not only on the football field, but also on the cricket green. With gratitude, Felix swiftly gobbled it down and looked up at Sara, hoping for more . . .

A short distance away from this scene stood Karl, Sara's colleague. Through smiling eyes, he observed not only the game but also his friend's affection for her feline colleague. Sara had so much love to give, he thought. As Felix successfully snatched a second treat, Karl and Sara shared a smile over Felix's head, like two siblings enjoying a well-worn joke.

Further down the platform, team leader Dan watched them too. He soon came over for a natter. He was a joker himself – albeit the cracker of bad 'Dad jokes', as Sara liked to tease him – and it wasn't long before the three of them were giggling away at something Felix had done. Dan bent down to stroke Felix and the cat curved her head lovingly into his hand.

Sara watched the two of them somewhat shyly, the last traces of her laugh still showing in her smile. She thought it was really, really sweet, the way Dan and Felix were together – whether they were cuddling or staging penalty shootouts on the concourse. Not all the blokes at the station were into the cat, but Dan wasn't ashamed to show how much he liked her. Through his affection-ate cuddles with the famous Felix, Sara could tell that he was a really loving and truly kind man. As if in agree-ment, Felix purred loudly as Dan rubbed firmly behind her ears.

Just then, the team leader's radio crackled into life. 'Base receiving,' he answered, standing up from Felix and walking off back down the platform to attend to his work, raising a hand in fond farewell to his two friends as he went.

Sara watched him go without saying anything. She was still watching when Karl came over to her side and not so subtly coughed.

'Nice bloke, isn't he?' he said knowingly.

Sara blushed. 'He's all right,' she said – knowing that she didn't need to say any more. Sara and Karl had no secrets.

Karl nudged her with his elbow. '"All right", eh?' he teased. 'Whatever you say, princess.'

That small seed in Sara's heart was not the only thing beginning to blossom at the station that spring. Felix's multi-platform media career was also sprouting new buds – as Mark Allan, who was always looking for ideas to pep up her Facebook posts, now began screening Felix's antics via Facebook Live.

He had wondered for a while what that button on Facebook labelled 'go live' did, and so he decided one morning at 6.30 a.m., as he was hanging out with Felix on the platform waiting for his train, to give it a try. What was the worst that could happen?

Famous last words. When Mark pressed 'go live', the first, alarming thing that occurred was that he saw his own face looking back at him. It turned out that his default camera setting on Facebook Live was for selfie mode! Rather than a beautiful pussycat filling the screen, being broadcast to hundreds all around the world, his own 'ugly mug' instead took centre stage! He did a rapid recoil and flipped it round, to where Felix was sitting patiently, ready for her close-up.

For that first video, he filmed her chasing after a treat – but despite the movie's simplicity, it went down really well. As it was live, fans could engage with her in real time, and Mark noticed that her international fans in particular – for whom it wasn't 6.30 a.m. – were especially enthusiastic. 'Greetings from Sydney!' came one message; 'Hello from Oregon!' was another; a third declared: 'Just going to bed in Utah. Goodnight, Felix!' A wave of hearts and likes swept across the screen, so fast that Mark couldn't keep up with them.

After that, he and Felix often 'went live' during Mark's early-morning commute. The whole experience was a learning curve for the mild-mannered commuter. During one 'broadcast', Mark's train arrived while he was still mid-shoot. Rushing to catch his service, he completely forgot to press 'stop', so that Felix's global fans were treated to a rather perplexing video of Mark's fellow passengers' legs. He had crowded on to the busy train and set off for Manchester, all without realising that he was still broadcasting live to over 400 of Felix's fans! On other occasion, he was busy filming a train coming in when Felix suddenly decided to jump down into the four foot – the railway-industry name for the deep man-made valley in which the train tracks run.

What do I do? thought Mark, panicking. Felix was perfectly safe, and he knew that she would get out of the way of the incoming train in plenty of time, but he was worried about the safety message her antics might send out. So, as soon as Felix had leapt into the abyss beyond the platform edge, he abruptly stopped recording.

Her fans, of course, had no clue as to what had

happened to their favourite feline friend. Had that train that they'd seen coming in actually made contact with the cat? Was that *why* Mark had ended the film – because of a terrible and tragic accident? It didn't bear thinking about it – but they had to know. Felix's Facebook page was soon flooded with messages from worried fans.

'I'm all right!' Mark wrote on her behalf, as soon as he realised their concerns. 'I just had to go and scare off some pigeons!'

The love that her Facebook fans felt for her was simply beautiful. Mark tried hard to make her Facebook page a place of warmth and goodwill and the fans responded in kind. People came for a laugh and a smile – and, increasingly, to chat with their fellow fans. It wasn't long before a sense of community sprang up between the 'Friends of the Floof' (FOTF). They had their own affectionate acronyms and words (flooftastic, pawsome, Huddersfloof station . . .), as well as regular traditions such as 'pub o'clock', 4 p.m. on a Friday, when Felix would officially declare that the weekend had begun. Too often these days the online world could be combative and full of rage, with trolls appearing more and more, but Felix's Facebook page was 'a beacon of friendly, cheerful, fun-filled light' – as one fan, Barbara Blackie, put it – and this loving community of fans soon found that friendship with Queen Felix opened up all sorts of other opportunities too. Across the ether, new friendships formed and hearts were healed, all thanks to Felix the cat.

Felix brightened up people's days. She entertained them. She made them smile – even at their very darkest times. People wrote to tell Felix that she had helped them through their breast cancer treatment, or made them feel that life was worth living again after they'd struggled with depression. 'I get very down sometimes,' one friend, Jennifer Adele Berry, confided in her, 'with depression, anxiety and panic attacks – but I don't tell people, really, as they always say things like, "Cheer up, it might never happen." I'm grateful to be here, but sometimes I just want to shut the door and close the curtains. Yet hearing your stories and seeing your beautiful face makes me smile from the bottom of my heart.'

Alyson Meadowcroft, meanwhile, found that when she was struggling desperately with having lost the man she loved after he tragically passed away, Felix was of incalculable help. 'On those days when I feel it most,' she said, 'Felix lifts me up.'

The sheer healing power that Felix had, even through a screen, was truly special. She touched hearts across the globe. She brought happiness to thousands. Some felt their involvement in her life, as they followed her trials and tribulations online, was like owning a cat by association; Felix had many international 'aunties'. Quite simply, they were her family, and she theirs.

And with such a depth of feeling focused on Felix, her fans kept on coming to meet the flooftastic one in person . . .

One afternoon in the summer of 2017, Angie Hunte's radio crackled into life.

'Base receiving,' she answered.

'Angie, there's somebody here to see Felix.'

'No problem,' she said. 'I'll be right out.'

Tap, tap, tap went Angie Hunte on the door of the

ladies' locker room. 'Felix . . .' she called gently. 'There is somebody here to see you . . .'

But when Angie tiptoed into the room, she saw that it was empty. Felix wasn't there.

Not to worry, thought Angie. *I'll check some of her other favourite spots.*

Felix did have a habit of getting all over; though she had a bed laid out for her in the shower room, she rarely used it, preferring to find another cosy spot for a catnap. Sometimes they found her in the old announcer's office, where the conductors still kept their in-trays; at other times, she would sneak into the former lost-property office, whose shelves were now lined with maintenance log books and blue-flashing mobile revenue devices set to charge.

'Felix!' Angie called now, as she stuck her head into the old lost-property office and looked for the cat. She was careful to scour the uppermost shelves of the room too, where a series of black conductor bags lay. On one occasion, when Angie had thought she'd lost Felix, the cat had, in fact, crept in there and curled up, way up high, on top of a conductor's bag on the third shelf up. So high had she been, and so well camouflaged – her black fur indistinguishable against the black bag – that Angie had not spotted her for ages. In the end, it had been Felix's ears that had given her away. As they always did, they had pricked up upon hearing Angie calling to her, and the slight movement of those pointy ears peeping above the bag had revealed to Angie exactly where her baby girl was hiding.

But while she had hidden there before, she was not there today.

'Dear, oh dear,' Angie muttered to herself. 'Where can she be?'

She went out on to the platform to greet the person who wanted to meet Felix. Today, it turned out to be a softly spoken lady in her sixties with short cropped hair. She hesitantly asked Angie if she might be able to see the cat.

'I've brought something for her,' she explained, holding out her hand. In it, two white ping-pong balls nestled. It turned out that the lady, who was from down south, had been attending a table tennis tournament at Huddersfield University – and she'd brought the balls that had been used in the contest for Felix to enjoy.

'Well, she's not in the back,' Angie told her. 'But let me see if I can find her for you out here.'

Angie had already checked the little lobby as she came out of the office, but she now scouted out the bike racks and the benches – to no avail. Felix did not seem to be around. Angie looked high and low, but could not find Felix. She asked Chris Bamford, who was out on duty, if he had seen the cat – but he had not.

'Felix!' Angie called with increasing desperation, but there was still no sign of the station cat.

Just then, an announcement interrupted proceedings – it was Andy Yarwood, a TPE colleague, who was working on platform one.

'Please stand clear of the incoming train,' he intoned in his deep voice on his portable microphone. Though the announcing system was now fully automated, for safety reasons the team still kept a portable capacity for making those announcements which required immediate delivery – and it was this system that Andy now used. 'Please keep back behind the yellow line,' he continued.

Angie scurried swiftly over to him as the scheduled train arrived and then departed, accompanied by the timid lady who so longed to meet the cat.

'Oh, Andy,' Angie exclaimed. 'This woman has come all the way from down south to meet Felix and I can't find her anywhere. Have *you* seen her?'

Andy was a well-built, characterful man in his fifties, with a cheery voice that always brightened up the station. When Angie asked him how he was of a morning, he would sometimes reply in his Lancashire drawl, 'Living the dream, Angie Hunte, I am living the dream . . .'

But, to her disappointment, she found he could not help this particular visitor live her dream today.

'I've not seen her, Angie,' he said, shrugging his shoulders helplessly.

Angie put her hands on her hips, wracking her brains. She'd seen the cat earlier that shift, so where could she be now? 'She can't be too far off . . .' Angie said.

Just then, her eyes fell on Andy's portable microphone, which hung round his neck on a black lanyard. It was a black tube, about six inches long, on which Andy could press a red button to speak to the whole station. An idea suddenly struck Angie – an idea that was a little bit crazy and a little bit kooky, but also an idea that *might just work*.

'Andy,' Angie said slowly, 'would you put out a staff announcement for Felix for me please?'

Andy looked at her askance, his big brow furrowed.

'You know,' Angie said with increasing enthusiasm,

as he looked rather lost, 'just put out a staff announcement: "Will Felix please contact the station supervisor?" Let's just see if she comes.'

Andy chuckled aloud, shaking his head at the silly idea. Nevertheless, he did as his boss had instructed. In his booming, jolly voice, he intoned into the small black tube, 'This is a staff announcement. Would Felix please contact the station supervisor?'

He, Angie and the lady all fell about laughing. But then, to everyone's surprise – including, it seemed, Felix's – a little black-and-white head suddenly came poking out from the bushes in Billy's garden on platform four!

Angie and Andy exchanged looks of complete surprise.

'I don't believe it . . .' Andy said, walking away down the platform, shaking his head. 'I do *not* believe it . . .'

Angie, meanwhile, was crowing with excitement. She waved her arms across the tracks at Felix with characteristic enthusiasm. 'Come over here, sweetheart!'

In a heartbeat, Felix dropped down on to the railway lines and trotted safely across, before leaping up from the four foot with expert skill. She looked nonchalant as she did so, as though answering a staff announcement was all in an ordinary day's work for the station cat.

The ping-pong lady looked from Angie to Felix in sheer admiration.

'If I hadn't seen that for myself, I would never have believed it!' the woman exclaimed in delight. 'She *responded* to a staff announcement! My oh my. She really *is* a very special cat.'

12. Fears for Felix

The summer of 2017 proved a busy one for the team at Huddersfield. Though the school holidays were a while off yet, the weekends were hectic as daytrippers made the most of the sunshine. The team found that the swell of passengers came in waves – and they all had favourite and not-so-favourite times as their customers sought out entertainment on the railway lines that summer. There was nothing lovelier, for example, than seeing an excited family heading for a day out at the seaside or to see men and women dressed up for a day out at the races. But all team members – Felix included – detested those Friday nights when the Real Ale Trail came to town.

The Real Ale Trail is a drinkers' voyage through the best real ale pubs in the region, all of which are located a stone's throw from a railway station, so that revellers can hop on and off trains while imbibing their favourite beverages all night long. It's rather like a traditional pub crawl on steroids. And though many fun-seekers pursued their passion for real ales with grace and decorum, others were not *quite* as considerate of their fellow passengers and more than a few ended up steaming drunk. (A poster of guidelines for the trail that hung at the station tellingly included the obvious advice: 'Use the pub toilets, not the platform!') Team leader Dan took to nicknaming the 'witching hour' when these pubs would kick out their worse-for-wear revellers as 'idiot o'clock'. It wasn't unusual for screaming drunks to holler at each other across St George's Square on such an evening, or to sprawl across the front steps of the station with pizza boxes and bottles of beer, before continuing their anti-social debauchery within the station, as they sought to get home via a late-night train. Felix, sensibly, always took this as her cue to clock off; she would tuck herself away in one of her hidey-holes to avoid a confrontation with the inebriated travellers.

The rest of the time, however, she usually felt pretty safe at the station. She had once had a bad experience, when she was much younger, which had made her wary for a while, but she had long since managed to get over that. So when a chap who had been on the razzle all morning, downing drinks in the sunshine, suddenly appeared at the station midway through one weekend afternoon, she didn't immediately sense any danger. It wasn't idiot o'clock, nor even night-time, and Felix thought there was nothing to fear.

She was out by the benches on platform one that day, twisting her way lovingly between the legs of anyone who would let her. As she wandered, she heard the familiar hiss of a train's brakes as a service pulled into the station. She was so used to the noise by now that it did not faze her, but she did glance up along the platform to observe passengers disembarking. Were any of them new friends, come to visit the station cat?

As she watched, she spotted a potential target for affection as he stumbled awkwardly off the train. Eagerly, Felix began trotting up to the young man, her attention also caught by the bright-yellow hi-vis vests worn by the two people who accompanied him, and who were now talking sternly to him.

But these people were not Felix's TPE colleagues – nor even Adam Taylor and the Friends of Huddersfield Station. The hi-vis vests belonged to two officers from the British Transport Police. And the man they were talking to was in deep trouble.

He had been taken off the train for fare evasion. He was trying to argue back, slurring his words, as the officers discussed the matter with him, their voices calm as they tried to de-escalate the drama. They sat him down on a nearby bench while they stood beside him, continuing to reprimand him for his crime.

Felix, watching, took the action of the man sitting down on one of 'her' benches as an invitation to come closer. She approached insouciantly, her interest piqued. The man within her sights was a young lad in his early twenties, who was casually dressed for his day out drinking. As Felix received attention from such a wide variety of people, it seemed to her that he was just as likely to be a fan of hers as a child or an elderly lady. Basically, in Felix's mind, anyone was fair game when she was in the mood for attention. She trotted nearer, quite happily, occasionally dipping her head to the ground to sniff out secrets, her fluffy tail flicking back and forth.

The young man raised his hands irritably, remonstrating with the male and female officers and getting more and more worked up. Felix, however, perhaps thought his gesture a game, for she walked even closer.

As she did so, the movement caught the eye of the young man. He watched her wander closer, his eyes narrowing tightly. His cross frown was etched fully into his forehead. His cheeks were flushed with rage. He was really angry, but somehow Felix did not seem to see it. Uncharacteristically unable to sense the tension, she merely drew nearer, her tail flicking lazily with the knowledge that she was queen of all she surveyed and no one could or would dare to attack her.

But that was where Felix was wrong.

Felix continued to walk nearer; the cops continued to rebuke the man. Further down the platform, team leader Dan suddenly noticed the way the fare-dodger's eyes were fixed meanly on Felix. Dan had been staying out of the situation, leaving the officers to do their jobs, but as he saw Felix step closer to the troubled young man, his heart began to pound with fear.

His instincts were justified. As soon as Felix was close enough, the man petulantly lashed out his leg at the innocent cat, trying his hardest to kick her.

Seeing the man's cruel, violent action, a switch flipped in Dan and he barrelled down the platform towards his fluffy friend, running as fast as he could. He felt rage rising within him, his fear for Felix making his voice sharp.

'You: off!' he shouted at the man. 'Off the station now. Officers, he needs to leave this station immediately. He tried to kick Felix. That's animal abuse! Get him off this station *now*!'

Colour flushed into Dan's cheeks, but he couldn't

help the way he felt. Though he had no children, he nevertheless felt a fatherly protection towards Felix. It was as if the young man had tried to kick his daughter – and he was not having it! While Dan had respectfully kept his distance, Felix had not known to do the same. She was a cat, after all. Yet the man had not seen that innocence. He had only seen red.

Now he saw only the station whizzing by as the officers acted on Dan's instruction, also outraged by the man's attack on Felix. He was urged to leave at once – and escorted off the premises sharpish.

Dan watched him go, but he felt no sense of triumph, only concern for Felix. He quickly bent down to tend to her. Very luckily, the man had not made contact, but an inch or two could have made all the difference.

'Are you OK, Felix?' Dan asked the cat worriedly, his fingers fumbling through her fur as he checked for any damage.

Felix pressed her head against his hand, as if to reassure him. She had darted out of the way of the man and had suffered no bruising at all. But it was a reminder that not all humans could be trusted.

That perhaps explained why, in June, she reverted to her old wary ways. That month, the Sky Sports presenter Jeff Stelling made a visit to Huddersfield station as part of his fifteen-day March for Men charity walk: a 400-mile trek through which he hoped to raise £500,000 for Prostate Cancer UK. As that was the same charity for which Felix had raised funds from her bestselling book, a suggestion was made that Jeff should meet Felix as he came through Huddersfield on his walk. A media photo call was duly scheduled and the two famous fundraisers were introduced on film.

It was the station manager, Andy Croughan, who brought Felix out to meet Jeff on the front steps of the station on that cloudy summer's day. She seemed a little grumpy, having just been woken from a nap, but deigned to pose for the camera in Andy's arms as the silver-haired Jeff grinned tiredly. He was absolutely exhausted after his endeavours, but valiantly tickled Felix on the cheek and beamed beside her. Unusually, Felix often turned her head away from the many cameras trained upon her. She seemed rather more interested in this man who was sharing her limelight. She sniffed hard at Jeff's face and looked him square in the eye, as though trying to determine who this interloper was. Felix was used to being a solo star.

Andy, perhaps sensing Felix's wariness, jiggled her gently in his arms, trying to calm her. Jeff, too, continued to stroke her. Felix accepted it – until, uninvited, Jeff cheekily tickled Felix on her snow-white belly as she sat up in Andy's arms.

Her reaction was instantaneous. Her jaws stretched wide, as though she was a panther on the hunt, and she swivelled her head sharply towards Jeff. Without warning, she went for him, apparently intent on taking a chunk out of his finger!

'It's all right!' Jeff declared, laughing despite his shock, as he backed away from her. Now he was the wary one. 'I've got four others!' he joked.

To calm her, a team member quickly gave Felix a treat. This, however, could only be a temporary measure – and, as it turned out, in more ways than one. That summer, to Felix's great displeasure, treats were designated off the menu . . . for good.

One afternoon that July, Angie Hunte took her not-so-little-any-more girl to the vet's. As Felix stepped on to the scales, the vet's eyes widened in alarm. 'Ooh!' she exclaimed. 'You're a very heavy lady, aren't you, Felix?' The vet gently felt her way through all the fluff on Felix's body to touch her rounded belly. 'Ooh! We all know what that is, don't we? It seems it is full of Dreamies, Felix . . .' She tutted her disapproval, and told Angie that a diet was required. This was beginning to become a recurring theme in Felix's trips to the vet . . .

Though Felix was not *too* obese in human terms – she was roughly half a kilo overweight at that time – for a cat that is still significant. When Angie communicated the news back at the station, the team knew they needed to take action. Everyone wanted to do all they could to get their fluffy friend back down to a healthy weight, so they decided that the team members now had to be included in the treat ban. No more football games on the concourse or treat-catching tricks for Felix! It was the end of an era, in a way, but Felix's health was far more important. They would just have to have treat-free adventures in future, that was all. Knowing Felix, that really would not be too challenging.

Yet the team knew that their own ban on treats was not enough. For even with the ban in place, Felix's struggles with her weight were likely to continue, both because of the free-roaming nature of her job and because of her insatiable appetite! The two elements made a recipe for disaster. Whenever she went on the platforms, Felix would be on the lookout for food. And given her celebrity status, she often didn't need to beg – snacks would be served up to her practically on a silver platter. The vast majority of her treats still came from her fans, who understandably couldn't resist the expert pleading in her big green eyes. Felix was her own worst enemy in that way, using all her skills of persuasion to get what *she* wanted, whether it was good for her or not. In addition, it was a pleasure for Felix's fans to meet her, and they wanted to treat her in return. *Surely just one won't hurt*, they all reasoned. And had they been the only ones thinking that, it wouldn't have hurt a bit. But Felix was by now meeting dozens of fans every week, sometimes dozens a day. And some were not so restrained; Angela Dunn had seen some people emptying entire packets of cat treats out on to the platform when they thought she wasn't looking. Felix, of course, was always quick to hoover them all up. If anything, it was a wonder that she wasn't *more* overweight, but her regular patrols thankfully kept her active.

The team knew, therefore, that they also needed to remind Felix's many visitors about their responsibilities to care for her too. Shortly after Felix's return from the vet's, team leader Dan carefully wrote out a sign to display on the concourse. Due to its importance, it was written on the traditional station whiteboard that was placed each day in a high-visibility area to inform customers of significant information. Beneath the classic i-for-information logo and the heading 'Important Customer Information', Dan handwrote the following message:

Our own little celeb-kitty loves all of the people who come to see her, and she's also rather fond of the treats people bring for her.

However, in order to keep our senior pest controller fit and healthy, the vet has recommended a bit of a diet for the floofy one!

If you have brought something along with you today, and you don't want it to go to waste, speak to a member of staff, who can help Felix share it with some less fortunate kittens.

Thank you for helping to keep Felix healthy.

The Huddersfield Station Team

An image of the sign was immediately posted on Facebook in order to spread the word. Mark Allan decided to add a comedy caption from Felix, one which no doubt reflected her real feelings on the matter.

'Dan,' the caption read, 'I need to talk to you about this sign . . .'

Well, the witticism made it Felix's most popular Facebook post to date – though it was undoubtedly Felix's least favourite adventure!

Her fans were quick to defend her. 'I remember the cat who used to live on Paddington station back in the eighties,' wrote one Facebook friend. 'Usually seen fast asleep in a comfy basket in the ladies' loos. It was amazingly fat and huge. Ginger, if I remember right. Felix looks positively dainty in comparison.' Another chorused, 'It's not fat, it's floof!'

Others took the chance to be cheeky. 'I mean, maybe if Felix did some work now and again, she would burn some calories,' quipped Craig Forrest. To which Charlotte Stockwell retorted wittily, 'That was a bit catty. She works very hard . . .'

Angie Hunte hoped that the message would do the job. She hadn't liked hearing the vet's latest warning about Felix's weight and she was worried for the cat's long-term health. Her health had to be the most important thing – and if that meant not giving her a treat, then all the mewing in the world had to be ignored.

Felix wouldn't like it, Angie knew, but it was for the best.

13. Happy Days

'Have you heard . . .?' was the refrain that began echoing around Huddersfield station in July 2017. 'Have you heard the good news?'

Incredibly, Huddersfield had been nominated for Station of the Year at the TransPennine Express Star Awards 2017 – and the team were over the moon.

The award winners were to be announced at a posh do in a hotel function room in Manchester that month. Many of the team wanted to attend, but with the station running 24/7 and only limited capacity, not everyone could go. In the end, the station manager Andy Croughan was joined by team leaders Angie Hunte, Geoff, Dan and Jacqui, as well as Sara and Karl, Andy Yarwood and Dale Woodward. (Felix, taking one for the team, decided she would work through the event, while they all went off and had fun. After the termination of her gravy train of treats, she wasn't really in the mood for celebration.)

Since it was a formal occasion, Sara and Angie both opted to wear little black dresses, while the men dressed smartly in jackets and waistcoats. It was rather like they'd traded places with Felix, who always looked such a glamourpuss at work, while they had to wear their workaday uniforms. Jacqui wore a stunning white trouser suit; they all gave Felix a run for her money in the fashion stakes that night.

While they looked their best on the outside, inside they felt anxious. It was a very nervous Huddersfield team who took to their round table in the hotel conference room, craning their necks back to look at the balloon decorations in the TPE corporate colour scheme of purple, blue and white. A spot-lit stage dominated the large room; this was where the awards would be presented. Andy Croughan sipped his wine anxiously, wondering if his team would triumph this time.

Huddersfield had won the award before, but years and years ago now. Andy had only been at the helm of the station since January 2016, so he could take little credit for that previous plaudit, but tonight's decision would reflect on him. The year before, Huddersfield had been nominated for Station of the Year in the national rail industry awards, but although they had won a commendation, they'd lost out to Nottingham. Would it be the same at these internal TPE awards? Was Huddersfield destined to be the runner-up again?

There had been a lot of changes at the station in the past couple of years. Losing Billy Bolt and gaining a celebrity cat had been just two of them. The team had changed shape too, becoming significantly more streamlined, and Andy had been working hard to build a talented team that could still provide top-notch customer service. Tonight, he and his colleagues would be judged on their performance.

They were up against Scarborough. As TPE's managing director, Leo Goodwin, read out the nominations and described the achievements of each team, Andy and the others felt proud of what they had built at Huddersfield. But would it be enough . . .?

Eventually, to rapt silence in the ballroom, Leo revealed the results – and Huddersfield had won! Everyone round the Huddersfield table was jumping up and down, hugging each other and yelling at the tops of their voices. Sara and Dan embraced along with the rest of the team, Sara holding her breath as the man she fancied squeezed her tight – before Dan released her to hug another colleague. Nonetheless, Sara felt as though she could still feel his arms round her . . . Karl, giving her a hug next, seemed to know exactly how she felt. As usual, she did not need to say a word; he understood her instantly.

But there was no time for any of that tonight. There was an award to collect – and the whole team had triumphed! Every team member present traipsed up to the stage to receive their award, which was a stunning rectangular glass sculpture imprinted with the purple-and-blue TPE logo and the slogan: 'Together, we're taking the north further.' Karl, with typical charisma, raised his hand triumphantly above his head as he reached the stage, punching the air with joy. As the team posed for a photo, linking arms, Karl embraced Angie Hunte and the two of them beamed broadly for the camera. In their grins and delighted eyes, you could see at a glance that everyone was immensely proud of their mutual achievement. Everyone was in good spirits that night – even Geoff!

Back at the station, the award took pride of place in the booking office, alongside all the Felix tributes – which by now included several foreign editions of her bestselling book. It seemed somehow right that the award had its home alongside all the Felix memorabilia – for it was a prize for teamwork, after all, and Felix the station cat was undoubtedly part of that team. Angela Dunn was also delighted by their win, feeling it gave everyone a bit of a boost. It brought the whole team closer together.

It was a whole summer of happy days, in fact. Returning from holiday, Karl came running into work one day with a smile that said *he* was the cat who'd got the cream. Sara hugged him instantly, her cry of 'Congratulations!' already crossing her lips. She already knew his news because he'd phoned to tell her; while abroad, Karl had proposed to his long-term girlfriend at the top of a mountain . . . and she'd said yes! He'd been planning the proposal for months – asking Sara for suggestions and ideas along the way – and everything had gone as intended. Sara was thrilled for them both. So close were she and Karl that he even asked her if she would be a bridesmaid at his wedding. His future with his bride seemed as sparkling bright as that shiny new team award hanging in the booking office. As he told all his colleagues his exciting news, Karl's brown eyes sparkled just as brightly too.

As for Felix, the two Angelas had been cooking up a little plan to ensure that Felix was not forgotten in this summer of celebrations . . . as if such a thing could ever happen! While Felix's diet meant they couldn't spoil her as they might once have done, it didn't mean they couldn't come up with new ideas. And though it had never been done before, Angie and Angela decided they wanted to organise a special Felix-focused day at the station that summer, both to honour their girl and to thank her many fans for their support.

Both women had long been touched by these fans.

Angie and Angela could see how much Felix meant to people, and they were also overwhelmed by their generosity. Whether it was Christmas or Valentine's Day or Felix's birthday, gifts and cards with well wishes regularly arrived at the station for the little cat. Sometimes there were also gifts for the station team themselves, Felix's 'hoomans', as a thank you for their care of the beloved station cat. The team were sent wine and chocolates and cakes and more . . . And now that Felix's weight had become such a well-publicised issue, some people sent cash, rather than Dreamies, directing that the money be given to a charity of Felix's choice. The sums regularly topped three figures by the time each month was out.

Felix's charity work was another reason to celebrate the railway cat. Her fundraising efforts had not been limited to her calendar and her bestselling book – not on your nelly. Back in May, she had worked with the Manchester branch of a charity called Cash for Kids, donating the proceeds of a Felix-themed colouring book and a limited-edition Felix cuddly toy to their work supporting disadvantaged children across the Pennines. The cuddly Felix wore a blue superhero cape, which was apt, given that Felix's charity work was now literally saving lives across the nation.

By now, Felix's fans had supported Cash for Kids, the Samaritans, Fairy Bricks, Prostate Cancer UK and many other charities by buying Felix products or sponsoring her in some way. The team at TPE were determined that everything she did 'commercially' had to be for charity, never to build their brand or to make money for money's sake. That wasn't what Felix was about. Yet they also wanted to be sure to *share* the wealth that Felix's fans so generously helped to generate. That was why, every time Felix did something new, she had a new charity partner. Her fundraising was divided among lots of charities, so that all sorts of different groups in need could benefit from the fairy dust being scattered by Felix the cat. This approach was why, each month, Angela Dunn would donate the financial contributions given in Felix's name to a different institution, whether it was a local cats' home, a school in need or a mental-health charity.

Angie Hunte, too, felt that changing the charities each time rather matched Felix's own approach to life. After all, Felix was indiscriminate in her healing powers, helping everyone from Adam with his MS to autistic children and a man with dementia who loved to have her book read to him each night (he was on his third read-through already, his wife wrote in to say). 'I just see it as her flowing through,' explained Angie Hunte. 'That is what she does as she walks through life: she touches everybody. And if we can do that with her charity work as well, that just seems right to me.'

In the summer of 2017, however, the two Angelas felt that Felix's fans had been asked to give enough. By now, Felix had raised well over six figures for charity. People were always coming to Huddersfield to meet Felix, yet they always left empty-handed, sometimes without even the memory of meeting the station cat to see them through the journey home. The two Angelas wanted to give something back to these dedicated fans. They wanted to say thank you on Felix's behalf.

So, on Saturday 22 July, they planned a giveaway day for Felix's admirers. A limited-edition Felix goodie bag would be given away to hundreds of lucky families who were travelling by train on that first weekend of the school summer holidays. Angie even persuaded Andy Croughan to let her upgrade to first class the first five families who received bags; they'd also receive a free copy of Felix's book. The goodie bags, meanwhile, would be stuffed full of bespoke goodies featuring photographs of Felix, as well as sugar-free lollies or sweets. When Felix said thank you, she did it in style.

The giveaway idea came from Angie and Angela alone, and both of them really enjoyed the creative process involved in organising it. It was very different from their usual work at the station, but they found themselves relishing commissioning the various Felix products and getting involved in design, as well as sparking off each other as they came up with the little details that they hoped would make the day a great success.

It wasn't all glamour and creative brainstorms. The night before the big day, Angela Dunn found herself on her hands and knees on the concourse floor, pressing black pawprint transfers on to the tiles and securing them with a damp squeegee. She and Angie had thought it would be nice to lead the children to the giveaway bags with a trail of Felix's 'pawprints'. It was a lot of work, but they looked amazing when they were finished – so much so that Angela told the cleaners to leave them there; twelve months later, you could still see the pawprints proclaiming that this was indeed the home of Felix the cat. It became another tell-tale sign and part of the 'Felix tour', alongside her 'oil' portrait, Billy's bench and her famous cat flap on the concourse.

With the pawprint transfers done, Angela's work was far from over. She and Angie then had to stuff the brown-paper bags, printed with Felix's paw-tograph, with all the goodies they had commissioned: magnets and key rings, postcards and colouring sheets, and crayons and sweets. Yet it was work that was full of camaraderie, as the two women worked happily together, Angie worrying aloud that they might have made too many bags . . . There certainly seemed a lot of them; hundreds were laid out in the Hub by the time they were finished!

Before the two Angelas left for the evening, they also set the scene on the concourse: moving the station's big black suggestion box to one side to clear space for their stall, covering their table in smart purple and black cloths printed with Felix's name, and erecting a huge, beautiful picture of Felix behind the stand. She looked glorious – eyes sparkling, fur fluffed, proud and regal as the queen she was.

But even after Angela had waved goodbye to Angie and driven home to her empty house, she still had more work to do – this time, making special Felix T-shirts for the five team members who would be handing out the bags: Amanda, Chrissie and Angela herself from the booking office, Angie Hunte and Sara, who was still working on the platforms, but who had asked if she could help them out. Angela was up till gone midnight ironing transfers on to the five shirts: they were white T-shirts, with black pawprints on the sleeves and tummy, and 'Felix' in big black letters over the right breast.

It was a funny thing, but somehow Angela found that her house didn't feel quite as empty as usual that night – not when she had such a hive of industry to focus on. Before she finally turned off the lights, she looked with pride at the T-shirts laid out ready for the morning. She hoped, after all their efforts, that people would turn up . . .

Angie Hunte hurried into work the next morning with a fluttering of butterflies in her belly. They had put out an announcement that the giveaway would start at 9 a.m. As she parked her car and walked across the square towards the station, it was not even 8.30 a.m. – so she was not looking out for any signs of action. The square did seem a little busier than usual, but she put that down to it being the first Saturday of the school holidays – everyone and their dog was out and about, stretching their legs and soaking up the sunshine, feeling that glorious first frisson of the freedom that was theirs for the next six weeks.

But as Angie scurried up the station's grand steps, she realised that unusual, buzzing busyness continued inside too. Next to the booking office was a large gathering of people. At first, Angie sighed wearily. *Oh, it's going to be one of* those *days*, she thought, *we're* already *rushed off our feet* . . . But then she noticed that there was an exceptional number of children in the crowd – and the penny dropped. *Oh my gosh. They're not queuing for tickets – they're here for the giveaway!*

After all Felix had achieved to date, it may sound naive of Angie not to make the connection immediately, but she was used to seeing Felix's fans come to visit in ones or twos. To see a whole mass of them all at once, all eager to take home Felix's thank-you presents, was rather overwhelming. It was perhaps the first time it really hit Angie just how many people Felix had reached. And to know that she and Angela had conceived this idea, to which so many people had responded, was also touching. As Angie bustled about, getting things ready and pulling on her special Felix T-shirt, she saw that the children on the concourse were already running wild with excitement. She handed out bottles of bubbles and a blonde toddler in a pretty pink dress enthusiastically got to work, blowing big fat bubbles all over the station, so that the bubbles' rainbow sheen sparkled in the sun.

Well, by the time Angie and Angela were ready to declare the day open, Angie could not see the door, there were that many people waiting! She quickly went from worrying that they had too many bags to worrying that they had too few!

'Karl! Karl!' she cried. The platform worker stood nearby. Helpful as ever, he swiftly stepped over to her side. 'Karl, we need to capture this day,' she told him, still reeling from the amazing turnout. 'You are hereby promoted to chief cameraman! Any time we need a picture taking, can you please do the honours?'

Karl was more than happy to oblige. He loved Felix – so much so that he made sure to get himself one of her key rings that day; it had a snapshot of Felix on one side and 'pub o'clock' on the other. So he was on hand to capture all the day's special moments – such as one of the first children in the queue: a girl of about six or seven with shoulder-length brown hair and wire glasses, who was wearing a blue jacket with floral embroidery and the most enormous grin. He was there to capture an anomaly among all the families in the queue: a plumpish man in his fifties who looked just as thrilled to get his bag as the children. ('Thank God I've got one!' he declared with relief as he finally reached the front. 'My wife would have *killed* me if I didn't come back with one of these!') And he was there to capture the memorable moment when the star of the show put in an appearance, all with her trademark professional poise.

The two Angelas came up with something pretty special for Felix's entrance. Of the five windows in the booking office, the top one on the far left is never used, so its white shutters always remain closed. Unbeknownst to the waiting crowds, Angela Dunn fetched Felix and popped her down behind those closed shutters. Then, as people milled in the booking office, eagerly claiming their giveaway bags, Angela pressed the button that made the shutters rise . . .

From the excited squeals that greeted the dramatic 'reveal', you would have thought those white plastic shutters were thick red velvet stage curtains, and that the cat standing behind them was the most popular singer on earth. As the crowds realised that the shutters were slowly showing off Felix herself, a collective happy sigh echoed around the booking office. It sounded like the sigh of the ocean lapping at the shore, a homecoming of sorts, as Felix met the fans and the fans met Felix.

The cat sat neatly between the two clear plastic shields of the serving hatch, so that she was not behind them but in the open air. She placed her two front paws together with a ballerina's precision and sat proudly upright, angling her head this way and that as she acknowledged the crowd before her and invited those taking photographs and videos to capture her very best side (both being fabulous, of course). Posing for selfies, her ears twitched as children chattered happily to her, as though she was listening hard to all the secrets they were sharing. She stayed for a full half-hour, soaking up the sunshine on the desk and allowing people to have their pictures taken with her – and generally glorying in their adulation. Despite her experiences the month before, when she'd encountered the kicking fare evader and snapped at Jeff Stelling, she coped beautifully with all the attention and didn't seem wary or lash out once. Instead, like everyone else, Felix seemed caught up in the joyful, celebratory feeling of the day.

Karl and Sara both enjoyed the event too. And Karl took the opportunity to chat with Sara about her feelings for Dan.

'Just tell him how you feel!' he urged her. Wanting to encourage her, he'd begun to make not-so-subtle hints to Dan about Sara's secret crush, but there was only so much a wingman could do. He thought his two colleagues would be great together and was trying to play matchmaker. 'You tell him,' he told Sara now, 'or I will . . .'

But Sara wasn't sure she was ready for that. What if Dan didn't feel the same?

'Don't, Karl,' she pleaded. 'There's plenty of time. I'll tell him when I'm good and ready . . .'

Eventually, the rush for the Felix bags died down and the giveaway day came to an end. It had been a resounding success. 'Well done, TransPennine Express!' people wrote on social media. 'Well done to the ladies for organising this! This is what a train company is all about. Well done, Huddersfield!' The two Angelas were tickled pink to see such praise, feeling a warm glow that people had taken the day in exactly the way they'd intended.

It had been such a success that they decided to reserve a stack of bags and do it all again the next day. So, as Angela Dunn packed up at the end of her shift, she left the cloth-covered table and the Felix picture on display, and simply returned the big black suggestion box to the table. It was better placed there than on the counter, as there wasn't really room for it there when the shutters were closed. Angela carefully adjusted its position on the centre of the black cloth. She would move it again in the morning.

The following day, they decided to start the giveaway later, so Angela began her shift by working behind the desk in the booking office. She was still buzzing from the day before, absent-mindedly smiling to herself every now and again as she remembered each child's joy. She had one such smile on her face when a lady came up to the desk to speak with her.

As she looked at the woman, Angela felt her previously happy expression slide straight off her face. The lady was clearly absolutely distraught. She had grey curly hair and glasses and was wearing a classic green mac. Even as Angela watched, the lady's tears dripped down her cheeks and on to the collar of her coat, staining it as dark as the woman's mood.

'Can I help you?' Angela asked, concerned. 'Are you all right?'

But the woman silently shook her head. 'I-I can't believe it,' she eventually managed to say.

'Believe what?' Angela asked.

The woman swallowed hard, trying desperately to contain her emotion. 'When did she die?' she asked, her voice breaking on the final word.

Angela furrowed her brow. She had no idea who the woman was talking about.

The woman began sobbing again. 'W-when did Felix die?' she asked, struggling to speak through her tears. 'When did your lovely little station cat die?'

14. Mystic Mog

Angela spoke gently to her. 'There's nowt wrong with our Felix,' she said. 'She's still around, I promise you. She's not dead.'

The woman blinked in shock, salty tears still caught in her lashes. She placed a hand on her chest, as though feeling for her broken heart that was now slowly being mended. 'Oh, thank *God* for that,' she said, with feeling. 'But – but what's all this, then? I really thought she'd gone.'

Angela looked to where the lady was pointing, at the giveaway table. She saw the sombre black pawprints leading up to the table. She saw the royal purple cloth covered over with its mournful black neighbour. She saw the huge picture of Felix behind the table . . . and then she saw the big black suggestion box slap bang in the middle of this 'shrine'.

'I thought her ashes were in that box,' explained the lady.

Well, on reflection, you could see why. If you didn't know about the giveaway, it did rather look as though the station cat was formally lying in state . . .

'Oh, no, no, no!' Angela reassured her. They both started to giggle at the mix-up. 'We were just doing an event for her, that's all. This was all left over from yesterday. Felix is alive, I promise you!'

'Thank goodness for that!' the woman exclaimed, and her face was suddenly sunny again.

For Angela, the woman's heartfelt emotion was yet another example of how deeply Felix's fans cared for her. As the summer drew on, Angela felt a continued connection to them, and a continued desire to do more to help. Though the Felix postcards they'd made for the gift bags had originally been intended just for the giveaway day, Angela now suggested that they become a permanent feature at the station. All the team members felt bad if people called for Felix when she wasn't available, but Angela hit on the idea of giving them a postcard of her instead. She printed a series of them, all featuring stunning black-and-white shots of the black-and-white cat, with slogans such as 'Sorry I missed you' printed on them. Angie Hunte joined in as well, arranging for Felix pens and pencils to be made. 'I've borrowed the senior pest controller's pen!' ran the slogan on the biros, which also featured Felix's fluffy face. It made the team so happy to be able to give visitors something, even if it wasn't time with Felix herself.

Angela wondered what more she could do as Felix's lady-in-waiting. Working in the office one day, her eye fell on yet another delivery that had arrived for Felix. Though Angela had taken charge of Felix's birthday gifts and charity donations, no one really had responsibility for all the post that she received. And people didn't just send packets of Dreamies or cat food, which were easily donated to a cat charity if Felix couldn't use them – they sent expressions of love, such as hand-drawn pictures, handmade quilts featuring Felix's face, and even hand-knitted pigeons to represent her long-time foe Percy. People spent hours, if not weeks or months, crafting things for her, and it didn't seem right to Angela that they largely languished forgotten at the station, perhaps eventually to be thrown away in a clear-out and dismissed as clutter. She felt someone should be caring for this growing collection of memorabilia. They did not have enough space in the booking office to display it all, as new things arrived almost every day, so only a very few items could ever end up in there; in truth, the room was already full to bursting.

So, that summer, Angela started taking the artworks home. She hoped one day that there might be a display she could create somewhere at the station in Felix's honour to commemorate all these bits and pieces. Until then, Angela packaged up the knitted items with love and securely transported them home.

That August, she surveyed her house, wondering where on earth she could keep it all so that her own home did not become cluttered. Then she had an idea. Arms fully laden, she climbed the stairs and pulled open the doors of the wardrobe in her bedroom. There was an empty drawer in there, she knew, where her ex-husband had once kept his shirts.

Well, he won't be needing this drawer any more! Angela thought and carefully laid the Felix-inspired artworks inside it. For decades, she had bent to place her husband's shirts inside that drawer, but its contents were rather different now. Yet Angela smiled as she shut the drawer, feeling a satisfying sense of purpose. It felt good to have that drawer in use again, with something new to occupy all the space that had been left behind.

Back at the station, Angela wanted to thank Felix for the way she was helping her to forge a new, independent life. So she bought her a special present that August: a fluffy white sheepskin-style radiator bed. It would hook over the radiator in the ladies' locker room and provide Felix with a toasty-warm snug to retreat to when she wasn't out working or meeting fans. Though she'd been given special blankets and baskets before, she had never really taken to them. Angela hoped that, for the first time, Felix might finally like to have a proper bed of her own.

The signs weren't promising at first. For about a week, ungrateful Felix merely assessed the new arrival from a distance, as though weighing up both what it was and whether it was friend or foe. The radiator bed was a little like a hammock that hung halfway down its heated wall: Felix would have to jump up to it from the floor, but once she was in situ it would give her an elevated, comfy throne from which to survey the world.

First, she had to get up there. For a while, it seemed as though it was a leap too far. She blinked her big green eyes at it instead. When she finally did try it, the bed wobbled on its metal hooks, so that she jumped back off it straight away, the powerful push of her hind legs saying in no uncertain terms, 'Oh no, I'm *not* keen on that . . .'

After a few weeks of this, however, Angela and her colleagues started to notice that Felix was spending an awful lot of time in her new hangout in the ladies' locker room. Now, when she leapt up on to the soft surface of the bed, she padded about on it happily, as though pressing the covers down – much as we might plump our pillows before settling down to sleep. She became so comfortable in it, in fact, that she would frequently lie with her limbs hanging right over the edges, splayed out in such a luxuriating stretch that her colleagues would yawn just to look at her, her evident comfort making them crave their own warm beds. If the ladies happened to be in the anteroom of the locker room, with Felix snuggled up next door, they noticed that she purred even when no one was in the room with her, taking audible pleasure from her comfortable spot beside the radiator. Now, if her colleagues had to go into the room while she was sleeping, they would tiptoe round her and turn the lights off as they left. It became a quiet and peaceful spot for the station cat, so different from all the noise on the platforms outside. Only a faint thrum of air conditioning – and a cat's contented purr – could be heard as Felix snuggled down to sleep. She looked utterly blissful blissed out in her bed. Before too long, her radiator bed became the first place that anyone looked for her whenever fans came calling. So that was where Andy Croughan found her that summer, as he came to ask her a very important football-related favour . . .

Earlier that year, on 29 May 2017, Huddersfield Town AFC had hit the headlines when they'd been promoted to the top tier of English football for the first time since 1972. It was an extraordinary day; half the station had headed down to Wembley for the play-offs and come cheering back again on the train – this time, as supporters of a Premier League side! Jean Randall in the booking office brought in a special blue-and-white Huddersfield Town scarf to hang up in the office to celebrate the lads' win – and Felix, agreeably, posed for pictures in it, wanting to do her bit for her local team. She frequently posted on Facebook during the football season, 'Congratulations to Mr Wagner [the manager] and the boys!' and across the whole of Huddersfield everyone was excited about their glorious achievement in getting to the uppermost league in English football.

Everywhere you looked, in fact, you could tell that the promotion was big news for the Yorkshire town – even Leo the Lion, the statue on the Lion Building outside in St George's Square, had got in on the act, having his own Huddersfield Town scarf draped round him and their blue-and-white flag flying behind him too. The council, meanwhile, decorated all the lamp posts in the square with metallic banners that tinkled in the wind, each emblazoned with the slogan 'Premier for Business' to encourage investment.

That August, the new football season was about to begin – and Felix was called upon to cast her judgement on the team's chances in the most competitive league in the world. Pre-season, Huddersfield Town – who were nicknamed the Terriers – were sadly favourites for relegation but Felix, as it turned out, had a little more faith in them than that.

Working in conjunction with the local paper, the *Huddersfield Examiner*, Felix was asked by Andy Croughan if she would predict for the lads whether they would win, lose or draw their first three games in football's top flight. Yet Felix was not expected to use a crystal ball or a set of tarot cards to make her predictions – she would be working with her favourite medium of all: *food*.

Out on platform one, Andy set up three dinner bowls:

one marked with the logo of Huddersfield Town, one with that of their opponent, and another marked with the word 'DRAW'. She could eat from only one. All Felix had to do was choose which bowl to eat from – and that would be her prediction for the result of the game. Between her tiny cat-toothed jaws, she held the fate of the newly minted Premier League side.

Andy watched nervously as Felix trotted up to the bowls for her first prediction. It was a toughie: Huddersfield were set to play Crystal Palace away at Selhurst Park. Felix seemed to sense the controversy; though she sniffed first at the Huddersfield Town bowl, lingering over its tempting scents, she later moved on to the Draw bowl without taking a bite from the local team's dish. Had the boys really lost her support so soon?

Once at the Draw bowl, she again lowered her head thoughtfully above it. She sniffed eagerly, assessing the aromas like an expert sommelier as she deliberated her difficult choice. But then, to the delight of Terriers' fans everywhere, she returned to the Huddersfield Town bowl – and chomped down hungrily on the food set out for her! Felix was backing the boys to win!

In fact, she did the same again for the other two games; on those occasions not even hesitating before heading straight for the Huddersfield Town selection. The bookies had the odds of three wins in a row at forty-one to one, but Felix defied those odds with her choices.

The cat's mystical abilities were immediately called into question by so-called expert football pundits, who unashamedly scoffed at her insights. Jack Kempf was invited on to the *Hawksbee and Jacobs* show on TalkSport

Radio to discuss Felix's predictions. After dissing Felix by initially getting her gender wrong, the presenter added rather dismissively, 'I think Felix has gone mad! She is being over-optimistic there . . .'

But, as the season began on 12 August 2017, it was Felix who had the last laugh. Against all expectations, on the first day of the season, the Terriers thumped Palace three—nil.

Seven days later, the team took to the field again, this time playing Newcastle at home. Once again, the Terriers triumphed, beating the Magpies one—nil.

They may have been pre-season favourites for the drop, but Huddersfield were now sitting pretty in the table in second place. Their impressive start had bowled everyone over — everyone, of course, except for Felix the cat.

'Mystic Mog' herself took the resultant flurry of media interest in her second-sight skills entirely in her stride, looking impassively at the sports journalists who now flocked to meet her. Such a laid-back stance was increasingly becoming Felix's default position. After her wobble in June, when she'd tried to 'attack' Jeff Stelling (as the *Huddersfield Examiner* dramatically put it), she seemed to be slowly becoming more and more tolerant of both fans and cameras.

It could be seen in her interactions with the travelling football fans. Many Huddersfield Town supporters regularly journeyed through the station on their way to and from games, and they now made a habit of coming over to their good-luck charm to give her a fuss. Sometimes fans would have a drink inside them and be a bit lairy, but rather than being frightened of them, Felix instead seemed to act as a calming influence. It wasn't unusual to spot a group of lads in their football shirts hunkered down on the ground beside her, stealing a shot or two of the famous station cat on their smartphones. And their loud cheering would diminish to a burble of baby talk as they greeted the cat affectionately. Their big, dominant gestures soon subsided into gentle, sensitive strokes of her fluffy black fur. It really was quite something to behold.

Of course, nothing in life lasts forever – and sadly Felix's winning streak came to an end on the Terriers' third game, when they drew against Southampton in a nil–nil draw at home. Mystic Mog hadn't seen that coming.

Coming to an end, too, was former announcer Chris Bamford's time at the station; he was soon to move on to his dream job within the company as a train driver, with his end date set for October 2017. Though he'd be passing through Huddersfield at least twice a day in his new role, as he'd be working on the line that ran from Liverpool to York, he knew he wouldn't be hanging out with Felix any more. The best he could hope for was that he might some-times glimpse her sitting by her favourite bike racks as he drove through the station. It was a rather sad thought. He really had loved working with the little cat.

So it was the end of an era for both Chris and Mystic Mog. It was a shame, in a way, as everyone at the station would have liked some warning as to what would hap-pen next. For dark times lay ahead for the Huddersfield station team – and they were dark times that no one, not even Felix, could ever have predicted.

15. Shocks and Sadness

'Come on, princess,' said Karl. 'Where's my hug?'

Sara squeezed her friend tight before heading home that September evening. She'd been a bit down of late, still pining for Dan yet persistently tongue-tied about saying how she felt, but Karl never let her go home feeling low. Every day as they said goodbye he and Sara would have a quick hug, and within his big, brotherly, bear-like arms, she always felt so much better, whatever had happened that day. Sara, at twenty-four, was the eldest of her real-life siblings; to have a work 'big brother' in the form of Karl, who was twenty-nine, was a lovely perk of the job.

Even after all these months, Sara really didn't know how Dan felt about her. They got on so well, but he had never made a move. Every day, they laughed their heads off together, but she wondered if he just saw her as a friend. Karl acted as a go-between, encouraging each of them separately, dropping hints and teasing them, but despite his cheeky words and the knowing twinkle in his brown eyes, neither Sara nor Dan had taken things further. Since Dan had joined the station, he had become heavily involved in Felix's Facebook page; a recent, popular video series he'd made, called 'The Floof Files', had included the following caption from Felix: 'Dan. Must you tell the world our secrets?' But when it came to the secrets of Dan's heart, he was keeping them under wraps.

For the newly engaged Karl, it seemed obvious that love was in the air – but for the time being he and his fiancée were on their own when it came to such affairs of the heart. All Karl could do, besides urging Sara to seize the day and tell Dan how she felt, was try to cheer her up. That September, he took her to her first football match at Old Trafford, where they watched his beloved team Manchester United roar to victory. Aside from his fiancée, Karl's passion was football, and Sara didn't think she'd ever seen him happier than watching his team play that beautiful game.

As for Felix, more game-playing was certainly afoot that autumn – not least when Jack Kempf organised an autumnal-themed photo shoot for her upcoming 2018 calendar, which would this time be raising funds for Cash for Kids.

At six years old, Felix was a pretty worldly-wise moggy. She'd been around the block a few times; she knew her four foot from her forests and her Dreamies from her supermarket own-brand treats. She knew, too, all the ins and outs of station life and had seen all the usual things that regularly got rolled out on to the platforms – suitcases and carry-ons, beer kegs and crates. So *what* – she must have thought that autumn – was this new, huge object? And what on earth was it doing in the middle of *her* train station?

For on to the platform that September rolled a massive orange pumpkin, the ideal prop for the October 2018 calendar image. Jack and the team had sourced it from a local veg shop in Huddersfield and it really was gigantic – about ten times Felix's size. She watched warily as it came closer – it was that heavy, it took at least three men to move it – and Jack plonked it down with some relief in the centre of platform one. He didn't think he could drag it any further if he tried.

'Come on, Felix!' he called out to the station cat. 'Come and check this out!'

Felix needed no second invitation. Curiosity soon sent her scurrying over to the mysterious orange globe, which had a thick green stalk in its centre that was almost as long as Felix's fluffy tail. Nose twitching furiously, she gave the pumpkin the once-over, walking all the way round its very long edge. Still no closer to deciphering its identity by the time she had completed one circumference, she decided to jump on top of it, launching herself at it with all the velocity of a space rocket. It was so high up when she landed that, really, she might as well have been on the moon, albeit a bright orange one.

Way up high, Felix continued her investigations. She seemed to decide that, whatever this ginormous object was, it was really fun! Before too long she was leaping all over it, as a professional photographer snapped away happily, capturing Felix as the queen of the pumpkin castle, as well as midway through her own private hide-and-seek game; the pumpkin made the perfect shield for the mischievous station cat. Squashed down on the floor beside the pumpkin, doing her best to conceal herself, Felix made the giant orb look even bigger than it really was. She seemed rather sad to say goodbye to it when the photographer finally finished the shoot and the orange moon rolled away into the sunset.

Luckily, however, that was not the last of the autumn fun. In October, a brand-new toy rolled on to the concourse: a black-and-white-keyed station piano to entertain the black-and-white cat! The new arrival was partly the brainchild of station manager Andy Croughan. He'd wanted to get one for a while, having seen the success of station pianos in places such as Leeds and London St Pancras. But they were expensive instruments; wishes weren't always so easy to turn into reality. That year, however, a local Green Party councillor had called him to discuss the idea: the councillor had links with the nearby Marsden Jazz Festival and was able to arrange for a piano to be situated at the station, as long as the station got involved with the festival. Andy was delighted to agree.

The new piano was a simple upright brown wooden instrument, accompanied by a smart wooden piano stool with a maroon-velvet cushion. It sat on the concourse, just beyond the gateline, and a sign on its top encouraged passing passengers to 'PLAY ME'. And so they did . . .

For Adam Taylor, working on the concourse on the information stand, his Friday-morning shift suddenly took on a new element after the piano arrived. A middle-aged man took to coming in to play the piano and Adam loved listening to him. The man was always dressed smartly, usually in a suit, and he would sit down on the velvet stool at around 11 a.m. and play sad, slow, haunting songs.

When a gifted pianist took their place at the piano, it

proved a truly beautiful addition to the station. The sound would sweep up under the corrugated-iron roof and out to the rolling hills beyond, soaring through the station skylights like a flock of melodic birds. The acoustics were astonishing, amplifying the music and translating the melody that flowed from the pianists' fingers into a sound that touched the heart. Passers-by would stop to listen, their schedule for the day suddenly put out of their minds. A gent in a flat cap and black media glasses might pull his headphones from his ears, wanting to listen instead to the live music. A lady in an LBD and her hair in a bun, meanwhile, would pause a moment, then linger longer. Her neatly pulled-together appearance seemed to unravel a little, somehow, as her foot began tapping to a jazzy tune and her head began bobbing in time.

It was no coincidence that the theologian Albert Schweitzer once said, 'There are two means of refuge from the misery of life: music and cats.' Huddersfield, it seemed, had nailed them both. Andy Croughan, witnessing these gifted artists at work, thought that their performances had all the makings of a new Saturday-night TV show: *Station Pianists Have Got Talent!*

The players were not *always* quite so tuneful, though. When children plink-plonked on the keys or drunken fools used it to have a laugh on their way home at night, it created a terrible racket.

'Bloody awful!' team leader Geoff would mutter at such times, shaking his head wearily at all that he had to endure.

As for Felix, it seemed she shared his reticence when it came to the bad players. Cats have very sensitive hearing – they can hear sounds from 45 to 64,000 Hz, whereas we humans are limited to frequencies between 64 and 23,000 Hz – so for Felix the noise was even more of a headache. She kept a wide berth whenever the piano was occupied.

When it first arrived, however, she did give the empty piano a thorough investigation, leaping up on to its wooden top and sashaying along it while her flicking tail kept time like a metronome. Though it would make a lovely story, the team had never actually seen her walking along the keys – as fun as it is to imagine Felix making up her own compositions at night, perhaps even following in the footsteps of her namesake Felix Mendelssohn. But this didn't stop Angela Dunn from joking, if ever asked if Felix liked to interact with the piano, 'Oh yes, she plays a lovely Mozart!'

That October, it was sad songs that seemed apt for the station. It was always emotional when much-loved members of the team moved on and a card now began circulating behind the scenes for the team to say good luck and goodbye to Chris Bamford, whose last shift was scheduled for 23 October 2017. He had been a key colleague through Felix's rise to fame and both the cat and her human companions would miss him dearly. Ironically, despite the station being the setting for thousands of goodbyes, day in and day out, it never got any easier for the team to say farewell to colleagues who had become nothing less than family.

Midway through the month, another card started doing the rounds among the Huddersfield team – this time for Karl, who had been taken ill on his return from holiday. He'd been admitted to hospital and the station rallied round one of their favourite team members at once in order to wish him a speedy recovery.

Angela Dunn came into work on Saturday 14 October feeling a bit miserable; she'd just had a week's holiday in Malta and had four and a half days of rain. She looked for Karl as soon as she got to the station, as with him having also been on holiday at the same time, they'd had a little joke before they'd gone away about who would have the most sunshine. She wanted to tell him that he had most definitely won! But Karl was nowhere to be seen.

In the office, she saw the get-well-soon card laid out on the desk.

'Who's poorly?' she asked.

'It's Karl,' her colleagues told her. 'He's not right well. He's been in hospital for the past couple of days or so.'

'Oh, that's not good,' said Angela, sympathising. She scribbled down her best wishes to him – 'Get well soon Karl, love Ange' – and then turned her attention to the grim reality of the first shift back at work. Even Felix couldn't help make that one fly by any faster.

But not two hours later, work at the station ground to a halt. The team leader on duty, David Jackson, called everybody into the office and told them to leave off whatever it was they were doing. *What's going on now?* wondered Angela. It was far too early for Chris Bamford's send-off, and there was no meeting in the diary.

David stood in front of his colleagues. His face looked ashen and shocked. Seconds later, so did everybody else's.

'I'm sorry to have to tell you,' he said, 'but Karl died this morning.'

Nobody spoke. The news seemed to have driven all words and all sense from the world. At first, the railway workers couldn't compute what David had said to them. Only after a minute or two was the spell broken, and the stone statues they'd become at hearing of Karl's death slowly began moving once more. First one colleague cried, then another. The team stood in shock, not knowing what to say or do. The news hit them very, very hard. Karl was everybody's friend: a warm, loving, funny, helpful, *young* man who had adored his job on the railway. For the rest of the shift, Angela and the others operated in a stunned state of disbelief and devastation. Angela kept thinking: *Why?* She'd only just been told he was ill, but now he had gone forever. It was extremely difficult to take in.

Everybody missed Karl. Everybody had had a joke with him or a memory of a time he'd gone the extra mile to make them smile. He was only twenty-nine and he'd been at Huddersfield for barely a year, yet he'd made a massive impact on the entire station. He'd had his whole life ahead of him. He'd had so many plans for the future. But now all that lay in the dust.

Sara, Karl's best friend, who was not on shift that morning, heard the news from the station manager, Andy Croughan. Knowing how close she was to her colleague, he'd phoned her as soon as Karl's family had told him the news. She'd been about to go and visit her friend in hospital, as she'd done nearly every day that past week, but as she listened to Andy telling her firmly that she must speak to Karl's fiancée before she left the house, she read between the words. In the spaces between them was a terrible truth that was somehow even worse for being unspoken. So she insisted that he tell her more and Andy broke the news.

It was a massive shock. A red-raw pain. Karl had been her best friend in the whole world. They had spoken every day. But, now, there was only silence.

Sara felt stunned. It had been so sudden, and so unexpected, that it was difficult to process. She stayed at home that first day, pretty much unable to function, but she forced herself back to work on Monday. But although she was there physically, her head wasn't in the right place. It was so horrible to be standing out on the platforms, where Karl had always stood beside her, and see another colleague trying to fill his shoes.

Sara found she kept bursting into tears at work. Everybody was so kind, knowing how close she and Karl had been, but in a way their kindness made it worse. Only Felix's cuddles were comforting. The cat seemed to pick up on her grief as she had done with others, so many times before. Sara found her attention reassuring, as Felix snuggled down in her lap for a stroke or simply sat with her as she cried. Felix was always there for her . . . and so was someone else.

Karl's death hit Dan very hard as well. The two men had been close friends, and with Karl being only a year older than Dan, his passing was like a blow to his belly that pressed all the air from his lungs. Dan was too young to be burying his friends – yet that was what he was soon going to have to do.

A few days after Karl passed away, Dan and Sara went out for a drink. Usually, Karl would have joined them, ordering Jägerbombs to get the party started, his laughing voice putting everyone in a positive mood. But as Sara and Dan collected their drinks at the bar and retreated to a table, laughing was the last thing on their minds. Instead, Dan found himself crying about his friend's death. Crying in a Wetherspoons – it was hardly cool, but he couldn't help it. Silently, Sara reached a hand across the table and held his own tightly. She didn't need to say anything; she knew exactly what he was going through. She was simply there with him, just as he was there with her.

For months now, Sara reflected, she had been putting off telling Dan how she felt about him. There was time enough for all that, she'd told Karl over and over; she would tell him when the time was right.

But Karl's sudden death was making her realise time was not an infinite resource. Why was she waiting, really? What was she waiting for?

As for Dan, he found that Karl's death made him re-evaluate many aspects of his life. Life was short. Too short. You did not know how long you had to live; Karl's tragic death underlined that with emphatic clarity. And if he could be happy with Sara – as he thought he could be, perhaps even *should* be – then what on earth was he doing in not acting on his feelings?

There was never an official moment when things changed. Dan never said, 'Will you be my girlfriend?' and Sara never asked him if he wanted to date. With Karl having passed away so recently, it wasn't the time for anything as trivial as all that. What was going on between them was somehow deeper; it needed no label, no articulation, no moment where a line was crossed. It was more that their friendship was heading in that direction and neither of them did anything now to stop those flourishing seeds from growing, an inevitability that Karl had long foreseen. Rather, it was that their clasped hands on those pub tables became a little bit more common, that their hugs when they said hello lasted just that little bit longer than the norm. When they laughed at work in the team leaders' office, watching Felix as she frolicked about on the floor, they kept smiling at each other long after the joke was over. Felix, in fact, was probably the first to know what was going on between the two of them.

It was just as well she was so good at keeping secrets.

There was a horrible bittersweetness in their coming together as a couple now, though. For, simply: *Karl should have been there to see it*. He, who had done so much for them both, would have been thrilled to see them happy. But, no matter how much they might have wished it otherwise, Karl was gone.

16. Time to Say Goodbye

Karl's funeral was held on a cold, dry day in November 2017. The temperature itself was sobering, but the bite on the team's cheeks that day was a wake-up call they did not need. Everyone arriving for work that morning knew the itinerary for the day. They climbed the stairs to the station with a hushed air of respect, walking the same route as Karl had once done, his forever absence present as they traced the steps he would never walk again.

Ascending the stairs that morning were the TPE colleagues who worked in the booking office, such as Angela Dunn, and those who had volunteered to cover the shifts of the staff who worked on the platforms. The latter knew Karl best of all and needed to attend his funeral. Naturally, they weren't coming into work that day. So the railway family pulled strings and swapped shifts so that all those who wanted to could be with Karl for his final journey.

When the railway loses one of its own, it is a tragedy that ripples all the way along the network. And as Karl had worked on the rail-replacement buses before joining the team at Huddersfield, he had made a massive impact on people all over the railway. Everyone wanted a chance to say goodbye, even if they had to work on the day of the funeral. Karl's family also wanted their boy to bid farewell to the place he had loved for so long. A special send-off was now devised for this very special man. It proved to be so special that no one who witnessed it would ever, *ever* forget it.

At about 1 p.m. on 6 November, Karl came to Huddersfield station one last time. The word went round, and people from all over the network came to pay their respects. They arrived in ones and twos and groups: drivers and conductors and even some executives from head office. As they stepped through the gateline, it was with very heavy hearts. The concourse at Huddersfield was often the setting for affectionate reunions of friends and family, who rushed at one another to hug, the excitement of coming home eclipsing all else, but that morning there was little warmth to be found among the travelling TPE workers. Colleagues embraced or shook hands or acknowledged each other with formal, gruff nods, but there was no joy in their being together. For the one person who had brought them together was painfully absent.

In the booking office, Angela Dunn was fighting her way through her shift. Then, at the appointed hour, she gently drew down the window on her serving hatch. All work at the station ceased. Before she left the office, she draped a bright red pashmina over her navy uniform; everyone had been asked to wear red today for Karl, in honour of his favourite football team, Manchester United. Angela planned to wear her scarlet scarf all day long. It was nice to feel that she was honouring her colleague in this small way, even though she couldn't go to the funeral. Customers would ask why she was wearing it, and she would tell them, and in speaking Karl's name there was a kind of comfort, as though it was helping to keep his memory alive.

As Angela stepped out on to the station steps that lunchtime, she saw that everyone else had got the memo: all the TPE colleagues were wearing ruby-red hats, scarves, jackets and jumpers as they ranged along the steps of the station – about fifty people or more, all told. The steps were absolutely full. The colourful clothing made for an incongruous burst of brightness. It seemed at odds with the solemnity of the day – and yet, somehow, it also perfectly summed up the man they were mourning, he who could always cheer his colleagues up, no matter what was getting them down.

Despite the numbers there, a hush soon fell among the gathered colleagues. At that moment a big black hearse pulled off the road by the taxi rank and crossed on to the regal sandstone floor of the square itself. Driven at a sombre pace, the car pulled up in front of the steps – and there it remained.

The square fell silent. Even the pigeons pecking in the fountains seemed to stop what they were doing and be still. Karl's coffin was wreathed all over with flowers; one that stood out in particular was a love heart made of pink roses from his fiancée.

Angela Dunn blinked back tears. It was a very emotional moment. Karl had been so young and his death so sudden, and he had been such a wonderful, kind bloke. His was a truly tragic loss; there were no words to explain how everybody felt.

And so, without words, everyone standing on the steps

simply joined hands and bowed their heads. Sara was there, and Dan, and Chrissie and Amanda from the booking office. Everyone wanted to pay their respects. That was testament to Karl, and to his character – how very many people he had touched in his too-short time on this earth. There was a shared, silent moment as they all looked down at Karl's coffin in the hearse, holding hands and thinking of him. They cried genuine tears for the loss of a much-loved colleague who had been taken far too soon.

For Sara, it was a very peculiar moment. For though she was distraught, there was also some strange comfort in the knowledge that Karl was surrounded by his colleagues. There was comfort in knowing how much he had been loved. And, in a way, his presence at the station made him feel part of the team for one last time. This was one last shift that they all could work together.

Eventually, though, and all too soon, the time came for Karl to move on to the crematorium, for his funeral service to begin. So many people were going that the company had laid on a coach, and Sara, Dan and the others went off to board it. Angela Dunn and those who had agreed to work remained behind on the steps, ready to wave Karl off on his final journey, just as he had waved off thousands of passengers in his time at the station.

As the hearse pulled away, Angela raised a hand in farewell, saluting a colleague who had given so much to the station, but who, they all knew, had had so much more to give.

Karl's funeral, as with all such services, was supposed to mark the end of mourning, but of course that is never,

ever the case. Though it provided an opportunity to celebrate him and say goodbye, afterwards the raw pain of
his loss still smarted. It was impossible even trying to
get back to 'normal'. In truth, Sara wasn't sure she ever
wanted *not* to feel that lurching pain when she stood out
on the platforms in the wintry weather without him. At
least her grief reminded her of him. But who was she
kidding – there were reminders everywhere she looked.

For Dan, it was the night shifts when he missed Karl
the most. Though the team leaders and platform staff
only coincided irregularly in the rota, he was abundantly
aware that the next time Karl and he were due to work
together it was going to be somebody else covering for
Karl. Dan had figured that one out, and it left a hollow
feeling in the pit of his stomach.

As she had done for so many of her colleagues before,
it was Felix who helped him through. The cat had such
an extraordinary sixth sense at picking up on people's
vulnerability. When Billy Bolt had died, it was Felix who
had comforted and consoled his colleagues, who'd felt
bereft without their Billy. Now, as then, Felix stepped
up when her team needed her. Death may have snatched
another member of the Huddersfield station family,
but Felix was determined to be there for those left
behind. Karl may have gone, but Felix could still care
for the friends he had loved, now he wasn't there to do it
for himself.

Dan found that it was the way Felix would come over
to say hello as if everything *was* normal that he found
reassuring. He would be sat at his desk, trying and failing to concentrate, and Felix would come and sit on his

papers and paw gently at his bearded face. Her claws would be tucked in, so that she prodded softly at him with her velvet paws.

If he did not respond, she would lean forward and delicately give him a little nibble on his eyebrow, as if to say, 'I'm here, Dan. Don't you forget me now!'

As if he ever could.

17. Not Yet Time

As time has a habit of doing, it passed, unstoppable as the seasons. Before too long, Dave Chin was dragging a Christmas tree along the platform, and Chrissie was once again draping it in lights and baubles. Felix missed it all, being out the back on her radiator bed, having a snooze. Unusually, however, even when she appeared on the concourse and cast her eyes upon the brightly lit tree, she still didn't show much interest. For the first time in Felix's life, that year she did not run up the trunk.

She still went over to it; she was a cat, after all. But she just sat at the bottom and batted a few baubles. Gone were the days of her athletic adventures bounding from branch to branch. She could not be bothered any more; she simply did not have the energy. She preferred to lie beneath the lowest branches on a bed of pine needles, where it was quiet and dark, and watch the wintry world go by.

Angela Dunn watched her fluffy friend from her serving window in the booking office. With Felix lying beneath the Christmas tree, she was much more 'accessible' than she'd been before. Yet these days Felix was much more tolerant than she'd ever been of all those who wanted to meet her. The team had noticed a real evolution in her character over the past year, as though she had slowly grown into her role. It felt rather as though the increasing numbers of fans who had come to visit since her book had been published had immunised her over time from any former fears of strangers. The Felix of old had perhaps been like a teen heart-throb; she'd loved the adulation on her own terms, but every now and then had thrown a tantrum and stormed off. Now, however, she was more like a national treasure: relaxed in her celebrity, come what may. On the whole, she was placid as she greeted people, and at times would sit for hours on the concourse, her whole attitude laid-back. 'The queen is here, and you may stroke her.'

Her newfound maturity was something Mark Allan had noticed too, both in person as he commuted through the station each weekday and in the pictures Angela Dunn had sent him for the Facebook page of Felix meeting fans. Felix was notably more used to meeting strangers now and seemed to humour them more than she would once have done.

As for Jean Randall in the booking office, she thought that perhaps Felix's increasing laziness played a part in it all. For in Felix's willingness to remain in situ for people's visits, Jean detected a classic upside for the station cat. To her, Felix's soporific, half-closed eyes communicated the message 'If you think I can be bothered moving, you are downright wrong, my friend. So if you want a photo, take one, but I'm not going to move an inch.'

Jean, unfortunately, was not working at the station that Christmastime. Back in the summer, she'd had a terrible accident falling over in her garden; she'd smashed her right arm to smithereens and broken her elbow too, as well as her left wrist. The doctors had likened her fractures to what would happen if you dropped a china cup on to a concrete floor from a height of about four feet. Both her arms were put in plaster casts for months and she had to have a series of operations as well, to try to repair the damage. There was simply no way she could work in such a condition, so she had been signed off sick.

She still came in regularly, however, every month or so, for catch-up sessions with Andy Croughan. Every time she did, she made a point of seeing Felix, but the little cat was confused by the plaster casts on Jean's arms, which left her unable to stroke her fluffy friend. For a time, Jean couldn't even have the cat sit up on her lap, which was devastating for both of them. Jean found that she really, really missed the cat.

Felix seemed to know instinctively that Jean was hurt. And Jean saw her own sad expression that they couldn't cuddle reflected in Felix's eyes. Ever since Felix had been a kitten, Jean had been someone who had always taken time out for her, to give her love and affection or a bit of quiet space – whatever the cat had dictated. Now it was Felix's turn to care for Jean – and she did it as best she could. She rubbed her neck firmly against Jean's legs, stroking Jean since Jean could no longer stroke her. She walked alongside her too, a permanent partner wherever Jean went. Her considerate attentions made Jean smile, and that made her feel a little bit better, despite all the pain she was in. In some ways, Felix was better than any painkiller – and she had no side effects.

Some weeks before Christmas, Jean had one of her casts removed. Relishing the ability to bend her fingers after so long without freedom of movement, she made sure to give Felix a chin tickle in her radiator bed on her next visit to

1. Felix at home on platform one

2. Angie Hunte (left) and Angela Dunn (right), two of Felix's oldest friends

3. Felix 'helping' the Friends of Huddersfield Station with their gardening

4. Mark's unwieldy globe and a nonplussed Felix

5. One of Her Highness's favourite spots…

6 ...and another

7. The professional portrait of
Felix, painted by Rob Martin

8. Felix has always known how to work the camera…

9. …from iPhones to the paparazzi

10. Another special friend, Sara, turning treat time into playtime

11. Sitting with an absent friend on Billy Bolt's memorial bench

12. Angela treated Felix to a snuggly radiator bed…

13 …which soon became the best place for a cat nap…

14 …and is where she met Gloria, the Bucket List Lady

15. A very happy Eva after finally meeting Felix for the first time

16 and 17. There's no Dreamie too big, and no box too small for Felix

18. The new kid on the block trying and failing to blend in

19. Bolt and Jacqui having a cuddle

20. In the end, it wasn't long before the two furry felines became firm friends

the station. Felix purred like a train engine, so happy to have Jean back in this way. And, as she pressed her fingers into Felix's soft fur, Jean rather felt like purring herself.

But while Felix was much more tolerant of fans than before, she still needed her downtime. There were still occasions when the staff had to apologise and inform hopeful visitors that their queen was indisposed. It meant that when Eva – the little girl with big pink glasses, who was no longer wearing a starry blue coat, as she'd grown out of that last year – came calling for Felix that December, she was again left disappointed. Felix was not available for visitors that day.

Eva pushed her spectacles up her little button nose and sighed deeply. She and her mummy, Helen, had tried several times to visit Felix over the past year, scouring the station for any sign of her, but all their attempts to see her had ended in failure. For Eva, who still drew Felix at her kitchen table, who still thought of Felix as one of her very best friends, it was a bitter disappointment that was really hard to bear. Her big blue eyes would fill with tears and it was all Helen could do to get her to leave the station; Eva wanted to wait there for as long as it took for Felix to reappear. But after half an hour or so of tears and deep sadness, the bubbly four-year-old Eva would emerge again – and always with an irrepressible message of hope. 'Next time it might happen, Mummy! When can we try again?'

Eva had this deep conviction that it was just a matter of time before she would meet Felix. She was always asking to go back to the station to look again. 'One day, we *will* see her,' she told her mother over and over again.

This day, 9 December 2017, was not to be the chosen date, but there was a new development in Eva's quest to find Felix. Previously, she and Helen had been somewhat limited in their searches, asking only the platform staff for help. On this occasion, they had happened to be at the booking office, buying tickets to Stalybridge for a family day out, so Helen had asked at the counter if Felix was free.

Well, she wasn't – but what was this the lady was bringing back for them? To Eva's delight, the TPE team member pressed a free Felix postcard and pen into her hands.

Just as Angela Dunn had envisaged in the summer, the gifts went a long way towards making up for Eva missing out on meeting Felix. The little girl stared down at the beautiful image of Felix with dumbfounded joy. Across the bottom of the postcard was written 'Have a purrfect day!'

'Mummy, *look*!' Eva cried in excitement. She was absolutely made up. 'I am going to take it into school for show-and-tell!' Then a new idea struck her. 'Mummy, I am going to put this in my bedroom in a *frame*! Have you got a frame I can borrow please, Mummy? I want to do it *as soon as we get home*!'

And that was exactly what they did. Helen gave her daughter a brilliant white picture frame that beautifully set off Felix's ebony fur. That same evening, the framed postcard took pride of place on Eva's windowsill in her pretty pink bedroom. She placed it next to a framed photograph of her beloved grandad, who had passed away earlier that year.

He and Eva had been very close; he had used to call her 'Grandad's girl'. They'd spent hours doing jigsaws together, Eva squinting through her glasses, trying hard to see the missing pieces, despite the fabric patch over her good eye, while Peter smoothed her blonde hair back from her forehead and watched her with loving concern. It had been her grandad who'd been the first family member to spot her failing sight, the first to try to get her help. Perhaps, in some ways, it was a blessing that he wasn't around to know that Eva's sight wasn't getting better at all – in fact, it was getting worse.

But, for the time being at least, Eva could still see her grandad in that framed photograph on her windowsill. It was one of the last-ever photos of Eva and her grandad taken before he died, of them riding the dodgems on a family holiday in Malta, so it was very precious indeed.

That night, as Eva snuggled down to sleep underneath her bedspread – which was printed with the smiling features of a cartoon cat – she glanced between the snapshot of her grandad and the new framed post-card of her very best friend in the world. And she decided to begin a new nightly routine.

'Goodnight, Grandad,' she whispered to the image of the smiling man. Eva touched his face gently, and then flicked both her eyes, the good and the bad, back to the fluffy black-and-white cat. She grinned suddenly, so happy to be able to say it to her face. 'Goodnight, Felix.'

18. Perfect Partners

It was the morning after the night before at Huddersfield station, the morning after the staff Christmas party, which had been held in a local Italian restaurant. There had been food and drink, and revelations . . . for Dan and Sara, at last, had come clean about their office romance, having kept it under wraps since it had started (they had told no one apart from Felix). They hadn't wanted anyone else to know till their relationship was on a firmer footing, and even then they'd wanted Andy Croughan to be the first to find out, just in case there were any problems with two employees getting together.

Dan had had a few drinks before he broached the topic with his boss. It was one of those situations where he was really asking for forgiveness more than permission. 'By the way, this is happening, and I hope it's OK because, well, it's already happened . . .'

But Andy was absolutely fine with it. 'I'm happy for you,' he said to Dan. 'Just don't do owt daft on shift.'

In truth, it had been fairly obvious to the station manager for quite some time now that there was a spark between the two team members – and who was he to stand in the way of true love?

True love was what one creature certainly had in mind at the station that December – but, sadly for him, his affection was very much *not* reciprocated. His name was

172

Charlie and he was the loveliest, friendliest and soppiest cocker spaniel in the whole wide world. Though perhaps not according to Felix the cat.

One late evening that December, Charlie and his human, Julie Swift, were coming home from Sheffield University, where Julie had been lecturing her students in dog grooming and Charlie had been a model 'model' dog. He was such a happy-go-lucky fellow that he had patiently allowed every student in the class to have a go at hand-stripping him, a grooming technique whereby they used their fingers and thumbs to pluck the dead undercoat from his fur. Under Julie's direction, the students had excelled at their work and Charlie's glorious golden coat now had a lovely silky sheen to it that was shining brightly under the station lights.

Julie walked along with her fake-fur-trimmed winter coat buttoned up against the cold. She was a short, dark-haired lady in her mid-forties, who described herself as a mad dog groomer with an even madder dog. Charlie, true to form, was enjoying his evening stroll as they disembarked from the Sheffield service on platform two and began walking up platform one towards the station exit. He trotted along on a blue patterned lead that was attached to his blue diamanté collar, his nose sniff-sniff-sniffing at the cold winter air.

Charlie was a very, *very* friendly dog, one of the kindest dogs Julie had ever known, an absolute sweetheart. If he met a person, he would wag his tail. If he met a dog, he would wag his tail. And if he saw a cat, he just went potty.

This was because one of Charlie's very best friends in the whole world was a cat called Ludo. He was a black-and-white tuxedo cat with a white-tipped tail who regularly allowed Charlie to smother him in wet-tongued kisses. Every time he saw him, Charlie would signal his excitement with a flurry of tail wags that silently cried, '*Yes*! It's Ludo!' And the two creatures would then greet each other warmly: Ludo rolling over and splaying out his limbs while Charlie excitedly licked him all over with his long pink tongue.

Julie had another cat, River, who was less enthusiastic. But any time River lashed out at Charlie, telling him, 'Gerroff!' Charlie seemed to take it as a term of endearment and covered him in kisses again. Charlie simply loved cats and every time he encountered one, he liked to stick his big, drooly, dopey face right up next to theirs to say hello. His eager greeting was always completed with an excited wag of his tail and a sudden slurp of his fat wet tongue.

So when, on this December evening, Julie spotted Felix the railway cat sitting further along the platform from them, calmly taking in the cool night air, she decided to give her plenty of time and room to move if she wished to. In order to get to the exit, Julie and Charlie had to walk past the cat – there was no way round her – but Julie hoped that if she held back a little, Felix would take the hint and get a head-start so their paths would never have to cross. Julie didn't know quite how the station cat might take to such a friendly hound.

Felix did see them coming. But, in keeping with her new chilled vibe, she did not move a muscle, even as the crazy cocker spaniel came closer. Felix had encountered dogs at the station before now, of course; both Angela

Dunn and Dave Chin had observed her with them. She tended to give them a right eyeful, warning them off with a fierce flash of her emerald-green peepers – and usually that was enough to see them heading for the Yorkshire hills. At the end of the day, the station was Felix's territory, and she would not be scared off it by such mere mortals as dogs. Felix viewed canines as the enemy, on the whole, but it was she that was generally the more confident aggressor. She would never lower herself to engaging in combat, as such, but did everything through silent diplomatic channels – a ploy that had always got her exactly what she wanted in the past, which was usually the dog's departure.

So, as she watched Charlie approach, his legs excitedly bounding along the cold concrete platform, his nose sniffing left and then right, Felix remained as cool as a cucumber.

Julie noticed that she had not moved. *I'm just going to slow down a little bit more*, she thought. *Perhaps she hasn't seen him yet. She might spot him in a moment and walk away – and then she won't get an earful of cocker spaniel slobber . . .*

While Julie was well aware of Felix, Charlie, for all his hound-dog sniffing, had spectacularly failed to notice the fluffy black-and-white cat sitting slap bang in front of him. But there was so much else for him to focus on! The plants in their pots! The bikes in their racks! The people walking past! He was using his nose more than his eyes, hedonistically lost in all the new smells, so he didn't see Felix until he was really very close to her.

But, as soon as he did spot her, that tail of his began wag-wag-wagging. 'Ooh!' it seemed to exclaim with great excitement. 'It's a *cat*! I LOVE cats! Oh my, oh my, oh my, oh my!'

'Charlie,' Julie said soothingly, as she sensed his rising anticipation at meeting a new friend. 'Just be nice, now – and gentle. She isn't Ludo, remember. She might not like it . . .'

Obediently, Charlie took her at her word. He slowed his pace right down and approached Felix ever so gently, as though she was a precious bairn and he was a night nurse checking on his ward. Julie was not worried about him hurting Felix – Charlie was such a kind-hearted soul through and through that there wasn't a bone of aggression in his body.

Felix was also calm and gentle as the dog approached her. She did not run. In fact, she did not even stand up to acknowledge his presence. She simply sat there and looked at him, seemingly unimpressed. 'Who are *you*?' her eyes sneered silently. She was giving him the dead-pan, dismissive look that she always turned on dogs – but it was having little effect on the dopey Charlie.

Julie, watching them carefully, was impressed at how cool and collected the station cat was. She'd seen other cats freak out at having a dog so close to them, but Felix couldn't be bothered even to have a reaction. She fixed Charlie with her bored green eyes. 'I'm not moving,' they seemed to say. 'So what on earth are you still doing standing there?'

Charlie's golden tail began to wag faster. 'Oh, oh, oh!' it excitedly declared. 'I'm going to say helloooo to yooooou, little cat!'

With a grinning, goofy expression, he stepped right

up to Felix. Then he lowered his friendly face to hers until the two animals were nose to nose. And then . . . he licked her, sloppily, right on her fluffy black face!

Felix looked absolutely appalled. She made a disgusted sound at the back of her throat. In an instant she batted Charlie away, smacking him firmly on his nose as though she was a strict disciplinarian doling out corporal punishment.

Charlie jumped back, taken by surprise.

He was not one to give up easily, though. While Ludo had never hit him, he knew that River sometimes did . . . Perhaps, he may have thought, this was how some cats said hello.

Well, in *that* case, Charlie wanted to say hello too! After only a brief pause, his tail started wagging again enthusiastically and he developed a kind of excited, dancing energy in all four paws. 'Hello, hello, hello!' he seemed to say as he bounced more buoyantly with every step. 'I want to say hello to you!' He swooped in again, his long pink tongue wiping all over Felix's face.

She looked absolutely outraged. 'How DARE you!' her indignant green eyes intoned loudly without words. She was Queen Felix – didn't this dopey dog understand that royal etiquette ruled that she should *never* be touched by lesser mortals? *Once* had been bad enough, but *twice*?! What on earth was wrong with this brainless ball of fluff?

Once more with feeling, she smacked Charlie on the nose – and, this time, she was not waiting around for a third unwanted kiss. She skipped a little bit to begin with as she walked away, at the shock of his affection, but then stalked off at a steady, much more unruffled pace. It was as though she was determined not to give him the satisfaction of seeing her run away; she made a dignified exit, her head held regally high.

'Charlie!' admonished Julie, as the dog looked sadly after the station cat, his nose feeling really rather battered after Felix's two well-placed swipes. 'That is what you get for sticking your nose in people's ears when they don't want it! When will you ever learn?'

But the answer, Julie knew, was never. Charlie was just too friendly a dog. Indeed, even as he watched Felix walk away, he noticed that two TPE staff were standing nearby, chuckling heartily to themselves at how adeptly Felix had dealt with him.

All thoughts of the cat were suddenly banished. With a scurrying stride that brought Julie with him, he bounded over to them. 'You stroke me instead!' his eager strides seemed to say – and they were more than happy to oblige.

It was a Christmastime full of cuddles. Charlie and anyone who would pet him . . . Sara and Dan – who marked their new relationship with a meeting of minds (and lips) beneath the mistletoe . . . And even Felix found her perfect partner too. She may not have had her own beau, but she would always have Angela Dunn. Her lady-in-waiting had been a constant companion ever since kittenhood – and now their steadfast friendship was feeling festive. For this pair of perfect partners had decided to spend the holiday season together. Boyfriends and husbands were overrated. This Christmas, the true love affair was all about feline fun.

19. A Very Merry Christmas

When she wasn't working at the station, Angela lived in a semi-detached three-bedroomed house in a nearby village. She really wasn't sure what Felix would make of it as she took her home for the holidays on 22 December 2017. Though Angela and Felix had long been friends, Angela had never taken her home before. After all, when Felix had first arrived at the station as a kitten, six and a half years ago, Angela had always had a house full of family over the festive season and it wouldn't have been fair. As for the past couple of years, with so much upheaval in Angela's life with her divorce going through, the last thing on her mind had been inviting a fluffy friend for Christmas. But this year it had seemed the right thing to do.

Angela had been facing another Christmas alone. When she'd first got divorced, her friends and family had rallied round, inviting her out or over to theirs so that she was never on her own. But you couldn't expect people to do that forever; her children had their own lives and families, and she didn't want to be a burden. She'd arranged to see her daughter on Boxing Day and her son for a few hours on the twenty-fifth, but the rest of the time she would be celebrating solo. At least, she would have been. But now she wasn't — not now that Felix was coming to stay.

Angela was hoping that Felix would settle in easily,

but she was concerned that the unfamiliar setting might send the railway cat running for cover. Back at the station, she'd managed to get Felix into her carry case, which was the first triumph – Felix was still as reluctant as ever to go travelling. The panting cat soon settled down on the journey, as Angela frantically adjusted the blower in the car up and down, wanting to find just the right temperature for the station cat. (Felix sat in her carrier in the front seat calmly, taking all this as her due.) However, being settled in the carry case was one thing, being comfortable in new and strange surroundings quite another.

With trepidation, Angela set down the carrier in her lounge and opened the lid. She left Felix to come out at her own pace; she didn't want to rush or scare her. Angela tiptoed back cautiously, doing everything in her power not to startle the station cat.

Well, Angela had never seen anything like it. Queen Felix stepped out of that carry case as though she was stepping out of a chauffeur-driven Jaguar. As she glanced around Angela's comfortable home, her tail went straight up in the air and she started purring appreciatively, as if to say, 'This'll be all right, this, for a while. This will do nicely.' There was no fear, no worry, no bolting. She made herself right at home.

She soon decided to go confidently into every room to suss out what was what, and every room soon got the Felix seal of approval. She liked the conservatory out the back, which looked out on to Angela's garden – including her tinkling, trickling, tiered water feature, which encouraged the birds to visit. She liked the lounge at the front too, which had a comfy brown leather sofa that she liked to lie along the back of, looking out the front at all the neighbours; Felix, it turned out, was as curious as any local busybody to see what was going on. And she liked the spare room upstairs as well, where she found that Angela had laid out a radiator bed for her; knowing how much Felix loved the one at the station, Angela had bought a second one for her to enjoy while staying at her home. Far from seeming out of place in a domestic setting, the station cat slotted straight in. However, there was one aspect of Angela's home that took her completely by surprise . . .

Angela was following Felix around as she explored, making sure she didn't get into any trouble. (The story of how Felix had nearly escaped up the chimney at Jean's one Christmas was by now legendary.) So Angela was on her tail as Felix tiptoed into her grey-slate-floored kitchen and did a double take.

Felix's brow furrowed in confusion. She already knew from her explorations that there was no other cat in the house . . . so who, then, was this spectacular-looking beauty staring back at her? She peered closer at the black-and-white cat reflected in the oven door . . . and her fellow pussy peered closer too. She blinked when Felix blinked. She twitched her ears and sniffed.

Felix sat there for quite some time: at first rather startled; later, simply admiring her reflection. She did not preen, but instead seemed quite comfortable. 'That cat looks nice . . . We're just going to sit here for a while, OK, Angela?' she seemed to say. She was there long enough for Ange to creep away and pick up her phone, so that she could snap a picture of the station cat being delighted by her doppelganger. Felix seemed to think that she had never seen such a lovely-looking cat!

Nor was that the only photograph Angela took that holiday season. Part of her reason for wanting to host Felix was to keep her fans updated via Facebook. Angela knew from first-hand experience just how much Felix meant to those who were lonely at Christmas, and she wanted to fill their newsfeeds with shots of Felix having festive fun. In truth, too, she knew it would give her something to focus on. So she snapped Felix standing next to an extraordinary turkey that was the exact same size as the station cat; and in the days to come would even attempt to capture her watching the Queen's speech on Christmas Day. (It took a while, but she succeeded in the end!)

Most of all, however, Angela wanted Felix to have some time to relax while she was with her on her holidays. It had been a very busy festive season at the station, with Felix raising money for Cash for Kids again, this time through sales of a new cuddly version of herself; rather than a superhero cape, the toy cat had worn Felix's famous hi-vis jacket that had so long ago been lost. The two Angelas, meanwhile, had raised around £3,500 for Dementia UK by creating a special Felix Christmas bauble for her fans to hang on their trees. They had been really touched by the response.

When Angela thought about all that the station cat had achieved and experienced that year, it took her breath away. Felix now had over 120,000 Facebook followers; she'd published a bestselling book; she'd raised hundreds of thousands of pounds for charity; she'd touched the lives of countless fans. The meet-and-greets alone were very demanding for Felix – being woken from her naps, meeting strangers day in and day out – and Angela thought she probably needed a bit of peace and quiet. She wasn't as young as she used to be, and Angela wanted her to take some 'me time' (or should that be 'meow time'?) to recharge her batteries. When Angela got tired, someone else would cover her shifts for her, but Felix, as the sole railway cat, had no such luck. Poor old puss. It really was an awful lot of work for one cat . . .

After a while, Felix left behind the beautiful cat who lived in the oven and re-entered the lounge. Soon the cat was busy bouncing all over the sofa, treating it as a trampoline. There was unmistakeable joy in her eyes to have such a soft and comfy place to sit and chill out . . . and with a contented purr that was exactly what she did.

Angela, feeling similar pleasure, happily joined her colleague on the sofa. 'This is none too shabby, is it, my sweet?' she asked the cat, giving her a long stroke, her fingers fumbling through Felix's fluffy black fur. Felix purred loudly again, as though in agreement.

As they sat together, companionably watching a spot of telly, Angela and Felix glanced around the lounge. They saw the soft sofa, the wide window . . . and the beautiful Christmas tree standing proudly in the corner. It was wreathed in brightly coloured baubles and twinkling with fairy lights. In fact, Angela had put up not one, not two, but *three* trees in her home that year: a little one in the hallway, a big one in the front room and a fibre-optic version in the conservatory. As she and Felix watched the television, their gaze also took in two toy dolls representing Father and Mrs Christmas, who stood sentry below the screen, like soft-tummied soldiers. With such loving and lovely details in place all over the house, Angela's home certainly looked festive and fun.

It was a total transformation – and not just from how it looked out of season. The year before, Angela hadn't bothered with any decorations at all, feeling there was no point when it was only her who was there to see them. But, this year, everything was different. This year she was spending Christmas with somebody very special indeed: Felix the railway cat. And she'd wanted it to be nice for her. Felix, she knew, was worth going the extra mile for. After all, although Angela had arranged to see her family over the festive period, it was Felix who would be with her every day, Felix with whom she would wake up on Christmas morning. And, in all honesty, it was Felix who had helped to get her through the past, rather difficult year.

Yet Angela's house wasn't the only thing that had been transformed over the past twelve months. She too felt different: more positive about the future, brighter overall. She knew it was due to Felix. Angela had a lot to thank that little cat for.

An Austrian study, carried out in 2003, had once shown that having a cat in the house was the emotional equivalent of having a romantic partner – but Angela totally disagreed with that. It wasn't equivalent at all. It was actually much, much better. And, with Felix by her side, it turned out to be the merriest Christmas that Angela had experienced in many a year.

20. New Year, New Felix

'Nice one, Felix,' said Mark Allan, Felix's Facebook manager, in January 2018. He lowered his phone, on which he'd been taking pictures of the station cat, and gave her ears a rough stroke. She tipped her head up into his hand, acknowledging the compliment – although, really, she was so consistently fabulous in front of the camera that it didn't need to be said . . .

Mark slipped his phone into his pocket with a heavy heart that morning, and returned to stroking Felix. He had only a few minutes before his train was due to arrive and he wanted to make the most of the time he had with her.

Felix didn't know it, but it was the end of an era. Mark's job had recently changed and would require him to work in London from now on. For the past three years, he and Felix had met every weekday morning; it was a daily appointment that Felix rarely missed. Her delicate ankles and wrists bore no trace of a timepiece but, even so, the TPE team knew they could set their watches by her – because Felix was always impeccably punctual for meeting Mark. Every day she would wait for him by 'their' bench. But from tomorrow onwards, she would be waiting in vain.

Mark didn't have the words to say goodbye to her. The only upside for him was that most Fridays he would be back up north for work. His bosses had given him the option of working from home that day – but Mark had a sneaking suspicion that the prospect of meeting Felix meant he wouldn't. He'd much rather come in to see her on his way to the Manchester office – so that's exactly what he did. He enjoyed his time with Felix so much that he simply couldn't go cold turkey, even if that was what everyone else was eating in those first few days of the new year.

Luckily for him, Felix did not seem to hold a grudge against him when his new job began and he failed to arrive to see her four days of the working week. She still waited for him on those Fridays when he caught the train from Huddersfield. Remarkably, on his birthday she even waited outside on the station steps for him before accompanying him inside, as though she knew it was a special day. (Perhaps she had a calendar as well as a watch secreted somewhere on her person.) Mark found that he really missed their daily interactions – but he also discovered that it made the shorter time they now shared together even more special. Absence makes the heart grow fonder, after all, and that was definitely what happened for Mark, who continued to run the Facebook page (with a little help from the station team) despite his change of job.

As well as cherishing his time with Felix more, he found that he noticed little details which might previously have escaped his notice, such as the change in Felix's name tag. The team leaders' phone number, which was engraved on the back in case Felix ever got lost, had recently changed, so team leader Jacqui had ordered a new tag for Queen Felix. Naturally, it had to be a glamorous design. Jacqui had opted for a gorgeous one: a silver circular tag with a pink glittery pawprint on the front, and Felix's name, address ('Platform 1') and the new phone number engraved on the back.

Felix took to it straight away, showing it off in her modelling shoots with her trademark style. Watching her pose and posture, the pink glitter at her throat sparkling under the station lights, it was more like seeing a diva on a dancefloor, lit by rotating glitter balls. Mark made sure to capture every sensational step she made.

On those Friday visits to the station he also noticed that Felix's famous cat flap on the concourse had changed. Unfortunately for Felix, it wasn't exactly an upgrade due to her ever-increasing fame. The original cat flap, which had been decorated with her name and cartoon image, had recently been vandalised. One Saturday afternoon in the run-up to Christmas, an angry man had decided to boot the plastic partition panel and badly cracked it; luckily, Felix wasn't around at the time. The team had taped it up and put in a request with maintenance man Dave Chin to repair it.

But, before Dave could get to it, half a dozen fare-dodgers got there first. A group of lads, rushing to get through the gateline without paying for their tickets, had decided to try to hurdle their way over Felix's personal entrance to the station instead. But their collective weight, combined with the original damage, was too much for the structure to bear. It had since been replaced, but it was 'only' a standard cat flap, brown and drab in design, with no decoration and no name of the famous railway cat appearing anywhere on it.

Felix, however, took as much notice of the 'substandard' replacement as she had of the original – which is to say, none at all. She had never used it anyway – she would squeeze awkwardly round the gaps at its sides, rather than swinging through the saloon door in its centre – and she wasn't about to start now. Still, the unused cat flap stood on the concourse as before, a not-so-secret sign that a railway cat lived here.

Truth be told, as 2018 began, such signs were needed more and more. It was perhaps Dave who first noticed the difference in Felix. As he didn't come to Huddersfield every day, he was struck by how Felix had gradually changed her routine. Once upon a time, when he came to the station, Felix would be out and about, sitting comically in a watering can belonging to the Friends of Huddersfield Station, stalking pigeons on the platforms or simply taking a breather on one of the metal benches. She was seemingly never off the platforms, and clearly enjoyed the fresh air and all the adventures of the railway. Back in the day, Dave had found himself unable to undertake a new task at Huddersfield without Felix trotting over to see what he was up to. Her inquisitive green eyes would drink it all in as he hammered or plugged or screwed or banged and she was fascinated by everything he did – by everything anyone did.

But, as the new year began, Dave realised that it had been quite a while now since Felix had done any of that. Her six years at the station had taught her what everyone was up to and she no longer bothered to investigate.

Why chase after Adam Taylor when he was watering the plants? She had seen it all before. Why race after Dave as he dragged a ladder along to change a light bulb? She was switched on enough to know that it was a waste of her time. She preferred to snooze on her luxurious 'chaise longue' in the ladies' locker room instead.

It was, in fact, rare, now, for Dave to see her out on the platforms during the day at all. He found he could spend all day at the station and never see her, whereas in years gone by he had seen her all the time. If he wanted a cuddle with the station cat now, he had to go and pay court to her in her radiator bed, just like everyone else. Nine times out of ten she would be sleeping, and Dave would tiptoe out of the room and leave her be.

When he mentioned the cat's change in routine to Angie Hunte, she could only agree. She too had noticed that Felix had got much more sleepy of late. Cats sleep for an average of fourteen hours a day anyway, but Felix was clocking up much more than that now. To her credit, she would still have bursts of liveliness, where she might stalk after a pigeon or play pouncing games with the on-duty team leader, and for those brief moments she would still be sprightly and springy. But as soon as she'd had enough, she would go and lie down – and that would be her adventure done for the day.

Jean Randall, too, noticed on her infrequent visits that Felix was much less frisky and playful. She had never been a big one for toys anyway, but they seemed to have lost any appeal they'd once had; Felix just wasn't interested in them. And if Felix did go out on to the platform during the day, she would settle herself down and watch the world go by, without any inclination to engage with it. It was rare that she went to explore the wildflower garden beyond the white picket fence at the bottom of platform one these days – or any further afield. Angela Dunn soon realised that when she went to look for Felix to introduce her to her fans, more often than not Felix *was* findable, even if not always in the mood to grant an audience. It was unusual these days for her to be off on a patrol somewhere during the daytime. She preferred to stay much closer to home – so much so that even her hunting trips to Billy's garden on platform four were much less frequent. Though it had once been a favourite spot, she hung out there only sporadically, even though the garden was just across the tracks.

But 'just across the tracks' could seem a very long way away when you were slowing down physically, as Felix now seemed to be. And there came an incident in February 2018 that underlined that with heart-stopping clarity.

It was a classic wet and wintry day. The passengers coming through the gateline looked battle-worn, having fought their way through the wind and rain even to reach the station. Commuters crossly dumped inside-out umbrellas that had been destroyed by the strong gusts blowing across St George's Square, while professional women mourned the loss of the smart hairstyles with which they'd left their homes. The bad weather lasted all day long, so that the platforms were soaked through by the time Felix decided to put in an appearance later in the day.

For the first time in a long time, she decided to pay a visit to Billy's garden, braving the bad weather to cross the tracks and have a sniff about in the long grasses.

Dale Woodward, out working on the platforms, watched her with interest, given it had been so long since he'd seen her explore the garden.

A train began to pull slowly into platform one and Dale turned his attention back to his work. Out of the corner of his eye, he noticed Felix jumping down into the four foot and crossing back towards her bike racks, but he paid her little mind; she was expert at crossing the tracks by now, and at knowing the timetables of the trains, and he knew she wouldn't put herself in danger.

Sure enough, as Felix reached the bottom of the four foot on platform one, she gathered her haunches beneath her and sprang upwards, summoning a single burst of energy from somewhere to propel herself to the top. Further down the platform, the train continued to pull in and Dale subconsciously admired her timing – she'd got it just right so that she would be safely on the platform by the time the train arrived.

But, on this occasion, something went wrong. Was it because of the wet platform? Was it slippy, perhaps? Or did Felix, sleepy Felix, simply not have the energy to make the leap?

Either way, something in Dale's mind registered that Felix hadn't popped up on the platform after her leap. He looked across at her directly, his heart beginning to pound. And all he could see was her little face peering above the platform edge – as her two front paws clung on for dear life. Try as she might, she couldn't pull her back legs up. She was hanging from the cliff edge of the platform, her hind legs dangling behind her in mid-air, kicking furiously but failing to find any traction.

Dale began to walk towards her, panic powering his own legs. But even as he watched, Felix the cat failed to find the strength to survive this leap. First her head disappeared from view, and then her white-capped paws, as she let go of the platform edge. Despite all her efforts, she hadn't had the ability to hang on for any longer.

Felix had fallen back down into the four foot. And the train was still coming in.

21. The Senior Station Cat

Dale's head snapped round to look at the train. How long did Felix have? Could he get to her in time? Had the driver seen her? There was a long-running 'joke' in crew mess rooms up and down the railway network which train drivers often said: 'My life wouldn't be worth living if I ran over that cat!' But it didn't seem so funny now.

The train, luckily, was moving at a snail's pace. Dale thought it very likely the driver had seen the cat – all the crews were vigilant as they came into Huddersfield as they all knew about Felix and how special she was. The driver could hardly have missed the sad spectacle of Felix bicycling her back legs as she clung desperately to the platform edge.

As for Felix, before Dale had even reached her, he saw her springing up again from the four foot as she gave it a second attempt. Like an action hero dismissed for dead who suddenly returns in the nick of time, she emerged in a spring of glory. This time, she managed to do it in one take as the station cat powered her whole self on to the platform.

The entire ordeal had lasted only a matter of seconds, but Dale was struck with fear. Felix herself seemed unperturbed. She strolled casually away from the edge of the platform as though nothing had happened. Perhaps she was just trying to style it out.

Although she may have glossed over that incident,

nothing could conceal the fact that Felix was growing undeniably older. That May, she turned seven, which in equivalent human years is about forty-four. It was hardly past it but, just like a middle-aged human, Felix found that she wasn't as sprightly as she used to be. She could still leap the four foot, but she'd to give it a bit more welly each time, and she was more tired afterwards than she once had been. No wonder she reduced her visits to Billy's garden after that. She was much more comfortable sticking to her favourite spots on platform one, so that was what she did. She reminded Angela Dunn of a grand old lady – no longer the mischievous kitten who had pranced about, but a mature, independent woman who knows what she wants to do and damn well does it.

On her birthday, Angela Dunn once again opened all Felix's presents and cards that had flooded in from all over the world. Felix's Facebook page by now had over 130,000 Facebook fans and many had generously sent her gifts. The power of the puss showed no signs of slowing; only a month or two before Felix had been honoured in the most extraordinary way with the news that she would feature on her own square in a special Huddersfield edition of Monopoly. There had been a contest to choose which English town would be next to get its own bespoke version of the classic board game, and word had it that Felix's fans had secured the win for Huddersfield by voting for her home town to triumph. It was a sign of how brightly her star still shone – and Angela Dunn could see that for herself as she opened card after card on 17 May.

As she did so, team leader Geoff banged open the

door into the booking office. 'Are all those for Felix?' he asked crossly. 'It's my bloody birthday as well . . .'

Angela exchanged a look with Chrissie, who was also working that day.

'Actually, Geoff,' said Angela slowly, 'this one is for you.' And she presented him with a card signed from all at Huddersfield station – and a bottle of red wine for good measure. She had remembered how upset he'd been the year before at Felix 'stealing' his birthday, so she'd nipped out to Sainsbury's in her lunch hour to make sure Geoff got something too.

It wasn't often that Geoff was lost for words, but Angela thought the kind gesture might just have done it.

'Well,' he said. 'Well. Thank you very much.'

He had a chuckle to himself and his cheeks went a little pink. While he didn't say much more than that, Angela could tell that he was right pleased.

When Felix visited the vet for her birthday check-up, however, 'pleased' was not the word that sprang to mind. To her great displeasure, the vet advised the station team that Felix was no longer classified as an 'adult' cat in the prime of life, but a 'senior'.

'Oh, Felix, love,' said Angela Dunn when she heard. 'You'll have to get on to TPE about your pension!'

Felix was especially displeased as the new classification meant a recommended change of diet. Older cats' kidneys cannot process the same amount of protein that adult cats can, so cat food companies produce special 'senior' ranges that are lower in protein and calories. Older cats – as Felix was already beginning to demonstrate – move about a lot less and are a lot more lazy, so they need fewer calories. It made logical sense, if you knew the science behind it – but Felix, for all her many talents, had never quite mastered that particular discipline.

So when the senior food was duly served up, Felix turned her nose up at it – just as we humans might turn up our noses at the passing of time, not wanting to admit that we have gone up an age bracket on a marketing form or transitioned to the next stage in our lives. Felix point-blank refused to eat any of it. They couldn't let her starve, so the team went back to the adult food for a little while. They cut down her portions, so her calories were limited, but they knew it wasn't a long-term solution. It was a battle that they would have to fight another day.

And it wasn't as if Felix was entirely immobile. Far from it. Though she no longer really clocked on during the day, it didn't mean she had retired from duty altogether – she had simply changed when she chose to be most active. And for Felix that was almost exclusively during the night shift.

Perhaps she took inspiration from her old colleague Dale, who had worked nights all his life and liked it. He slept like a baby in the daytime and enjoyed the peace and quiet of the station when it was silent and still. On nights such as those, you could hear the grasses in Billy's garden rustle in the wind even over on platform one. It sounded like a whisper of gossip that spread from one end of the garden to the other, a rumour that was taking hold. Felix liked to listen, too, to the noises of the trains coming in to sleep in the station at night. They sounded tired themselves, after their days of carrying passengers about, and the scrapes of their brakes and their wheels against the rails sounded rather like the sighs of senior citizens as they heaved themselves from their armchairs and wearily climbed the stairs to bed.

At night, the station was populated not by the commuters of the day, but by the engineers in their orange hi-vis outfits and white hard hats and by the cleaners with their bottles of bleach. Felix liked to listen as they shouted to each other across the tracks or whistled while they worked. She listened, too, to the clinking sound of bottles as the cleaners removed the rubbish to the big Biffa bins, and to the rumble of Henry the Hoover, which they dragged behind them. But on the night shift, listening was only half her duty.

Felix liked to conduct her own patrols in the evening, as though seeing what people had done with her domain during the day. In contrast to her slip in the four foot during daylight, she was much more sure-footed when she was stalking solo in the shadows of the night. She would assertively investigate each new development, such as a puddle that had formed on the platform from a daytime shower that had long since ceased. Felix would pad alongside it on the dry ground, then carefully test the damp patch with her paw. She would then nod knowingly, as though her suspicions had been confirmed, and ensure she avoided stepping in the water, valiantly leaping over the puddle instead.

When Dale locked the big blue doors at the front of the station at half past twelve each night, bolting them with a long brass pole, Felix would often be there.

'And that's the station locked,' he would say emphatically, and Felix would look up at him from the floor, blinking her big green eyes in considered approval.

On the night shift, Felix was at times like her old self. She'd join her colleagues on security checks, wait out on the front steps to greet those passengers arriving for the night-time services, and oversee the arrival of the *Metro* newspaper too, copies of which were delivered each working day around 3 a.m. The delivery man would haul in his big bundles of newspapers, bound up in brown paper with plastic ties, and begin slicing at the ties with a Stanley knife to liberate the papers, before throwing them into pink display holders. Felix would always sit to one side of these holders, closely inspecting the man's work. He thought her far more professional than the tabby station cat at nearby Todmorden, who, he said, tended to climb into the holders and thereby stopped him from putting the papers inside. Felix, of course, was far too professional to mess about in such a way.

But that didn't mean that *all* her games were over. In the spring of 2018, Felix was known to instigate the odd game of hide-and-seek with Dan on the concourse. With a mischievous expression on her face that was like the Felix of old, she ducked and dived in and out of the local information leaflets that the Friends of Huddersfield Station had left out on display. Dan, who had not played this game with Felix before – she'd mostly played it with Andrew McClements, back in the days when he'd been a team leader – had been confused by her behaviour at first. Every time he tried to move around the display of leaflets, she had hidden behind them, deliberately crouching down low so he couldn't see her. It took him a good couple of minutes before he realised she was doing this on purpose. After that, Felix found him a willing accomplice if ever she was in the mood to let off a little steam at night.

It was perhaps good practice for Dan anyway, to be reconnecting with such childhood games, because there had been a recent development in his relationship with Sara that made the likelihood of him playing them in the near future all the more certain. Sara was pregnant. A TPE baby was on her way.

The pregnancy may have come as a surprise to Dan and Sara, as it was still relatively early days in their relationship, but they could not have been more thrilled. Sara soon moved back into the booking office to work, as her platform job required her to lug ramps and lift luggage and the physical labour was not advisable; she also had very bad morning sickness. It helped her physically, but it was also perhaps an emotional boon too, as it meant she was no longer out working on the platforms where she had spent so much time with her best friend Karl.

She still missed him so much, every single day. She so wished he could have been around to hear their news. She knew he would have been over the moon for them; he would have been the best Uncle Karl that her daughter could have wished for. It was really, really hard to know that her child was never going to meet him, but Sara was determined that her little girl would still get to know him through her memories. Karl meant so much to her that, for a long time, she debated with Dan naming their baby after him in some way. But, in the end, her instincts told her that Karl would not have wanted that.

She could picture his brown eyes twinkling at her, full of love and good-willed guidance. 'Don't do that just because you miss me,' he would have said, with his big brotherly wisdom and a big brotherly hug. 'You must name her what you want to name her because *you* want to name her that.' In the end, and well ahead of arrival, Dan and Sara decided on Maisie.

One day, shortly after their news had been announced to the team, Sara came into work to find Felix in the locker room. As she was fond of doing, Sara took a seat and allowed Felix to leap up on to her lap. Felix could be a bit grumpy from time to time, but Sara always took the risk of having a cuddle, because Felix was like the little girl in the nursery rhyme: when she was good, she was very, *very* good.

Normally, if she was in the mood, Felix would quickly settle down for a cuddle with Sara, and that was that. But, on this day, she looked rather quizzical as she got closer to her colleague. She did not sit down. Instead, her velvet nose quivered, as though she was smelling something new. Very, very gently, she placed her white-capped paws on Sara's belly.

Maisie was about twelve weeks old inside Sara's tummy at the time. Sara had not started showing yet, but it was as if Felix knew, all the same, that there was something different about her. It was as if she knew there was a new colleague sleeping away in there that she needed very much to say hello to.

So softly, very softly, Felix picked up one of her paws and placed it gently down on Sara's belly. Then she did the same with her other front paw. Then she did the same again. Felix kept on padding Sara's stomach with a beautiful and caring conscientiousness, as though she was stepping out a message in Morse code – a message that was intended just for Maisie.

22. Poorly Puss

After that day, Sara noticed that Felix never once showed her diva side to her again. It was as if she was on her best behaviour. She was kinder. Nicer. Maisie's impending arrival seemed to make the station cat suppress her occasional flashes of fierceness and bring out her more maternal side – one that Angie Hunte hadn't seen for a very long time, not since Felix had used to carry her brown bear around in her mouth many years ago.

Angie Hunte was feeling pretty maternal herself that summer as her friend Jacqui, her fellow team leader, came into work in June with an irrepressible smile on her face and a series of snapshots on her phone that Angie melted to see.

'Look who's moved in with me, Mrs H,' said Jacqui with great excitement.

On the phone was a photograph of the tiniest little black-and-white kitten. He was eight weeks old and absolutely adorable, a new brother to Jacqui's existing three cats.

'This,' Jacqui said, with all the pride of a new mum, 'is Romeo.'

'Oh, Jacqui . . .' breathed Angie. 'He is *beautiful* . . .'

It may have been that Jacqui heard the wistfulness in her voice. It may just have been that one idea snowballs into another. But as they chatted about the new arrival,

Jacqui asked Angie, offhand, 'Have you ever thought about getting another cat for the station?'

'Oh yes, I have,' said Angie honestly, for she adored cats. 'But the company have been so great about Felix, I really don't want to push my luck. We never thought we'd be allowed to get a cat in the first place! And how lucky are we to have Felix?'

Jacqui nodded. Lucky indeed.

'It's a shame, though,' Jacqui added lightly. 'I think it would be really good for Felix.'

Jacqui knew how much her own four cats liked each other's company, and it seemed to her, in comparison, that maybe Felix was a little lonely – and perhaps even under pressure, too, with the responsibility for pest control falling entirely on her shoulders.

Whether it was good for Felix or not, Angie had to put the idea out of her mind. She had other concerns that summer – and foremost among them was Felix.

The summer of 2018 was a sweltering one – what proved to be England's hottest ever on record. For Felix, swathed in her fluffy fur coat, the heat was pretty unbearable. Angie watched her with concern; everything seemed such an effort for her. The station cat slept even more than usual and seemed very lethargic, totally lacking in energy. Though she still went out at night, her daytime excursions dwindled to the absolute minimum. When she did rouse herself from her extended sleeps, rather than sitting outside, where the heatwave had made even the fresh air boiling hot, Felix tended to prefer the cooler climate of the interior corridor or the ladies' locker room. Though Felix had never really been one for drinking from her water bowl before, it was so hot that Angie noticed that she was going for her water more and more. She made sure to keep her blue plastic water bowl topped up.

At times Felix would sit in her old favourite spot on the grey-carpeted floor of the little lobby by the former customer-information point. It was shady there, and it was really the only place outdoors that Felix seemed able to sit that summer where she didn't melt in the heat. So it was there that her fans found her when they came calling. Though Felix barely had the energy to greet them properly, they didn't mind.

The law had been laid down about treats from visitors the year before, but not everyone followed the rules. Lethargic Felix was just pleased that she didn't have to lift a paw to be fed; as she reclined on the mat, people would give treats directly to her, much as a toga-clad goddess in ancient Greece might be fed peeled grapes by a minion. Felix, delighted, kept the secret, and only the widening curves of her hips gave her away . . .

The hot days passed by. Out in Russia, the England football team began their World Cup campaign, with their goalkeeper Jordan Pickford becoming one of the stars of the team. Only a year earlier, Felix might have given him a run for his money, but it was impossible to imagine her skidding across the concourse floor saving goals these days. She became more and more stationary. She explored less and less. More and more often, when Angie went to see if she was in the mood for meeting fans, Felix would allow it only if they came to her; she would not bother moving to the platform to see them.

Visitors curtseyed by the radiator bed and Felix wearily allowed them a few minutes of stroking before sleepily closing her eyes again and drifting back to sleep. More and more often, she did not even wake when Angie entered, or would growl with grumpiness at having her nap disturbed, so her colleague would have to tiptoe back to the hopeful visitors and apologise for the fact that Felix was indisposed. There were simply too many visitors for Felix to be able to keep up. *If only*, Angie thought, *there was someone else to help Felix share the load . . .*

Someone else was watching Felix that summer with concern. And as he yelled at her to get out of his office, playfully stamping his foot like a starting gun to launch a new game, Geoff, the team leader, was worried to note that Felix did not respond to him at all. Before now, she had loved her 'banter' with him. Usually, her interaction with Geoff would get her going – she would leg it down the corridor with delighted skips at his raised voice, before returning to do it all over again. She loved to tease Geoff playfully, scampering back and forth as he criticised her, clearly egging him on, as though she was charmed that someone would still stand up to her despite her fame. She liked to taunt him, too, by peering in through the low window in the office door. Knowing he had banned her from the team leaders' room while he was on shift, she would nevertheless prop her snow-capped paws up on the window ledge and gaze in longingly, like a child at a sweetshop window dreaming of sherbet lemons and chocolate limes. Geoff could shout all he liked – she was sticking to the rules yet reminding him who was really in charge. But these days, when he put on his cross voice and shouted out her name, she just blinked lazily at him and didn't move a muscle.

'She's not right,' he fretted to Angie. 'She's not like she used to be. I think she's overweight again. I promise you, she's not right well.'

Due to the dynamic nature of their games, Geoff was often the first one among the team to notice if Felix wasn't well, so Angie listened when he raised the alarm. And on 19 June 2018, his dire predictions came true.

Luckily, Angie was on shift when it happened. Midway through the day, word reached her that Felix had vomited in the back-office corridor. It was Terry from the platform team who drew the short straw and went to mop up the mess.

Soon after, he came to see Angie with an ashen face. 'Angie,' he said. 'Do you know . . .?'

'Know what?' she asked lightly.

'Do you know there's a bit of blood in Felix's sick?'

'You what!' Angie cried. She abruptly sat up straight, all thoughts of work forgotten.

Terry explained gently that the little cat's vomit had been red with blood – and not just a fleck of it. It had been very, *very* red. Felix, it seemed, was very, very sick.

Angie felt the bottom fall out of her world. Surely nothing could happen to her Felix; she couldn't even compute the idea of harm befalling her. Without missing a beat, she marched straight into action, running quickly to the station manager's office.

'Andy!' she hollered at the top of her voice.

The station manager glanced up from his paperwork in alarm. 'What is it?' he asked.

Angie felt her panic trying to overwhelm her, but she swallowed it down. 'It's Felix,' she burst out. 'She's not well, Andy. She needs to go to the vet's at once. There's blood in her sick, Andy. Oh my gosh, *there's blood in her sick* . . .!'

Andy raised a calming hand to stop the anxious flow of words. 'Just do what you've got to do!' he exclaimed. Felix always came first.

Angie, released from duty, rushed Felix off to the vet's. They fitted her in straight away, even though she didn't have an appointment. The vet carefully examined her and soon called Angie back in to discuss his diagnosis. Angie crept into the sterile room, which was lit with fluorescent lights, and felt as though her own heart was on the operating table. Was the vet about to slice it open with his scalpel – or bring her back to life?

'First things first,' he said. 'She's fine. She's going to be OK.'

Angie felt the breath that she didn't know she'd been holding release from her lungs in a rush of air. *Thank God for that*.

'It's not internal bleeding,' the vet went on. 'If she keeps vomiting, we should get her back in to do some scans, but I don't think that's going to be necessary.'

'What was it?' Angie asked in trepidation. 'What made her so sick?'

'Well, we can't be certain,' replied the vet. 'I think it could well be that she ate something that was bad for her – perhaps something left out on the station that she shouldn't have had?'

Angie nodded, remembering open tins of tuna and bright orange Wotsits . . .

'Or it could have been a mouse she caught, that perhaps had some poison in its system,' he went on. 'It basically could have been anything that disagreed with her, but there's nothing specific I can tell you, I'm afraid.'

'What can we do? How can I make her well again?'

'Well,' said the vet, 'I'm going to prescribe some medicine to help her recover, and I want you to put her on some special food. She really mustn't eat *anything* else for the next two weeks at least, so I recommend that you keep her indoors. OK?'

'OK,' said Angie, feeling relieved it was not *too* serious. But at the back of her mind she was thinking: *Felix is not going to be happy about this.*

Angie was right. Felix was not happy about it one bit. Against character, she actually coped with the change in diet quite well. The vet had prescribed some special gastro biscuits, which were crunchy brown balls. Felix sniffed at them cautiously when they were first served to her. Previously, she would never have touched biscuits in a million years – she had always insisted on a moist meal – but Angie was amazed to see that, after some initial reticence, Felix was soon eagerly gobbling down the biscuits from her white china dish, her little pink tongue regularly flicking out to lick her lips with satisfaction. Her demonstrably good appetite undeniably gave the dry biscuits her royal seal of approval. Perhaps, with a more mature palate, she was developing more refined tastes.

She was not a fan, however, of the medicine itself. It was a liquid that had to be administered from a syringe into a special wet food the vet had also prescribed. And her dislike of taking her medicine quickly led to the biggest problem of all: trying to keep Felix confined to barracks.

In some ways, one wouldn't have thought that she would have been too bothered by the new rule to stay indoors, given she now slept most of the day in her radiator bed. But, as with all of us, the moment Felix was told she *couldn't* go outside, there was nothing she wanted to do more in the world. Kept indoors, Felix's only option was taking her medicine. Outdoors, on the other hand, was a whole new world of opportunities and forbidden treats from passers-by. Felix soon became determined to win her freedom.

It was a battle of wits between her and Angie Hunte. Felix made the first move. She would lie in wait in the back-office corridor, biding her time until a colleague came along and unwittingly opened the door.

But Angie was one step ahead. She put up eye-catching posters on both sides of the door that led out to platform one, which featured two huge eyes urging people to look out for the station cat. The message exclaimed: 'Please be careful and watch out for Felix as you come in. She is trying to escape because she doesn't like her medicine, so please be very careful. DO NOT LET FELIX OUT!'

In response, Felix upped her game. Rather than loitering in plain sight, she took to concealing herself behind the hulking structure of the reservation printer close to the exit, where she could cleverly camouflage her ebony fur against its firm black sides. Thus concealed, she would then make a mad dash from her hiding place as soon as the door was opened.

She also tried a brand-new tack. So Angie thought she was going to exit via platform one, yes? Well then, in that case, Felix would go a different route. She took to loitering 'innocently' close to the kitchen, whose door, as it happened, was right next to that of the booking office. When the office was open to the public, Felix knew only too well that the shutters would be up – and she would have a clear path through to the concourse. So, as soon as the booking-office door was opened, she made a beeline for the narrow gap that had just appeared, dashing through it with more speed than she'd displayed in months. Angie therefore found herself fighting a battle on two fronts.

Yet the team soon got wise to the wily cat's ways. Angie put up yet more signs, this time also on the booking-office door, so that Felix's secondary route was also closed off.

Nevertheless, despite all their best efforts, Felix did outwit the team every now and again. But, in a sign of the times, the escape artist's victory was muted. If she did get out, the station cat went no further than platform one. She would go and sit on one of the benches – a sign she wanted attention. She would flop down with a sigh and merely lie there, much as a nineteenth-century lady who is weakening from consumption might cast herself upon her chaise longue and press a pale hand to her fevered brow. People would come over to the famous cat and Felix would gaze at them sadly, clearly feeling sorry for herself.

To Felix's frustration, however, no matter how much she turned her molten, pleading eyes on her fans, making her large black pupils tempting pools into which her followers could fall, on the whole they resisted all her powers of persuasion. Felix couldn't understand it.

Unbeknown to her, her old friend Dan had been up to his sign-making tricks. Dan, who couldn't wait to be a father when his baby daughter Maisie arrived later in the year, found that he didn't have to wait, after all; he could use all his fatherly instincts to care for Felix now. So he put pen to paper to protect the station cat, making new signs for the public's attention, for those rare occasions when Felix slipped the net and managed to break out, Houdini-style, during her two weeks confined to barracks.

'Felix and the station team need some help to make sure we can keep our resident celebrity happy and healthy,' he wrote on the typed sign, which was displayed all over the station. 'I'm afraid that Felix has been a bit unwell recently and the vet has prescribed her a special diet, one that we hope should make her right as rain. Understandably, this diet does not include treats of any kind, scraps from anyone's dinner, or leftover takeaways discarded on the station . . . If you do see Felix, please don't give her any bits of food, even if you think that you're the only person doing it. We can almost guarantee you wouldn't be, and it is very important that her meals are firmly managed to ensure she remains healthy and ready to receive her loyal fans again . . . Thank you for your help in looking after our girl.'

It was Felix one, station team two.

23. Felix Transformed

Dan was right to act with his signs. For although Felix soon got the all-clear from the vet for her stomach problems – she did not have to go back for any scans and she was not sick again – the vet did tell them that her weight was increasingly becoming a problem. In the summer of 2018, Felix was almost a whole kilogram overweight, the largest she had ever been.

Her more sedentary lifestyle inevitably played a part. Dale remarked that it had been a while since he'd seen Felix leaving any mouse gifts for the team too; whereas once she had caught mice regularly, she was really slowing down on the pest-controlling front. Her age was also a factor and, that summer, Felix found the switch to a low-calorie senior food was non-negotiable, as both the vet and the team insisted that she had to do what was best for her health.

In fairness, the vet said that Felix was in pretty good health overall, her weight aside. Her world-famous fluffy coat was glossy and thick. Her emerald eyes were bright. She also had good mobility – when she could be bothered to get out and about. But an overweight cat may be storing up health problems for the future, including arthritis, diabetes and heart disease. It was in Felix's best interests for them to try to get on top of it as soon as they could. Even after Felix was free to move about the station again, Dan and Angie kept the signs up on the concourse, urging visitors not to give her any treats.

Angie Hunte fretted about her not-so-little girl so much that summer. She couldn't bear the thought of anything happening to Felix. She was such a special cat; she was irreplaceable. If only there was some way to give her a break, Angie thought, some way of helping her to take things a bit easier . . .

Angela Dunn also watched the fat, fluffy cat as she lethargically lounged around through those hot summer days. Angela had taken over management of Felix's trips to the groomers of late, and she now decided that she had to take her for a haircut to try to shear off some of her thick fur coat. This was, in fact, an idea she'd already tried to help Felix feel less hot and bothered that record-breaking summer. Felix had gone for a grooming session earlier in June, but unfortunately the groomers hadn't done a very good job.

Knowing how hot the cat was, Angela had specifically asked them to give Felix a really thorough going-over, stripping out the dead fur that really bulked out her fluff and combing through her knotted pelt. Once at the salon, however, diva Felix had kicked up such a terrible fuss that she managed to throw a well-aimed spanner in the works of Angela's carefully laid plans.

'She wasn't right happy today,' the groomer had said, tight-lipped, as she'd handed back the carry case to Angela, 'but we've done the best we can.'

Sadly, their best was nowhere near what Angela had hoped for. She couldn't believe it when Felix stepped slowly out of the carry case back at the station and showed off her new hairdo. Angela had watched her strolling about wearing the pained expression of one who doesn't quite know how to tell her best friend that her new look was really *not* working for her. Frankly, the formerly beautiful cat looked deformed: she had one tiny hip, where the groomers had cut out a chunk of knotted fur from her side, and one huge hip, where Felix had not allowed the groomer to touch her. She looked completely lopsided. But worst of all her pelt was still as thick as ever, knotted and tangled and threaded through with dirt from the railway tracks. Poor old Felix. Her glamourpuss look was a thing of the past. She really was in a bit of a state.

Angela had straight away tried to find an alternative groomers – but then Felix had got sick and all thoughts of tending to her personal appearance had taken second billing until she was properly on the mend. When she got the all-clear, however, it was time to get back on the job.

One day, at the very end of June, Angela came into the ladies' locker room and announced to Felix that they were going on a trip to a new grooming place. Angela was careful, as she always was, that she did not show Felix the carry case until the last possible minute. Show the station cat the carrier too soon and you would never get her inside it. Felix would swiftly pull her old Houdini tricks and be off into the distance.

Back in the day, only Dave Chin had been able to get Felix in her carrier. Angela wasn't one for scooping Felix up off the floor in her arms as Dave did, so she'd had to develop her own technique.

The first rule was that you had to choose your clothes

213

very carefully in the morning. Some days Angela changed three times before heading out to the station, having to identify the perfect practical outfit: clothes that wouldn't snag or pull or expose too much skin, just in case Felix scratched. Second was to do everything in the right order, so that Felix didn't run for the hills. Third was to take everything nice and slow and easy, trying to make Felix feel as calm as she possibly could.

Despite the 'rules', when Angela lifted down the carry case from its home on top of the ladies' lockers, Felix backed away slowly. Angela moved ever so gently as she placed the carrier on the floor and opened its detachable door, but Felix had such fear in her eyes that you'd have thought Angela was asking her to step inside the mouth of a whale, and not the mouth of a basket that was already lined with a soft fleecy blanket.

Angela knew how much Felix hated the carry case. She'd recently invested in a new one for her – a grey carrier with a wire mesh door at the front – which she'd purchased with a voucher that one of Felix's fans had sent her for Valentine's Day. The new case was larger than Felix's previous carrier and Angela had hoped that having more space might help the cat feel better about it. But whether it was large or small, Felix still hated it.

That morning, she ducked her head as Angela lifted the box down and tried to hide in plain sight on the locker-room floor – almost as though she was a toddler playing hide-and-seek, who thought that closing her eyes made her invisible.

When Felix realised that her dastardly plan had failed, she turned tail and ran into the ladies' loo. Her too-fluffy tail flicked crossly, as though she was using it to signal 'No, I am *not* going in there!'

As though she sensed that her tail was not emphatic enough for this particular desperate scenario, her voice soon joined in too. Angela never heard Felix be more talkative than when she had to go in her carry case. She hissed and she howled and she squeaked and she growled . . . even though all Angela did was pick up the carrier and take a small, slow step towards the station cat.

'In you get, Felix,' Angela urged. 'Please go in.'

'Miaow!' shouted Felix, her voice high and shrill.

'Just go in, and then it's finished with,' Angela encouraged her. 'Come on, my love . . .'

But Felix darted round her and headed straight towards the locker-room door, where she mewed loudly, hoping someone would come to her aid.

'You're not getting out, Felix,' Angela told her. 'You're getting *in.*'

Eventually, Angela somehow managed to 'scoop' Felix into the carry case. The station cat gave a final little squeal and then there was silence. As Angela attached the wire mesh to the front of the carrier, Felix scooted forward until her fluffy black face was pressed right to the edges of the metal grille. She looked rather like a convict then, trapped behind bars, her green eyes looking gloomily out. But, funnily enough, now that the battle was over she calmed down and adapted to her situation. By the time Angela had pushed on her sunglasses and collected her car keys, the cat was sitting contentedly in the case, watching the world go by through the metal bars. Angela knew, after all the fuss, that Felix would now travel quite happily in her car to the new grooming destination.

The sun beat down hard on their heads as Angela and Felix crossed St George's Square to reach the station car park. It was more than 30 degrees that day and both Angela and Felix panted a little in the heat. As Angela cranked up the air conditioning in her car, cooling them both down, she wondered what Felix might make of the place she had found. She was rather intrigued to know – because it was like nowhere Felix had ever been before.

Felix gazed out through the bars of her carry case as the car began to climb steeply up a hill. They had been driving for about twenty minutes and were now out in the rural countryside surrounding Huddersfield. All around were rolling hills and valleys, their lush grasses green under the hot summer sun.

Felix's curiosity was piqued as Angela brought the car to a halt and came round to open the door for Queen Felix. As Angela pulled it open, Felix's senses felt suddenly assaulted by all the unusual scents that rushed in from the outside. Where *had* Angela taken her this time?

Angela lifted Felix out of the car in her carry-case chariot and the station cat's nose went into overdrive. What were all these new smells – and sights and sounds? What had happened to the familiar roar of the trains and the rumble of suitcase wheels on platform one? And what on earth made a noise like *that*?

'Moo!' heard Felix.

For the first time in her life, Felix the railway cat was on a farm.

It was a working farm, with cows bred for their meat, and Felix's nostrils twitched in trepidation as the earthy smell of manure and animal hides hit her fully in her fluffy black face. Being a city cat, used to the stink of engine oil, it was a very different smellscape for her out here. Her green eyes peered eagerly out of the wire-mesh door, trying to identify all the different elements.

Felix saw that she was at the top of a very steep incline. A drystone wall bordered the track that she and Angela had driven up, beyond which was a severe drop down into a plunging valley. Angela had parked beside a traditional farmhouse with duck-egg-blue doors and brightly coloured flowers in pots; on the opposite side of the track were farm buildings and garages. Hay was strewn across the farmyard in thick yellow strands, while mud-splattered wheelbarrows and tractor buckets cluttered up the drive.

In the distance, Felix heard a dog barking excitedly, its clarion call brought to fever pitch by the sound of the car on the track outside. Meanwhile, closer to home, her attention was caught by a white-and-tabby cat who prowled possessively among the plant pots. But the cat paid little attention to Felix, being used to the comings and goings of animals at her home.

Felix's nose twitched again. Further down the track were the cows she could smell: a herd with pale brown hides, who chomped mindlessly on the green grass of the fields that surrounded the farmhouse. And now she smelled something else, too: a new human, coming to say hello to Angela.

'Good morning!' said a cheery female voice.

'And a very good morning to you!' replied Angela. 'Thank you so much for being willing to take her – despite her reputation as a diva! As I explained on the phone, she really needs some help, bless her. She needs all the lumps and bumps and the loose fur taking out. Can you help her, please?'

The woman in her early forties with close-cropped blonde hair smiled easily, smoothing down the red tabard she was wearing. 'Well,' she said, 'I'll give it my very best shot.' She bent down and she and Felix gazed at each other through the bars of the carry case, as though sizing each other up. 'Hello there, Felix,' she said warmly. 'I'm Louise. Welcome!'

Louise was the cousin of a friend of Angela's. She had come highly recommended as a wonderful pet groomer. A shy, rather unobtrusive person, she had never advertised her services, but had nonetheless built a successful pet-grooming business over the past twenty-five years simply through word of mouth. She'd been grooming animals ever since she'd left school. Louise actually groomed more dogs than cats, but when Angela had phoned to ask specially if she might give Felix a makeover, she'd agreed to give it a go. Cats were very familiar to her too – two of them officially lived at the farm, but at one point they'd had more than twelve in residence, as strays often found their way up the steep lane and subsequently set up home in the farm's outbuildings. Louise and her family never had the heart to turn them away.

Angela was very pleased to notice that Louise had a lovely calm demeanour. Angela knew that Felix needed a firm touch, but she also needed a kind one; Angela hoped that, in Louise, she might just have found the perfect person for the job.

As Louise took Felix from her and walked with her new client into her grooming 'parlour', Angela felt increasingly confident. For 'parlour' wasn't really the right name at all. Rather than operating in some soulless salon or a clinical room that smelled scarily of chemicals, Louise worked in a small, neatly proportioned garage that was attached to the main farmhouse. It had a homely feel to it, despite its concrete floor, and smelled distinctly of animals. There was a black table for the grooming; a white bath within a dark green exterior; and a couple of cages for the animals to wait in, although these were empty today. It was anything but a sparkling poodle parlour with bells and whistles, more a practical establishment where Louise simply got the job done. To Angela's mind, it was exactly what Felix needed.

'Well, I'll leave her with you,' Angela said. She bent down to the carry case and locked eyes with Felix. 'Now, madam, behave yourself, please!'

Felix watched her go, then turned back to face Louise. She squinted at her through the bars of her carrier. Louise may have been the loveliest woman in the world, but Felix felt hot and bothered and hated the indignity of anyone grooming her luscious pelt. Even as Louise began to unclip the wire mesh from the front of the cage, Felix began to growl. And by the time she came out, she was in full-on panther mode, hissing and biting and scratching.

'Whoa, there!' said Louise calmly. 'It's all right. I'm not going to hurt you. Let's just take a look at you.'

Felix, grumpily, submitted to an examination. And Louise could see she had her work cut out for her. Felix was such a long-haired cat that it was easy for her fur to become knotted and there were several big tangles cluttering up her coat. Her belly in particular was filthy – the fur there dragged on the tracks as she crossed them, and although the Angelas always asked the groomers to trim her belly fur in particular, in order to keep it short and practical for her railway adventures, it had been a while since anyone had done it, so the white fluff of her stomach was long and bedraggled. With her former grooming session having ended so abruptly, her main pelt was exceptionally big and bushy, verging on wild.

As Louise peered at her haunches, where the fur matted around Felix's intimate parts, she wasn't sure that anyone had ever had the courage to get in there and de-mat the diva before. On the upside, Louise was pleasantly surprised to find that Felix was not especially dirty – she had wondered if a railway cat might get more greasy or oily than her domestic fellows, but that did not seem to be the case.

Felix growled constantly throughout the examination, almost like a guttural snore. She seemed to take Louise's interest as an affront. In keeping with most adult cats, Felix spent about half her waking hours grooming herself, and perhaps she felt human intervention was unnecessary – an undermining of her natural talents.

'Right,' said Louise briskly. 'First things first: let's take off your collar and get you combed.'

Louise used two combs for the grooming. She had one with teeth that looked like metal nails, which was good for pulling out the lugs in Felix's fur, and another that looked more like a human comb, for smoothing out her fur after the tangles had been removed. It was important to comb first, otherwise they'd waste time washing dead fur that really needed to be removed.

'All right, Grumbles,' she said to the growling Felix. 'Let's get going.'

She began trying to comb Felix with firm, regular strokes of her comb, but she could barely complete a single stroke as her coat was so full of knots. Louise really needed to spend time on each one, teasing them carefully so as not to pull her fur too hard – but Felix was not going to allow her the time she needed.

Hiss went the cat. *Swipe* went her paw. *Slash* went a sudden swish of her sharp, bared claws.

'Mum!' Louise called out across the farm, as she tried to hold Felix steady. 'I've got a bit of a wild one here. Please can you come and help?'

Louise's mother, a no-nonsense farmer's wife with sparkling eyes, short grey hair and glasses, came bustling into the garage. Louise rarely needed help with her grooming, but Margaret took one look at the wildcat on the table and reached for her heavy-duty freezer gloves, instantly understanding the situation.

'She's like a panther, isn't she?' she exclaimed. 'Just look at those jaws!'

'It's all right,' said Louise, reassuring the cat. 'Good girl. Try to calm down now; we're not going to hurt you.'

But Felix was not in the mood to listen. As Margaret held the cat still and Louise began tackling her tangled nether region, Felix let out an infuriated yowl at the indignity of it all.

'We're nearly done,' Louise soothed, combing as quickly but as thoroughly as she could. She was amazed at how much fluff was coming off the cat as she teased out the tangles. 'Just hold still for me please, Felix. Come on, sweetheart. It's all right, calm down now.'

But Felix would not calm down. Around her bum and belly were big clumps of matted fur and she couldn't bear to let Louise touch them. She let out another huge snarl.

'Dad!' Louise called out across the farm, as she and her mum held the cat steady. 'I've got a bit of a wild one here. Please can you come and help?'

So then Louise's father came into the garage too. He was in his seventies: a stockily built, muscular farmer with short dark hair. He was an easy-going, friendly man for whom nothing was ever a problem, so when he saw the wildcat situation unfolding in his garage, he simply rolled up – or, rather, down – his sleeves and pulled on his thick elbow-length gloves. They were more likely intended for falconry than Felix-handling, but he could see at a glance that they would be required.

Louise had never known anything like it. Most cats didn't like to be groomed, and she was used to that; they were less tolerant than dogs. Yet Felix's behaviour was on another level. As in all things, it seemed Felix was determined to outshine them all – and that was how she ended up with Louise's whole family tending to her, as if they were a Formula One team and Felix was a very expensive, very valuable racing car. Her constant under-score of growls certainly sounded like a turbo-charged engine setting off at 200 mph.

Margaret was absolutely astonished at her diva-like behaviour. 'I can't believe they make all this fuss about this cat!' she whispered to her daughter above Felix's head, as though not wanting to enrage her further. 'She's a nightmare!'

But the three-man operation was slowly bearing fruit. As Louise patiently helped to clear Felix's coat, teasing out the seeds and lugs and tangles, they cleared the way to a new Felix. Soon a much sleeker panther was sitting grumpily on the table, while a huge puff of grey old fluff piled up next to her, which had all come from her coat. Louise tried hard not to cut the tangles, which would have left Felix with a very patchy coat. Instead, she took the time to comb and comb and comb through her fur, taking however long was needed to rake out the lugs. Finally, she picked up her pet-grooming scissors and trimmed Felix's long white belly hair so she'd be better able to travel on the railway tracks, just as Angela had asked.

'It's OK, it's OK,' she told Felix, as the cat tried to wriggle away. 'You'll feel so much better afterwards, I promise.'

But Felix did not believe her – not least because after the combing came the shower. Louise didn't always bathe her feline clients – if you bathed them too often it could strip all the natural oils from their coats – but Felix really needed the full works this time. On the count of three, Louise, her mum and her dad carried a fighting Felix over to the white bath in the corner of the room and switched on the shower hose. She fixed them with a glare – a fierce look that endured for the next five to ten minutes, as Louise soaped her up with a hypoallergenic shampoo to get her coat nice and clean. It didn't really smell of anything, as scented soaps can aggravate animals' senses, but nevertheless Felix turned her nose up at it.

Bless her, she did look sorry for herself, as the water splashed on to her coat and weighed her down. Many cats famously hate water and Felix was no different. She was used to being dry and would really rather have preferred to stay that way. She looked bedraggled, sitting glumly in the big white bath, as the three humans fussed around her, Louise carefully wielding the shower hose as gently as she could. The water flattened Felix's fur until she looked more like a drowned rat than a famous Facebook cat who had captured the hearts of thousands.

At least there was no conditioner to follow; it can leave a residue on a cat's coat, and as Felix would soon be washing herself with her tongue, it wasn't a good idea to use such a product. But, to Felix's great displeasure, the job still wasn't over; next up was the blow-dry.

She was such a fluffy cat, it took a good twenty minutes to complete. Louise, sensitive to her new client's mood, worked as quickly as she could, blasting Felix with the long tube of the hairdryer-on-wheels as her parents turned the station cat this way and that to make sure her coat was fully dry. Towards the end, Louise decided to towel off her white-tipped paws. They were still a little damp, but they would dry off soon enough, and it was better to leave Felix like that than to stress her out with too much blow-drying.

'Nearly there!' Louise said cheerily to Felix. Felix glared back at her, sulking. Her Formula One team then 'drove' her back to the black grooming table and Louise gave her a final comb-through, to ensure they'd fully got out all the dead undercoat and tangles. To Louise's astonishment, yet more fluff was still emerging from the station cat.

She carefully continued to groom Felix, all over – lifting up her front paws to get to her armpits, smoothing out her intimate nether regions and brushing down her fluffy black back. After all Louise's careful work, each comb stroke now was smooth. Felix's coat looked gorgeously silky, shining in the bright lights of the garage. Though she'd fought it every step of the way, Felix had been transformed. The dirty fluffball was now clean and sleek. And the thick, heavy pelt that had been weighing her down for so long was gone.

Angela returned to collect her after a full ninety minutes of grooming.

'Felix the Tiger is ready for collection!' Louise had texted her, in order to summon her back to the farm.

'OMG!' Angela had replied, aghast at the nickname. 'Hope all is OK?'

'Still got fingers attached,' responded the groomer, 'but only just!'

As Angela walked into the garage to collect her friend, she couldn't believe the difference. The grooming may have taken ninety minutes, but my goodness they were ninety minutes well spent. Angela's real shock, though, came when Louise handed her a carrier bag.

'What's all this?' asked Angela in confusion. She peered inside it and did a double take; Louise seemed to have given her an unmoving second cat.

'That,' said Louise, 'is all the fur that came out of her. No wonder she's been too hot. She's been wearing the coats of at least two cats!'

Angela looked again at the huge amount of fur with utter astonishment.

She couldn't wait to tell Angie Hunte about it all when she got back to the station. She emptied the bag of fluff out on to the floor and stood Felix next to it, so Angie could see just how successful Louise's grooming had been.

'Bloody hell!' cried Angie. 'That's another cat! You could literally make another cat!'

The two women looked at each other in amazement.

But while the big pile of fur was certainly a talking point, the real conversation centred on Felix. And it wasn't about how marvellous she looked – although she did. Nor was it about how much she'd been physically transformed – although that had happened too. It was about the fact that Felix – the old Felix – was finally back.

'The best thing that ever happened to her,' said Angie Hunte with glee, 'was when Angela took her to the groomers. The difference in her when she came back . . . When they removed that "other cat" from her, it was like she got the spring back in her step. It was as if she'd taken off a heavy fur coat and put on one of those lightweight cagoules instead. You could see her thinking it: "Phew! Thank God for that. *This* is what I've been waiting for!"'

Everyone could feel the difference – especially Felix. She felt so much better that her behaviour changed. Though she was still hot, she was much less lethargic. It was as if she could breathe again. She perked up. She walked better. She moved more easily.

The cat was back – and not a moment too soon. Felix was about to be needed more than ever.

24. A Day to Remember

Nobody was happier to see Felix back to her usual self than her Facebook fans. For lots of them, checking her Facebook page each morning had become the highlight of their day. They loved to see new portraits of the beautiful cat or to watch one of Dan's 'Floof Files' videos. Felix was an incredibly photogenic pussy and a single snapshot of her patrolling the platforms or sitting up on the counter to check that a passenger's Metrocard was valid was more than enough to send people away happy, their hearts a little lighter thanks to the station cat.

She helped people all the time, even those many thousands of miles away. In the mountains of Switzerland, for example, a woman in her fifties found Felix online while she was still grieving for the loss of her own cat, Pauli, a black pussy who had passed away aged fourteen in September 2017. Gisela missed Pauli so much it felt like her heart had been torn out. She cried many tears and was in a very dark place. She was still in it when she first discovered Felix on Facebook about eight months after Pauli's death.

But then a strange thing happened. As she began following Felix on Facebook, the darkness seemed to subside. Reading Felix's posts and the lovely comments of her friends from all over the world made Gisela's own world seem brighter. Looking in Felix's eyes through her photographs seemed to show her that there was still potential for her to find lightness again. She felt full of thankfulness to be part of the Floof Fan Club. She loved being a member of such a warm and loving community – and at the centre of it all was a cat who seemed to have such wisdom and love in her big green eyes.

Slowly, Gisela felt that Felix was giving her back the strength that she'd lost after Pauli had gone. Her neighbours commented that the light had come back into her eyes as she told them stories about this wonderful cat she'd met online. And, after a while, Felix made the biggest difference of all. Gisela had always felt she could never give another cat a home, as Pauli was just too special, but she began to realise that she did have a lot to offer, after all. Felix made her want to offer a cat from a shelter a cosy home and it became something she was determined to do. Really, Felix simply made her want to live again.

It was a gift indeed.

Another woman who had fallen hard for Felix was a lady called Gloria, who lived in Tiverton in Devon. She had always loved cats, though she'd never had one of her own, something she regretted. After making friends with Felix online, she eventually made plans to meet her in person in October 2018 – almost to her surprise. Initially, she had thought Felix was 'just' a cat and hadn't necessarily felt the need to take their friendship offline; it had seemed strange, back then, even to think of travelling five hours to meet a cat. But over the months that Gloria had been following Felix on Facebook, the cat had slowly grown on her and she had come to realise how very special she was – until meeting her not only seemed sensible but desirable, even essential. Seeing her online every day – getting to know her through her pictures, captions and charity work – had made her a big part of Gloria's day-to-day existence and she was really looking forward to visiting Huddersfield. But on 2 July 2018, Gloria's life changed forever – and the fallout affected her distantly scheduled trip too.

Gloria had gone to the hospital that day for what she thought was a regular check-up for a condition she had – pulmonary fibrosis. While she was there, the consultant had asked to speak with her. And he had bluntly said, 'This is the end now, Gloria. I'm going to arrange palliative care for you from this point forward.'

Gloria was shocked to her core. She knew she had been ill, but she had never been told it was a terminal condition. 'Am I *dying*?' she asked the consultant.

He wouldn't answer her directly, not at first. But she kept on at him, until he conceded that she was.

'How long do I have?' asked Gloria numbly.

It was only a matter of months.

Gloria was stunned. Had it been longer, she thought she would have coped better. The suddenness was too scary. That cliff edge of nothing seemed too perilously close. It focused her brain in peculiar ways, giving her a crystal clarity on what was important in life. And she realised that the one thing she really, really wanted to do before she ran out of time was to visit her beloved Felix.

She messaged her privately on Facebook. 'I was planning to meet you in October,' she wrote. 'Please could we bring this forward? I got told today that I have less than a year to live. I really want to meet you before I go.'

She couldn't die, she told herself, before she'd met Queen Felix.

Her message came through to Angie Hunte and Angela Dunn. They put their heads together and, just as they'd done for the giveaway day the year before, they came up with a way to make Gloria's visit a very special day – a day that neither Gloria, nor Felix, would ever forget.

On 16 July 2018, Gloria sat on the train heading north, feeling a buzz of excitement flowing through her veins that was even more enlivening to her than the oxygen flowing into her nose from the cannula taped beneath it. She clutched the heavy black bag that held her portable oxygen tank tightly to her side, knowing it was helping to prolong her life and energy – knowing that it was allowing her to take this special trip to meet the station cat. Meeting Felix, in fact, was the number-one item on the emergency bucket list that she had hastily pulled together since receiving her prognosis just fourteen days before.

There were other items on the bucket list. She wanted to fly in a helicopter; to ride on the Orient Express; to travel first class; and to see the Blackpool Illuminations. But Felix trumped them all. Gloria felt that she wouldn't be able to relax – to face what was coming – without first meeting her furry friend.

Somewhat anxiously, she adjusted the settings on her oxygen and tried to settle back in her seat for the long journey. She was a pale woman in her mid-fifties with short black hair, much slimmer than she once had been, as she'd recently lost weight. Though it had been immensely difficult adjusting to her prognosis, now that this special day had arrived she mostly felt excitement, rather than the fragile vulnerability that had haunted her since leaving hospital. It was a good feeling, a feeling that Felix herself had brought about. Though Gloria knew she wouldn't have long with the station cat – knew, from pictures posted online of other visitors' experiences, that it would most likely be a quick five-minute stroke if she was lucky, as the solo station cat was so much in demand – she nevertheless sensed in her weary bones that it would still be worthwhile. Just the idea of seeing the cat with her own eyes felt special. She turned to the lady sitting next to her as the English countryside flashed past the window outside, and her excitement suddenly bubbled over into speech.

'I'm going to meet Felix today!' she told her gaily. 'Felix, the Huddersfield station cat!'

Even saying the words, it didn't seem real – too much a dream come true.

Her fellow passenger gave her a thin smile – she clearly thought her a bit mad – but Gloria didn't let her reticence affect her. 'She means a lot to me,' she confided further. 'And this is something that I have to do . . . while I'm still well enough to do it.'

Speaking to strangers was out of character for Gloria who was, on the whole, a very shy woman. So, as she arrived at York station from Devon – where the two Angelas had told her they should meet – she felt extremely apprehensive about rendezvousing with these two un-familiar women who had promised to take her to Felix. She clutched her oxygen closer and walked slowly along the platform. To her frustration, she was already finding that she couldn't walk far without needing a rest. It was a very,

very difficult thing to notice your own deterioration, and to know that your fate was just round the corner.

Further along the platform, Angela Dunn nudged Angie Hunte. 'I think that must be her,' she said, pointing out the slim figure.

They went over and introduced themselves, and Angie Hunte carefully took the heavy oxygen bag from Gloria, so that she could carry it for her instead. 'Now, let's go to Huddersfield!' the team leader said brightly.

'Oh, but I need to get a ticket,' burst out Gloria. 'My ticket was only to York.'

Angie smiled at her warmly. 'Don't worry about that, sweetheart,' she said. 'We've got all that sorted out for you.'

And to Gloria's surprise, she was escorted on to a TPE service as a guest of honour – without having to pay her fare. Not only that, but the Angelas ushered her into first class.

Gloria couldn't believe it. Travelling first class was on her bucket list! This was turning out to be a bigger adventure than she could ever have imagined.

The three women sat quietly as they travelled, taking their lead from Gloria. Gradually, however, the Tiverton lady started to talk. She told them shyly that she recognised them from Felix's book, which she'd loved reading. She told them how very, very sick she was. And she told them that all she wanted to do was get to Felix.

'Well, we're nearly there now,' Angie told her reassuringly, as the train pulled into Leeds. 'Next stop: Huddersfield.'

Gloria gazed out of the window with rapt attention.

Having read Felix's book, it was like seeing a story spring to life as the train drew closer to Felix's home town. There was the iconic landmark of the Emley transmitting station . . . There was the corrugated-iron roof of the station, where the pigeons lived . . . There was the Huddersfield station sign, declaring that they had arrived. Gloria disembarked with a buzzing in her belly, feeling excited to be breathing the same air as her favourite cat.

But even though she felt a surge of excitement, she could manage only staggered steps as she stepped clumsily off the train. She inhaled deeply, but her lungs relied more on the oxygen under her nose to help her catch her breath than the magic air she was finally sharing with Felix. The two Angelas exchanged glances. Rather than taking her straight to meet the cat, they first invited her into the first-class lounge.

There, Gloria said that she wanted to change. Though she kept on her ripped jeans, she slipped off her black top and revealed a white T-shirt with pink lettering that she'd had specially made. Its hot-pink words read 'THE BUCKET LIST LADY'.

Neither Gloria nor the two Angelas made any comment on her clothes. Angie Hunte sensed that Gloria did not want that, did not want their commentary. She had a very clear awareness of Gloria *preparing* to meet Felix – not only sartorially, but emotionally too – and there was an intensity that was palpable. Gloria had a nervous energy about her now. She kept putting her hand over her mouth as though she couldn't quite trust herself to speak, couldn't quite trust her senses that she was here at last, about to live out her dream.

When Angie sensed that her preparations were complete and she was ready, Angie beamed at her. 'Right then,' she said brightly. 'Let's go and meet Her Majesty.'

Gloria smiled back at her, feeling such a strong sense of anticipation that it was quite overwhelming. *Will Felix be friendly?* she wondered. *Will we share any kind of connection?* She felt a rush of nerves again, fearful that the visit might not live up to her expectations.

The two Angelas led the Bucket List Lady along platform one and through the door that led into the back office. Team leader Dan was on duty and said a warm hello to her. Thanks to his heavy involvement in the Facebook page, Gloria knew all about him – including about his and Sara's baby, as they'd announced their pregnancy on Felix's page – so she said a warm hello back.

'You're a VIP today, Gloria,' Angie told her. 'So you have to give us your autograph in our signing-in book.'

Angela Dunn – who had been designated official photographer for the day – snapped a photo of Gloria signing the official TPE paperwork. It said Gloria was a VIP and that she had come to see Felix. And then it was time.

Angela Dunn went ahead to check that Felix was ready. 'Please let madam be in the mood for visitors,' she muttered under her breath. You never could tell with Felix how that might play out. As the only station cat, Felix had so much to do, and now she was older she didn't always have the energy required for meeting fans. Yet when Angela opened the door to the ladies' locker room, Felix was lying comfortably in her radiator bed and the look in her green eyes said clearly to her lady-in-waiting, 'Yes, you may enter.'

'Gloria,' Angela called. 'She's ready for you.'

Gloria entered the room on tenterhooks, not knowing quite what she would find. As she crossed the threshold and saw Felix sitting in her radiator bed, it was as if time stood still. The nervous energy that had been building up swiftly dissipated. All tension drained away. In its place, an intense calmness seeped into their souls, as Gloria stared at Felix, and Felix at Gloria.

The station cat was bigger than she'd been expecting, absolutely massive with fur and fluff, even after her recent haircut. Yet she was also much friendlier than Gloria had been expecting. In those glorious green eyes was a sense of acceptance, even an invitation. Eyes fixed firmly on her feline friend, Gloria edged fully into the room and walked towards Felix.

She was so focused on her that she barely noticed as Angela Dunn fetched a chair for the frail woman to sit upon. It arrived just in time as Gloria bent her legs to sit beside the station cat, in such a way that her lap was almost under Felix's bed, so it seemed rather as though the cat was on her knees.

'Oh, you are lovely,' Gloria whispered to her, her soft voice close to breaking as her dream came true.

Felix raised her head, all the better to hear her.

'I'm so happy to meet you,' Gloria whispered. 'I've always wanted to meet you, Felix. You are just so beautiful, do you know that? You are so very, very fluffy!'

Felix's ears pricked up as she listened to Gloria talk. Her standard response to such greetings was cool agreement. 'Yes, I really am gorgeous, aren't I? I one hundred per cent agree . . .' But Angie and Angela, watching closely, realised that Felix was not, in fact, communicating with Gloria with her usual sense of arrogant self-satisfaction at all. Instead, they both felt that there was an instant, and deep, connection between the two.

Gloria felt it too. It was powerful. It was as though Felix sensed that Gloria was different from her other visitors, as though she sensed she had a problem. Later, after Gloria had gone, Angie Hunte would whisper fiercely to Angela, 'I swear to you: *Felix knew*. I swear she knew she was dying.'

It was not a far-fetched idea. There are several well-documented cases of cats sniffing out their owners' cancerous tumours or their hidden, internal illnesses, even one case of an American care-home cat, Oscar, who seemed able to predict the deaths of residents – he would curl up with them in the hours before they passed away, giving them a final piece of comfort before they crossed to the other side. Scientists reasoned with typical verbiage that cats' superior 'olfactory discrimination' might be behind these sixth-sense skills – but whatever the science, Gloria only knew that it felt amazing to be truly *seen* by Felix.

There is an Irish proverb that says, 'A cat's eyes are windows enabling us to see into another world.' Looking in Felix's eyes that July afternoon, Gloria felt as though she had glimpsed that other world, which was, perhaps, the world that lay ahead for her all too soon. Somehow, though, through her calmness of spirit and her generous love, Felix made her feel able to accept it.

It was incredibly comforting to be with her. 'Therapeutic' was the word that Gloria later thought summed it up best. As she stroked the fluffy cat and whispered sweet words to her, she realised that she had never felt so calm and relaxed in all her life. It was as though Felix took away all the badness, all the fear and doubt, and left behind a peaceful acceptance of whatever was coming next. Gloria fixed her eyes on her hungrily, as though she was committing the entire experience to memory, not wanting to miss a single detail. *This* was how Felix looked as she gazed back at her with total, unconditional acceptance. *This* was the exact position of the black blob by her heart, which she showed to Gloria as she invited her to tickle her tummy. *This* was the width of her wide white whiskers; *this* the texture of her fur.

As Gloria enjoyed her audience with the station cat, the two Angelas exchanged looks of silent astonishment. They had never, *ever* seen Felix behave in quite this way before. And as Gloria's visit went on, and then on, lasting longer than any previous audience, their surprise deepened further. Felix was generally patient with fans, but she usually gave them a finite length of time with her before indicating – by walking off or falling asleep or through an ill-tempered swipe of her sharpened claws – that their time was up. Yet she showed no such impatience with Gloria. Angie Hunte could not believe her eyes. Felix let Gloria take as long as *she* needed.

Angie could tell that the visit meant a great deal to Gloria, so much so that Angie felt as if she was intruding. A dying woman's wish was being played out in front of her; the emotion was intense. Gloria was whispering to Felix, telling her how much she meant to her, telling her how honoured she was to have the chance to meet her before she died. Angie wasn't sure she could take it. It was such a sobering reminder that you never knew how long you had on this earth, a reminder to be grateful for everything you'd got. Angie decided that she should leave Gloria and Felix to it and slipped quietly out of the locker-room door. Gloria, caught up in her conversation with Felix, did not even notice that she'd gone.

Only Angela Dunn remained with them, quietly documenting the meeting through photographs, as Gloria had asked her to. So she was there as Gloria whispered softly to Felix, in a voice that was tight with emotion, 'Have you ever had anybody visit you before who is dying?'

It was Angela who answered on Felix's behalf, as the cat kept her eyes trained on Gloria, trying to calm her as she frankly faced the truth of her prognosis.

'No,' Angela said softly. 'No, Gloria – you're the first.'

Gloria gave a wry smile, and the bitter twist of her lips spoke of time lost and wasted opportunities. 'Well then,' she said, 'I might be famous for something.'

Angela couldn't help the tears that pricked at her eyes. 'Oh, Gloria,' she said, helplessly. 'You have to give over; you're making me cry . . .'

But Gloria did not cry. Meeting Felix, somehow, stopped her from feeling sorry for herself – even though that was how she had spent much of her time since receiving her prognosis. It made her realise that she needed to dwell not on her death but on the life she had left.

So, in the end, it was Gloria who broke away from Felix. The station cat had gifted her however much time she needed – time that was hers to grant, even if she couldn't stop the larger clock that was inexorably ticking down. Gloria sat with her for almost half an hour, gradually absorbing the magic of the cat, and when she stood at last and told Angela she was ready to go it seemed that Felix was not quite finished with her yet – not with this woman with whom she had felt such a deep connection.

For the station cat followed Gloria out on to the platform, keeping her steady eyes locked on her, as though she didn't want to let Gloria out of her sight. She lay down on the platform and once more Gloria bent to stroke her. It was hard for her to do, because bending over took what little breath she had left in her damaged lungs, but she persevered for as long as she could, before she came upright again with a gasp, breathing deeply from the cannula running under her nose.

As she sat back, Angela noticed how tired she looked. Angie Hunte had now rejoined them and suggested that Gloria use the station wheelchair for the final adventure of the day: touring the station with all its Felix hidey-holes and secret spots that had been described in her book. Normally, Gloria was embarrassed to use a wheelchair, but the two Angelas made her feel so comfortable with the idea that she accepted their offer.

They took her all over the station, ending up at Billy's bench in front of his memorial garden, where Felix had spent so many happy hours playing as a youngster. In the softly fading light of the summer evening, it made for a truly peaceful place.

'How are you feeling now, Gloria?' Angie asked her.

Gloria smiled. 'I feel like royalty,' she said gratefully. 'You've treated me so well. I wasn't expecting any of this. I don't think I've *ever* been made to feel this special my whole life long. I can never thank you enough for giving me such a brilliant day to remember.'

Angie patted her hand. 'It's been our pleasure,' she said. 'We were glad to help.'

By now, it had been hours since Gloria had set off from her home in far-away Tiverton. The battery on her oxygen tank would soon need charging, and after all the excitement she found she felt exhausted. Though part of her wished she could stay at the station forever, she knew it was time to go home. She had come, and seen, and conquered her fears. There was just one thing left to do.

Her farewell with Felix, out on platform one, was as bitter as it was sweet. Sweet because she had finally met her and fulfilled her dream. Bitter because she knew, in her heart of hearts, that she would probably never see her again. It was very hard to leave her. But, with a final, loving stroke, Gloria whispered her goodbyes.

As she waited for the train to take her back to York – she would again be travelling in first class, with the Angelas accompanying her – she had one final message for her hosts.

'It's been such a lovely experience,' she told the women. 'It's been everything that I wanted – and more. And when the time comes,' she went on, trying to retain that calm that Felix had given her, 'I'm going to try my hardest to remember these moments.

'This is what I want to remember at the end.'

25. Dream Come True

It was visits like Gloria's, Angela Dunn thought, that summed up everything good about Felix. While some people focused on her staggering number of Facebook fans or the power of her 'brand', for Angela it was the near-miraculous, deep personal connections that Felix forged that made her special. Felix changed people's lives. She saved some people's lives. For Angela, that was what she was all about. And so it was a pleasure for her to help make people's dreams come true. In that way, Angela was not just a lady-in-waiting: she had a whiff of fairy godmother about her too.

On 1 August 2018, she waved her magic wand once more . . .

She was working in the booking office that day, serving customers their tickets and dispensing information. It was another sweltering day so Angela wore a short-sleeved white shirt with her navy-and-purple TPE uniform, occasionally flapping the purple scarf round her neck in an attempt to cool herself down.

She glanced up as a blonde-haired mother and daughter approached her. The little girl was about five, wearing turquoise shorts, a pale-pink T-shirt and a nervous, hopeful smile. As she and her mum came up to the counter, the girl lifted a finger to her face and pushed her big pink glasses up her nose. Angela smiled down at her. She couldn't help but notice that the little girl was wearing a skin-coloured patch stuck over her right eye, which had some kind of drawing on it. The railway worker asked the family how she could help.

'Is Felix about today?' the mother asked, somewhat wearily, as though she already knew that the answer would be no. She seemed unusually emotional to Angela, although it wasn't anything too evident – more like a deep seam of sadness that had clearly touched both mother and daughter.

'Bear with me a minute,' Angela said brightly, always happy to go the extra mile. 'I'll just go and see if she's free.'

Helen watched her walk away, feeling no hope that her little girl's wish to meet Felix would be fulfilled that day. She and Eva had been coming to the station for the past eighteen months now in the hope of meeting Felix and they were still no nearer to success. With only one station cat, Felix's time was spread too thinly to be able to accommodate meeting all her fans. All Helen and Eva had to show for their efforts was the framed postcard that still sat on Eva's bedroom windowsill, next to the photograph of her late grandfather. Every morning, she said, 'Good morning, Felix! Good morning, Grandad!' and she bid them goodnight at the end of each day. But she'd never got to say hello to the station cat in person.

Helen glanced down at her daughter standing beside her in the booking office, her heart lurching to see the eyepatch stuck firmly over her good eye. This was a new development that the doctors had prescribed only the day before, and both she and Eva were still adjusting to it.

It had been a very sobering appointment at the hospital. The doctors had told them that the fabric patches Eva had been wearing for a limited time each day were not working. They had hoped that her bad eye, forced to work hard by being the only eye Eva was using, would have started to correct itself from its turned-in position by now – that her vision would have improved. But everything they'd tried so far had failed to work. The doctors confided that they now suspected her bad eye was never going to be any different. Eva, they said, was likely to go blind in that eye.

Helen couldn't really process that bleak prognosis. She'd been focusing so much on helping Eva – encouraging her to draw so that she really used her bad eye; being diligent about following the specialists' instructions – that she couldn't compute that all their efforts seemed destined to fail.

The doctors said they wanted to try one last thing, a last-ditch attempt to try to save her vision: a permanent patch, changed daily, that she would have to wear all day over her good eye.

Eva, normally such a bubbly girl, was very upset about the idea. Her poor eyesight, to her, was normality, so she didn't take in the ramifications of the wider prognosis. But she did understand having to cover up her good eye all day long. She knew other people didn't wear patches and she became very quiet and down in the doctor's office. It broke Helen's heart to see her.

The doctors showed Eva the patches she could choose to wear. There were pre-printed designs for children, covered all over with colourful cars or birds or tractors.

'Or you could try these,' the specialist said, showing her a range of blank sticky patches that, to Eva, represented a pale-pink canvas.

For the little girl who loved to paint and draw instantly saw their potential. 'Oh, wow,' she said, brightening up. 'I could draw on these!' Then a lovely idea struck her. 'I could draw Felix!'

So, that morning, as Eva and Helen began the new regime, that was exactly what she did. Sat at her kitchen table, Eva plucked a blue biro from her pencil case and carefully sketched out the station cat on the medical patch. Eva's very favourite part of Felix was her long fluffy tail, so she paid particular attention to that.

When she was finished, Helen helped her seal off the sight in her good eye, gently pressing the patch to her child's soft skin. As she sat back and looked at Eva, rather than her daughter's beautiful blue eye looking back at her, she instead saw a jaunty sketch of Felix the cat. Helen asked Eva to go and gather her things, and when they were ready they headed into town.

Helen had planned the day trip as a treat for Eva, to try to cheer her up as she still seemed very low. She'd been such a good girl, wearing the patch even though she didn't want to, that Helen felt she deserved a treat. They'd gone for a milkshake and then – as they always had to do when they were in town – they'd swung by the station to see if they could see the cat.

Helen thought it likely they'd be disappointed again, and she didn't know quite how Eva might take the news this time. Eva was convinced that Felix would be fast asleep. As it turned out, they were both wrong.

Angela Dunn came bustling back into the booking office, having checked on Felix in the locker room and received the all-clear from the queen herself. She sensed that this visit was important to both Eva and Helen. That was evident as they both looked up as she came back through the door – and stared at her with such hope it almost seared her.

'We've been coming in for months now and not seen her,' Helen confided, already anticipating the crushing disappointment.

But there was none to be had.

'Today, Eva,' announced Angela Dunn, with a dramatic sensibility that could have given the station cat herself a run for her money, 'you're going to meet Felix!'

Helen couldn't help it; she started crying. Of all the days for Felix to be there!

'Go on to platform one,' said Angela, more gently. 'Come to the office door and I'll bring her out to meet you both.'

Quickly, Helen ushered Eva through the gateline and they made their way to the former customer-information point. Neither of them could believe this was really happening, especially after so long searching for an audience with Felix. Every day, Eva chattered away to her postcard of Felix; every day she looked on the Facebook page. The idea of meeting the real station cat, warm and fluffy, was absolutely overwhelming.

Eva and Helen stood nervously on the platform, excitedly anticipating the moment they had waited months to experience. As Angela Dunn opened the back-office door and came out, carrying Felix in her arms, Eva's little face lit up. Bad eye or not, she could see who had come to say hi to her and she was absolutely made up.

'Felix!' she cried, and the sheer, bouncing happiness in her voice made Angela and Helen laugh with joy. Eva was beaming with such unadulterated elation that it was hard to see where her big smile ended and the little girl began. Angela didn't think she'd ever seen a happier child in all her days.

Carefully, Angela laid Felix out on the mat and the station cat looked up to see who had come to visit her. She could sometimes be skittish around children, finding them unpredictable, but she was very chilled that day. She even allowed Eva to stroke her.

Eva was soon chattering away to her, crouched down next to Felix on the floor. She shared all the secrets of her heart with her, just as any best friend would do.

'So I have to wear these patches now,' she confided to the station cat. 'But, Felix, you know what? I don't mind it. I really don't. And I'll tell you why: because every morning I am going to draw *you* on them. And I don't mind wearing them if you are on my eye.'

Angela Dunn, hearing this, felt herself melt a little inside.

'You take my mind off all of these eye things,' Eva told Felix. 'You make me so very happy.' Then the little girl with big pink glasses gently petted the station cat, her fingers fumbling through her fluffy fur. She wanted to say more, but in the end she simply told her, 'Thank you, Felix.'

Helen, watching her, wanted very much to say the same. Seeing her child, who had been so sad yesterday, even just hours ago, suddenly beaming and bright, had made her year – if not her whole entire life.

She bent down and stroked the station cat too. 'You've made her smile again,' she whispered to Felix. 'Thank you so much, Felix. I don't think I can ever thank you enough.'

Felix accepted their adulation as her due. She was very, very good with them. It was as though all her experiences over the past few years – learning greater tolerance and growing up herself – had been building up to this one moment, where she could make a little girl's dream come true. She patiently waited as Helen took a snapshot of her daughter meeting her best friend; her child's smile was so bright, Helen did not even need a flash.

'You don't know how perfect this timing is,' Helen said to Angela as she put her phone away, and she filled her in about Eva's eye and the patches and Eva's desire to draw Felix on them – an idea that came about so that her friend would always be there with her, helping her through her challenges. Angela felt so happy that she had been able to help them meet.

'Eva, just think,' Helen added, 'now you've seen Felix in person, you can draw exactly what you've seen!'

As though she'd overheard her, Felix suddenly seemed determined to showcase to Eva the full gamut of her emotions, so that Eva would have all the source material she needed for the many days of patch-wearing ahead. By now, during their meeting, Felix had perfectly performed 'patient', she had resolutely rendered 'regal' and she had excelled at 'beautiful cat lounging on the floor'. Now, as Eva went to stroke Felix one final time, the dramatic diva added 'wild' to her repertoire and announced rather abruptly, with a tossing of her head, that the audience with Queen Felix was over!

But Eva didn't mind; she had her own cat at home, Sooty, who could be a very scratchy little cat, so Felix's feisty spirit didn't faze her in the slightest. In fact, it made her love her even more.

Though the young girl might not have grasped it yet, Eva would most likely need a bit of that fighting spirit in the weeks and months that lay ahead. Perhaps Felix would inspire her in more ways than one.

26. An Unexpected Arrival

Felix sat on the concourse with a justified sense of satisfaction. She was a cat at the top of her game: inspirational and professional in equal measure. And, yes, OK, she was still a little slower than she used to be; and, yes, OK, she might not catch as many mice these days, but, overall, she had never felt more proud of her position as the Huddersfield station cat.

She prowled about the station that summer with proprietorial prowess. Huddersfield had never looked better. As Felix picked her way carefully down the front steps to gaze out over St George's Square, her ears pricked up to hear the musical giggles of little girls who were darting in and out of the modern fountains. Each time a jet of cool water caught them, peals of laughter echoed around.

Everyone seemed in a good mood that summer, whether they were off to the races or to a music festival. Felix went to investigate one day as an odd rumble sounded loud across the concourse; it was a group of four lads shepherding a heavily laden skateboard through the gateline. They'd strapped an entire surfboard to it, laden with beer, as they set off for the Leeds Festival at the end of August. Other festival-goers were easily identified too, with flowers in their hair and red Wellington boots. They bought ice lollies from the station shop – raspberry ripples or white choc ices – and wolfed them down before the melting ice cream could stickily drip down their fingers. It perhaps all inspired Felix to reconnect with her fun side, to try to recapture her own lost youth.

One day in the booking office, she wound her way along the back shelf and was delighted to spot that bastion of entertainment that can keep children all over the world occupied for hours on end: a cardboard box. Felix had made games of cardboard boxes in the past, but this one was different. This one was no bigger than her two front paws.

Felix started sniffing around it. It had contained a delivery for her, so she perhaps felt some sense of ownership as she investigated it thoroughly. And perhaps she decided that she ought to assert squatter's rights too – because Felix decided to climb into the box.

Sara and Angela, who were both on shift that day, watched her with absolute disbelief. Felix was a large, full-size adult cat who was still (unfortunately) overweight – and she was trying to force her rather large frame into the tiniest cardboard box.

'She's not going to try to get in that . . .' Angela said incredulously. 'Felix, love, use your eyes!' Felix was about four times the size of the box!

But Felix was absolutely determined. She put her front paws in first; the box was essentially now full. Then she tried to get her back legs in, without success. She'd lift one up and try to squeeze it into the small gap left, but it would flop down again, simply unable to fit. Nonetheless, with the feisty determination that Eva had so admired in her, Felix tried again.

Felix ignored all evidence that she might be too big and kept on picking up her back legs. In the end, defying physics, she somehow managed to squeeze all four paws inside. But, of course there was now no room for the cat herself. Felix looked rather like a top-heavy tree, with all her roots squished into a teeny-tiny pot. When Angela Dunn took a picture of her, Felix, cheekily, stuck out her pink tongue childishly, as if to say 'Ha! I told you so! I've still got it, Angela!'

But if Felix thought she was still the baby of the station, she was about to get a rude awakening.

On 1 September 2018, Felix completed an outdoor patrol on platform one at about teatime. Hungry for her (low-calorie, senior-food) supper, she smoothly sashayed into the back office and made her way to the kitchen, where she knew she could stand and miaow until someone came to feed her.

As she walked along the corridor, she could hear her beloved Angie Hunte in the team leaders' room, talking to Jacqui. There was an excited murmur to their voices, but Felix thought nothing of it. The station cat, no doubt, may have thought they were just excited soon to have the honour of feeding her. She appeared at the doorway with her usual flair. 'Ta-da! Here I am, ladies!' she announced with a flick of her long fluffy tail.

But neither Angie nor Jacqui even noticed her. A second later, Felix saw why.

Her head flicked sharply to the right. And her back arched as it hadn't done in a very long time. 'What on *earth* is going on here?' said that swiftly rising spine, as Felix tried to process what she saw.

For tottering about in the corridor – *her* corridor – was a tiny black kitten. He was so young, he could barely walk, and was weaving a little as he tried out this new mobility malarkey.

Felix blinked as though her eyes were deceiving her. She didn't hiss. Instead, after only a second or two, she turned round and went outside again, as though she had mistakenly stumbled into a parallel universe and needed to go back and reconfigure where she came from.

Not five minutes later, she returned, the call of her grumbling belly perhaps bringing her back. She walked very slowly and very calmly down the corridor, as though returning to the scene of a nightmare that she knew full well, in the light of day, should hold no more fear. But, to Felix's dismay, the unsettling parallel universe into which she had stumbled seemed destined to stay.

The black kitten was still there. He was in the team leaders' room by then, wandering about and sniffing eagerly at all the new and (to him) unfamiliar scents. He was a gangly little thing with an athletic torso, extremely long legs and a tail in the shape of a tick. His ears were absolutely huge on him. As Angie Hunte sympathetically called, 'Felix . . .' they quivered atop his short-haired head to hear her lovely Yorkshire accent.

Felix glanced at her mum for only a moment before her shocked green eyes returned to focus on the little kitten tottering about in *her* team leaders' room. Yet in that short glance, Angie read the unmistakeable question: '*What have you done?!*'

'Felix . . .' Angie called again.

But once more her cat gave her only a passing glance, far more focused on the new arrival.

Felix refused to come into the room at Angie's call. Her back began to rise again as she watched the interloper walk about, as she processed the peculiar shock of another cat on her home turf. And – unusually for Felix – she let out one short hiss, a sound more of disgust than of warning, rather like a sigh. It wasn't nasty, but it was very guarded. Felix didn't know what was going on.

Angie went over to her. 'Felix,' she said, as the cat glared at the kitten. 'Please don't be like that. He's only little.'

Felix flashed her eyes only briefly upwards to connect with Angie's. She didn't want to listen. She didn't want to know. She had to keep her eyes on this imposter who had invaded the station . . .

But, as Angie now explained, he wasn't an imposter at all.

'This is your new apprentice,' Angie told her gently. 'You've got to teach him now, Felix. You've got to look after him. You've got to pass all your knowledge on.'

Seven years after joining the station, Felix had won another career advancement. The senior pest controller was now a line manager too.

27. Welcome to Huddersfield

Though her new responsibilities were news to Felix, they had been a long time in the planning for Angie Hunte. The idea that had been sparked by Jacqui's new kitten back in June had soon led to a forest fire of discussion between Angie and Jacqui over that long hot summer. In whispered conversations in the team leaders' office, they had batted the idea back and forth, as though they themselves were kittens and the idea was a catnip mouse on a string.

'Oh, wouldn't it be nice to have a little station kitten?' they would sigh wistfully. It was more of a pipe dream than anything else – a fantasy that flourished between them. 'We should so get another one,' they would enthuse. 'He could be a junior pest controller!'

Angie and Jacqui joked about it every time they handed over to each other on their shifts. It soon became a favourite topic of conversation and, as the weeks passed by, became so well-worn that the joky edges rubbed off.

That change in approach was prompted, too, by Felix's experiences over the summer. When she'd been so sick and lethargic a few months before, Angie had worried about her so much. As much as she hated to admit it, Felix wasn't getting any younger – and the demands on her time were only increasing as her fame continued to spread. Angie felt that if Felix wanted to sleep for ten hours straight during the day, she should be able to without interruptions. Yet she also knew how much meeting the Huddersfield station cat meant to people and how heartfelt many of the visitors were. She began to think that an apprentice might do Felix the world of good, taking some of the pressure from her.

Angie was conscious, too, of how much knowledge Felix had of the railway in her clever little head. Over the past seven years, she had learned so much: to master the initially scary sounds of the roaring trains, to cross the tracks, to hunt those pesky pests. Wouldn't it be something if she could pass all that knowledge on? And wouldn't it be better to start that process sooner rather than later, before Felix got too set in her ways to share her wisdom with a younger cat?

It definitely wasn't about retiring Felix – Angie was adamant about that. She was only seven, after all. It was more that, as the cat had now slowed down, Angie wanted to help her in that chosen course, so that Felix could enjoy her golden years – whenever she became ready for them. She had seen this kind of thing happen again and again on the railway network, when an old-timer, rich in wisdom, mentored a younger colleague until they were ready to step up. Perhaps Felix, already so much a part of railway history, was ready to shadow her human colleagues in this way too. The fact that a new kitten could hopefully be a friend to Felix as well, a bit of company for her, was an additional boon.

Angie and Jacqui both began to think more seriously about getting a new kitten at Huddersfield station. At times Jacqui's enthusiasm would get the better of her and she'd say to Angie, 'Let's just do it. What are the powers that be going to do – make us take it back?' But Angie, matriarch of the station that she was, was absolutely determined that – as with Felix's arrival seven years before – everything should be above board.

So it was that, one hot summer's day, around the time that Eva came to visit Felix, Angie paid a visit of her own to Andy Croughan, the station manager. She managed to waylay him in the back-office corridor one day and asked him outright if they could get a second cat. Before Felix had come to the station, there had been a long campaign to secure the authority to give a kitten a home, a crusade full of subterfuge and smart thinking, but this time Angie just came straight out with the suggestion. 'What are our chances?' she asked.

When Felix had first arrived, the then manager had been none too keen. But times had changed. And, in fact, Andy Croughan had played a key role in bringing Felix to the station in the first place – including green-lighting her 'hiring' as the pest controller when he was only acting up to the role of manager – so when Angie raised the idea, he had no qualms about doing it all again. He and others had separately been thinking something similar.

But, to tell the absolute truth, when he agreed with Angie that it would be a good idea to get another kitten, in his own head he was thinking that it would be a good idea about ten years down the line . . . He'd assumed it was a bit early to be devising succession plans, yet he enthusiastically agreed that, yes, a kitten was definitely something they would want to do. So he gave Angie the green light she was waiting for, and he did not clarify exactly *when* he had been envisioning hiring a new cat.

But that was all Angie needed. She tried not to show her absolute elation in front of the manager, but the moment she was alone in her office she started jiggling with excitement, almost dancing on the spot with glee.

Later that day, Jacqui arrived for their handover.

'Jacqui,' Angie said as soon as they were alone in the office, her tone deadly serious. 'I've got something to tell you.'

Jacqui's brow automatically creased in concern, but then Angie let her trademark beaming smile show. 'Andy said yes!' she declared.

Jacqui immediately knew what she was talking about and her jaw dropped. 'You are joking,' she said. She had never expected it to be so easy.

Angie shook her head emphatically: joking she was not. She whispered the next words, as their secret plan was highly confidential, but her delight was nonetheless loud and clear. 'We're gonna have a kitten! We're gonna have a kitten, Jacqui!'

The two team leaders began bouncing on the spot with joy, yet their celebration was entirely silent. The idea of Huddersfield getting a second cat was such huge news that they knew they had to keep it under wraps. Operation Kitten was now underway, and the two secret agents at the heart of the mission were determined to succeed.

They swung into action straight away. Jacqui had got her lovely little kitten Romeo from a local animal shelter, and Angie also liked the idea of giving a home to a rescued kitten, so Jacqui visited the same shelter as soon as she could.

They did have kittens available – but they told her they were not comfortable with the idea of letting one of them live at the station. Angie and Jacqui understood their position – they were only thinking of the welfare of the animal – but given how Felix had thrived in her domain, there wasn't much empirical evidence to justify their fears. So they tried another shelter – but they too said the same.

'We're going to have to go private,' Jacqui announced. And, in the last week of August 2018, that was exactly what she did. 'Kittens for sale near me,' she typed into a search engine – and a flood of results came back.

Angie and Jacqui, during their whispered top-secret conversations, had already identified some criteria by which they would choose the newest member of the Huddersfield team. Though it flew in the face of gender discrimination laws, he had to be male, for a start. This was because male cats were believed to be much more accepting of other moggies, which had been Jacqui's personal experience of integrating multiple cats in one home too. Felix, of course – despite the initial confusion on the issue – was female and they knew it wouldn't be a good idea to have two ladies, as they would be more likely to catfight, literally. Some research in Switzerland had also shown that opposite-sex pairings were more likely to accept one another.

They were also adamant that the junior pest controller should be a kitten and not an adult cat. This was partly for his own safety – so that he could learn from the very start of his life how to live safely on the railway and thus grow up used to all the hustle and bustle – but also because the same research study in Switzerland had shown that adult cats were more likely to accept the introduction of a younger individual than they were a cat of the same age or older. Angie and Jacqui wanted to do all they could to ease the transition as the two cat co-workers got to know one another, to make the shock of Felix sharing her home with another cat as easy as possible for her.

Angie really didn't know how Felix would take the addition of another feline member of the team. As evidenced by Felix's 'romantic' relationships with the feral black cat and the smarter white pussy, she was not averse to interacting with other moggies. Angie anticipated that, initially, she would not be too happy, because Felix ruled the roost at the station and no monarch likes to share power. But she hoped that the maternal instinct she had seen her display in the past would ultimately kick in. In her dreams, she loved the idea of Felix showing the new apprentice around the station, teaching him the role of railway cat. How wonderful would it be to see them sharing a shift together, both of them patrolling the platforms side by side? A new kitten might even be persuaded to wear a hi-vis jacket just like the one that Felix had so long ago jettisoned! She hoped they would be able to find a kitten who was easy-going and confident, friendly and fun, and who would become a character in his own right.

As Jacqui scanned the results that had come up onscreen, she noticed there was an advert for a young male kitten being sold from a home that was not five miles away.

She texted Angie the details. 'What do you think?' she asked.

Angie texted back just three words. 'Go for it.'

So, on Friday 31 August 2018, Jacqui found herself walking up the driveway of a semi-detached, newly built house and ringing the doorbell. It belonged to a Polish family with two blonde daughters, one aged eight and the other five. As Jacqui chatted with their parents about the eight-week-old kitten they had advertised for sale, the girls went and collected the kittens to show her.

There were two kittens: a light, tawny-coloured female and her brother, who was black as coal. They were both little cuties, but Jacqui didn't even hold the female. From the moment she saw the male kitten, Jacqui only had eyes for her boy. She knew he had to come home with her.

His eyes were open. They were a khaki-green colour and full of curiosity as this new lady reached out her hands, which were almost the same size as him, and pulled him closer for a cuddle. As she stroked his short-haired fur, so different to Felix's long-haired fluff, he remained calm and didn't wriggle once. Rather, he was friendly, peering at Jacqui intently, using his very pointy, very large ears to listen as she greeted him warmly and told him over and over just how gorgeous he was. He didn't look over her shoulder while she held him or get distracted by anything at all; it seemed he wanted to focus only on her.

Jacqui gave him a lovely long cuddle for twenty minutes or so, stroking him from his head right down to his pointy tail that tapered to its end. It was wiry and gristly, like a baton for a drum, and she had no doubt at all that she wanted him to join the Huddersfield band.

She FaceTimed Angie as she stood holding him. Angie

had the same immediate reaction: that he was 'the one' and that he needed to join them at the station at once.

'We'll take him,' Jacqui told the family.

Oh, the little girls did look disappointed to see him go! A crestfallen expression crossed their faces as they realised they now had to say goodbye to their little kitten. Even in his first eight weeks on the planet, he had clearly made an impression. The smallest child snuggled into her daddy for comfort with a very sad face indeed.

But the tiny black kitten was not destined to be a family cat. A greater fate awaited him. Jacqui unfolded the black-and-yellow fabric carry case that she had brought with her (just in case) and slipped him swiftly inside. Given his age, he had probably never been inside a carrier before, but he certainly didn't have an issue with it. As Jacqui was soon to learn, nothing fazed this little superhero.

She took him back to her house for an overnight stay before his first day on the job. Not wanting to overwhelm him, she kept him confined to her large bedroom, which had shiny wooden floors and lots of room to run about in, should he wish to do so. Immediately, however, he showed his preference for lounging about on the soft cherry-red blanket she had laid out over her bed.

Jacqui's four cats were terribly interested in the new lodger. They were off doing their own thing when he first arrived, so it was only as each of them returned from their adventures that they began to sniff their twitching velvet noses and notice him.

For Jacqui's youngest, Romeo, who was then about four and a half months old, the little black kitten became an immediate playmate. The two cats became best buddies in the blink of a khaki-green eye – playing together, sleeping together and even grooming one another. They were so sweet.

Pickle was Jacqui's one-year-old. He was a looker, with similar leg markings to Felix, but he was more uncertain. 'Ooh, what's going on?' his quizzical expression seemed to say – yet he was absolutely fine with the younger cat regardless. Ginger Deanie, the old man of the house at nine years old, almost rolled his eyes when he saw the new arrival. '*Another* one?! Really?'

The only sticking point was Smudgie, a three-year-old female calico cat who was disabled (she had four legs, but only three paws). She was also similar to Felix in a way, but only in temperament – for Smudgie was a diva. And, true to form, she hated the kitten on sight, hissing constantly at him whenever he came near.

But the kitten could not have cared less. Tumbling about on the floor with his new mate Romeo, he totally ignored the hissy fits being thrown by the female cat in whose home he was staying.

Jacqui was rather reassured to see it. She feared the little cat was going to have to learn how to live with a temperamental female . . . After all, if diva Smudgie wasn't a fan – then how on earth would diva Felix react?

Jacqui kept Angie constantly updated with pictures and videos of the new little kitten. Angie loved seeing the snapshots coming through on her phone, especially the ones of Jacqui's cats each welcoming their new friend: the kitten and the cat in question would stand nose to nose as they enjoyed getting to know one another. As her phone beeped again, Angie excitedly turned to attend to it – but, this time, it wasn't a picture Jacqui had sent. Instead, Jacqui had texted, 'We're going to need a name for him . . .'

Angie hadn't been thinking about names. Had Jacqui suggested one herself, she'd most likely have said yes to it straight away. Or if Jacqui had not mentioned it at that moment, perhaps they'd have done what they did for Felix and invited all on the railway network to suggest a name for the new cat. But the moment Angie read that message, the most perfect solution popped into her head.

'Jacqui,' typed Angie, 'can we call him Bolt?'

She was thinking, as she so often did, about her beloved former colleague, Billy Bolt. Though the little kitten was everything Billy wasn't – cute, friendly, black – the idea of having a Bolt back on-site at the station, of again being able to call that name, was too tempting to resist. It was her way of paying tribute to him. Angie didn't quite know what Billy might have made of it, but given his grudging love of cats, it was perhaps a fitting way to continue his legacy.

And there was another reason it was a fitting name – because the ladies' secret mission was about to blow its cover, and news of the apprentice was certainly going to be a bolt out of the blue for the rest of the world.

Their mission was completed the following afternoon. Angie got to the station first and waited for Jacqui and Bolt in the car park. It was a sunny September day and the weather more than matched her excited, happy mood. As she saw Jacqui's little yellow car coming round the corner she gave a thrilled squeal. She couldn't wait to meet her new baby. She was very restrained, though. As Jacqui parked up and lifted out the carry case, Angie didn't rush to peek through the mesh. She wanted to get the kitten safely into the office before anything else happened. So she deliberately didn't look for him, even though the case was rocking a little, focusing instead on getting through the gateline with their charge.

Neither Angie nor Jacqui was officially working that day, so their colleagues immediately clocked them as they walked on to the concourse. There was a young man called Joe on shift that afternoon – a very tall ginger-haired gentleman who was known for being thoughtful. As Angie and Jacqui tried to rush through, he noticed not only them but also the carry case that Jacqui was carefully shepherding through the gate, which clearly contained some kind of creature. He gave them all a puzzled look, which they had to ignore. The moment for announcing the mission was most definitely not now – not on a busy concourse, where the Saturday-afternoon shoppers were thronging through the gates. Heads down, Angie and Jacqui scurried straight through without speaking to anyone, turning left down platform one to make their way to the back office. Little did the passengers surrounding them know that a new chapter in Huddersfield station history was being written at that very moment.

Felix was not around as they entered the back-office corridor. Angie didn't know where she was, but she was glad that Bolt was going to have time to adjust to his new surroundings without his manager breathing down his neck. No new worker deserves that when they first clock on for duty.

The team leaders' office was empty, thank goodness. Angie, Jacqui and Bolt entered and shut the door behind them. Then Jacqui carefully laid the carry case on the desk.

Angie knew that in the next few moments she would be meeting a very special little boy. Her loving heart was already pounding in her chest. After all the planning and preparation and top-secret discussions, he was finally here. Her little apprentice. She couldn't believe it was real, that they had done it. She placed her hands over her mouth, not trusting herself to speak.

Jacqui gently opened the carrier. As she'd been looking after Bolt for the past twenty-four hours, she wanted this to be Angie's time, so she graciously stepped back and let her colleague come forward.

Oh my goodness, *what* a cutie! As she peered into the carry case, Angie saw his ears first. They looked bigger than him. 'Oh!' she cried in delight.

She cupped her hands and lifted him out. He was as good as gold, the moment just as precious. Close up, she saw that, actually, he wasn't all black, despite first impressions. He had a few little white tufts, barely noticeable, under his chin, and a slim flash of white on his belly too, just slightly left of centre. When he stretched, it looked like a horizon or a spaceship travelling at warp speed. With his long, gangly limbs, he was one of the most beautiful creatures she had ever seen (the other, of course, being Felix).

Though the love that Angie felt for him was identical,

he didn't remind her of the original station cat. They just looked too different. Felix as a kitten had been a big ball of fluff. Bolt, in contrast, was short-haired and all ears.

Already in love, Angie placed him tenderly on her chest. Bolt, clearly comfortable, nestled his head against her shoulder and sleepily closed his eyes. Just before he drifted off to sleep, he heard the loveliest Yorkshire voice whisper softly to him.

'You're home, Bolt,' said Angie. 'Welcome to Huddersfield.'

28. Meet the Apprentice

It was this cosy trio that Felix walked in on a short while later. Bolt, having woken from his nap, was beginning to explore his new home, confidently striding out into the corridor – even though his long legs couldn't quite keep up with his desire to explore, and he wobbled as he walked.

Angie and Jacqui had been so caught up in the moment that they weren't aware of Felix's arrival – so when she appeared in the corridor it was completely unexpected. They would probably have done the introduction in a different way, given time and opportunity, but it was suddenly taken out of their hands. Felix stayed only a few seconds, clearly not ready to engage with the new arrival, but when she returned about five minutes later and hissed at him, Angie spoke to her gently.

'This is your new apprentice,' she told Felix. 'You've got to teach him now, Felix. You've got to look after him. You've got to pass all your knowledge on.'

She remembered her vision of the two cats trotting companionably along the platforms and held her breath as she watched the senior pest controller. Was Felix going to rise to the occasion and assume her managerial duties straight away?

Felix was not. She gave a long, low hiss through her teeth, slow and steady, and then she turned on her white-capped heels and walked huffily away.

Angie let her go. She knew she would need time – possibly lots of time. Like any only child who gains a sibling, she needed to adjust to the new situation. Yet Angie was confident that she would eventually come round.

In the meantime, Bolt had to meet the rest of the team. The first person Angie let in on the secret arrival of their second cat was Angela Dunn. Angie sloped alone into the booking office and tapped her on her shoulder.

'Angela, have you got a minute?' she asked.

'Of course,' her colleague replied.

'Just step out of the office a moment with me,' Angie went on. 'Shut your window, please.'

Angela did as she was told, more intrigued than worried.

When she walked into the team leaders' room, she gasped. A little black kitten was sitting on Jacqui's lap.

'Meet Bolt,' announced Angie.

Angela made a beeline for him. Long ago, Angie had briefly mentioned the idea of a kitten to her, but nothing about Andy's green light. Nevertheless, Angela had heard enough to understand immediately that this was their newest member of staff. She was in full support of his arrival. Angela perhaps knew better than anyone what a busy old girl Felix was these days; anything that might give her a break could only be a good thing in her opinion.

She scooped up the kitten and held him against her chest like a baby. Bolt simply curled up against her and went to sleep again, and Angela felt her cheeks flush pink with happiness.

With Angela now in the know, it was time to let the cat fully out of the bag. The wonderful news soon spread around the station like wildfire – and everyone fell crazy in love with the new kitten. One by one, all the team members came into the room to meet him. There was a huge fuss made over him as each employee had a special moment with their new colleague. It was explained that, eventually, he would be helping Felix – and, by so doing, would give her a bit more peace and quiet.

Angie Hunte particularly remembered Joe from the gateline coming in on his break – the colleague who had been so suspicious when they'd first arrived at the station with the mysterious carry case. Now he knew the full story.

'Joe,' she said. 'Meet Bolt.'

Angie watched his reaction closely as she revealed the name, as she had been doing with all the members of the team. She wanted to see what they made of it. Would other people think it appropriate that she had named the kitten after their Billy? Would they be in favour – or against?

Joe had been at the station long enough to have known Billy before he passed and immediately made the connection. The moment he heard what the kitten had been called, he looked up to heaven and stared skywards for a beat, thinking of Billy Bolt. When he looked back at Angie, he was smiling. 'What a fab name,' he said. 'You could not have picked a better name.'

That was how everyone seemed to feel. Jacqui, who'd joined the station after Billy had died, soon found herself regaled with stories of the old-timer. The kitten prompted colleagues to recall their own favourite anecdotes so that Billy again loomed large in the minds of the Huddersfield team, even as his namesake gambolled on the carpet.

There was also a bit of ribbing about the new arrival, given what had happened with Felix. 'Are we *sure* it's a boy?' several members of the team joked.

But the confusion with Felix had arisen due to her long fluffy fur. With Bolt, they had no such difficulty. 'Yes!' cried Angie and Jacqui. 'He is *definitely* a he!'

Station manager Andy Croughan was duly informed of the kitten's arrival too, via text message. Well, the news came rather as a surprise to him, of course! But he could not have been more chuffed, especially about the name.

Someone else who needed to be informed was Mark Allan, Felix's Facebook manager. He was cycling over in Morecambe when he received a message from Angela Dunn: 'I've got something important to tell you.' Worried, he pulled off the road and called her, fearing the worst. Imagine his relief when he learned the team had recruited a new kitten! Angela sent him a snapshot and he could see at once that this was going to be one popular little pussycat.

The station staff were so excited about their new arrival that they wanted to tell the world. That very same day, they announced their staff update online, sharing a photograph of Bolt sitting on Angela Dunn's lap, as Jacqui and Angie peered over her shoulder like the proud parents they were. The message on Felix's Facebook page read: 'I would just like to let all my Facebook friends into a tiny secret . . . I've got an apprentice. Please meet Bolt, our new junior pest controller.'

And the world went wild.

As for the senior pest controller, she had not been seen since she'd met her new colleague. While everyone had been crowding round Bolt, cooing over his arrival, Felix had quietly slipped away. It was Angela Dunn, in the end, who went to look for her.

'Felix!' she called softly. She checked the ladies' locker room, in case Felix had retreated to her radiator bed. Yet her beloved sheepskin 'hammock' was hollow and bare. Angela double-checked the kitchen, in case Felix had returned to have her supper, but there was such a to-do about Bolt in the nearby team leaders' room that, hungry or not, the senior pest controller was avoiding it like the plague. Angela searched the in-trays in the old announcer's room, the shelves in the booking office and even the conductors' bags in her former lost-property home, but nowhere could she see the fluffy black-and-white cat.

Concerned, Angela pushed open the door that led to platform one. The cat wasn't sitting on the former customer-information point, but as Angela emerged she noticed Felix almost at once. And she wasn't on the benches or by the bike racks – she was somewhere she hadn't gone for a very long time. Felix was on platform four – sitting underneath Billy Bolt's memorial bench.

When Angela saw her, taking shelter under its weather-beaten wooden slats, she felt tears pricking at her eyes. Angie had told her that Felix had been shocked by Bolt's arrival, and Angela knew she must have been frightened, too. Where had the cat gone when she felt so scared and unsettled? She went to the place she had once been happiest, to the person who had always been hers. She was laid out under the bench on a bed of green moss that grew there, seeking comfort and support from a station ghost. She looked over at Angela when she called, but she did not move. She was with her Billy, and he would see her right.

29. A Confident Cat

For the first week or so after Bolt's arrival, Felix kept her distance. She came in to eat and sleep, but the rest of the time she avoided the new kitten as studiously as she could. He was spending most of his time in the team leaders' office, where he had a fleecy brown cat bed about ten times his size. Felix would consistently do a double take every time she saw him, as if she still didn't believe that this particular parallel universe could possibly be permanent. She would walk past the doorway, swivel her head to look in, and then continue on her way, almost shaking her head in disgust, her fluffy tail flicking haughtily.

Angie Hunte was very patient with her. Some of her colleagues were saying, 'Oh, what a shame, Felix doesn't like him,' but she knew that wasn't the case.

'You've got to remember that someone has come into her domain. Everything she's ever known here has always been *hers*. She's thinking, "We've got a little intruder here." Of course she's on edge. Of course she doesn't like the situation. But it's not that she doesn't like *him*. We've just got to give her time to adjust.'

In keeping with expert guidance on integrating cats, Angie declared that each cat would now have their own personal, defined space. Bolt would live in the team leaders' office, while Felix occupied the ladies' locker room. Bolt was not allowed to place one tiny paw over the threshold of Felix's room, so the senior pest controller always had a safe and undisturbed space to go to whenever she needed peace.

In fact, Felix had the run of most of the station, at least for the time being, as Bolt was so young that he was being kept strictly in the back offices. This was partly for his own protection, too – for ever since his new role had been announced, his instant fame had made him in demand. Within five days of his arrival, his first Facebook photo had garnered 7,000 reactions and hundreds of comments and shares. Meanwhile, cat fans rushed to the station in person to request an audience with Huddersfield's cat crown prince.

Well, Bolt was only nine weeks old. (No one knew exactly when his birthday was, but a best guess put it around 6 July.) He was far too young to be meeting strangers. He hadn't yet done a single day of training, either! The team needed to get him settled calmly and safely – and that meant no visitors. A polite message went up, requesting that people did not ask to see him, and the team were advised not to share any personal pictures that might whip up the social-media storm. TPE promised to post the odd 'official' portrait of him on Felix's Facebook page, but otherwise his introduction to the wider world had to be slow. The team decided that they would keep Bolt largely under wraps until the new year at the earliest, so that he could have a chance to settle into his new home.

Yet, truth be told, Bolt *already* seemed right at home. Angie had never seen such a confident cat. Nothing seemed to faze him; he took everything in his stride. He loved the office environment and took to transforming every administrative detail into a game. A laptop case became a ski slope he could slide down; a clipboard became a sledge. A rolled-up train ticket was an instant wonky football for him, while a stack of papers transformed into a tumbling trampoline.

One of his favourite tricks was to surprise Angie Hunte. She would walk in and put her small handbag down on the desk while she got herself settled. Imagine her surprise when she later went to fetch something from her purse – and who should be inside but a little black station kitten? Bolt's khaki-green eyes would merrily twinkle with mischievous amusement. Bolt soon took to climbing in regularly; he would scurry inside the bag and then snuggle down until not even his ears poked out of the top. He was the perfect fit – for the bag, for the station, for the team.

It wasn't long before his personality started to show itself even more assertively: Bolt, it turned out, was playful and cocky, energetic and fun. And he was full-on, too, the complete opposite of the laid-back cat that Felix had become. That promised another difference, Angie anticipated; while Felix had always sat out on the platform and *waited* for her audience to come to her, Angie suspected that Bolt would perhaps actively go *looking* for his – once the time was right.

The differences between the two cats became clearer as they continued to meet each other in the corridors behind the scenes at the station. In the early weeks, the size difference was striking. Bolt, who could curl up almost in the palm of your hand, looked like a David meeting Goliath as the huge, fluffy Felix loomed into view.

Bolt seemed aware of the situation. As Felix glared at him and hissed, he would shrink back into an inversion of his usual confident self. Yet Jacqui characterised his cowering as not motivated by fear, but by an awareness of the current state of play. Felix was far too big for him to take on at the moment, but give him time and he'd be up for it. He didn't seem scared at all – in fact, he became rather wily.

One afternoon that September, Felix came stalking down the corridor, her movements hallmarked by the grumpy, disconsolate moodiness that was her current default state. Recently Angie, Jacqui and the others had begun to open the office door for the kitten, so that he too could get a run in the corridor. Bolt lost no time in stretching out his long, gangly legs. He was gaining confidence and control by the day and no longer wobbled when he walked. But as he strolled into the corridor that September afternoon and laid eyes on Queen Felix, he very possibly felt a little wobble *inside* as her glowing green eyes focused firmly on him. Everything about her was dripping with disdain.

As Angie Hunte watched the pair of them, Bolt did the most remarkable thing. It was as if he was reading the situation and knew instinctively that he had to endear himself to his difficult boss.

Queen Felix tossed her head regally as she glared at him. Every move she made asserted her right to be there, her right to rule the station. For seven years, she had reigned supreme, uncontested. If this little upstart planned any kind of coup, her flashing eyes communicated, Queen Felix was determined to crush it. Her glare was a timely reminder that the kitten should not even dare to try usurping her authority.

Yet a coup was the furthest thing from little Bolt's mind – something to which his tiny black body soon bore witness. For in response to Felix's laser-like stare, Bolt – slowly but surely – lowered his head to his front paws before her.

The crown prince bowed to his reigning monarch.

As he did so, the queen drank in his submission, as though she was sipping from a golden goblet, and she clearly savoured every single sweet mouthful. Perhaps this kitten wasn't *quite* as stupid as she'd thought.

30. Sparks Fly

'What collar shall we get him, Angie?' asked Jacqui as she scrolled through some options online. Bolt was too young to wear a collar yet, but she was already planning for the future.

Angie clapped gleefully. 'A sparkly one!' she cried. 'Let him get his sequins on! Let's get him a diamanté one!' Angie loved a bit of sparkle; it matched her sparkling personality.

'No,' replied Jacqui, bluntly. Diamanté was definitely not *her* personal preference.

'Just a little bit of sparkle?' Angie pleaded, crestfallen.

'No,' said Jacqui again.

'*Please . . .?*'

In the end, it was Jacqui who caved. Bolt the junior pest controller was duly ordered a jet-black rhinestone collar and a very smart name tag. The latter was circular, its front yellow enamel with a silver lightning bolt, the back engraved with Bolt's personal details. When the time came for him to go outside, he would look hot to trot.

Orders were also soon placed for more official items – such as Bolt's official TPE name badge. This would say 'BOLT' in big letters in the middle and then underneath – cementing his position as a trainee learning on the job – 'APPRENTICE PEST CONTROLLER'.

Bolt was not the only TPE apprentice – although he

was certainly the most famous. TPE actually ran a very successful apprenticeship scheme whereby young people could join them for two years, in partnership with Manchester College, and gain experience and qualifications while working in role. TPE offered apprenticeships for those looking to get into careers including customer service, commercial, train planning and engineering – and, now, pest control too.

Bolt's name badge hadn't yet arrived, but Angie couldn't wait to see it when it did. In the meantime, she hoped that the two pest controllers could soon begin working together. But as Bolt grew more confident, his ceremonial bows began to lessen – and then the sparks really started to fly.

Bolt was, frankly, a bit of a lunatic. He was so full of energy that he always wanted to play – with anything and anyone. And that included Felix. To Bolt, she had the potential to be the perfect playmate. His previous interactions with other cats – such as with his fellow kitten Romeo at Jacqui's house – had been fun, fun, fun, and now that he had settled in at the station he wanted to let the good times roll. Literally roll. Ideally, all over the corridor in a wrestling match. He just had to get Queen Felix to join in . . .

Bolt started inviting Felix to play with him – sometimes after he had bowed to her, as though this was a formal precursor to his game, just as two sumo wrestlers will respectfully acknowledge each other with a bow before beginning a bout. Having made the introduction, Bolt would begin bouncing about playfully. Cheekily, he would dart up to Felix, as though he was a boxer, edging near to her on his tiny toes and then bottling it at the last minute and bouncing back.

Felix looked at him as though he had gone quite mad. Blithely, he dallied and danced around her. She wasn't angry at him any more; she was perplexed. There was something deeply thoughtful in her expression, as though she was trying to figure him out. 'What on earth are you doing, you foolish kitten?' her green eyes asked, but he did not answer. Eventually, she would turn away, almost rolling her eyes at his ridiculousness.

That was when Bolt would strike. He had no fear. He would literally launch himself at the adult cat, gymnastically hurling himself at her like a wild wrestler. He would sneak up on her and jump on her back. He would tumble over her. He would stretch out a paw and try to touch her, or force a face-to-face encounter by popping up suddenly between her two front paws, having tangled himself into a neat knot between her legs.

Felix would pull away from him sharply, horrified. If he leapt up in her face, she would stretch her neck back artfully, as though he was a paramour attempting an unwanted and unwarranted snog and she was recoiling from his garlic breath. She tolerated him for longer than anyone might have expected, usually with a disdainful shrug. There was very much a sense of her not lowering herself to his level; she would expend no more energy on him than she absolutely had to.

Eventually, Bolt's tireless entangling with her came to a head. She had to show him who was boss. So out popped her white-capped paw – and she boshed him on the head.

It was only a light tap – just hard enough to remind him of the pecking order. It made Bolt desist for a moment – but then he would bounce back. 'Young and dumb' Angie called him; for no matter how many times Felix physically told him 'No!' he did not learn. Again and again he'd get a light knock on the head – because every time he came back for more.

Whether she knew it or not, Felix was handling him just how her mother, Lexi, had once handled her as a kitten, when she and her four brothers and sisters had got out of hand with their unruly games. Just like Felix, Lexi had endured her kittens' mum-centred gymnastics for a while, but then she'd issued a backhander or grabbed them by the scruffs of their necks to keep them in line. Perhaps Angie Hunte's hope that Felix would discover her maternal side was not so far off the mark, after all.

As the weeks passed, Felix persevered with her boxing-based discipline, wearily hoping it would one day bear fruit. She reminded Angela Dunn of a world-weary big sister having to chastise an annoying little brother. Watching her apprentice, Felix would often toss her head, superiority shimmering through every hair on her body, as – for example – Bolt gaily skidded head-first into a door, too caught up in his game to notice he was running short on space.

But while Felix was taking some time to appreciate his talents, for the rest of the station the newcomer was a bona fide hit. Andy Croughan proudly posed for a photograph with his newest employee; it looked almost as though he and Bolt were formally shaking hands in the shot, as Andy welcomed him to the station.

For Jacqui, watching her fellow team members inter-act with the kitten was a revelation. Their instant affection for her little boy showed a softer side that she had not known they had. One brusque Yorkshire lad in yellow hi-vis almost visibly melted; Jacqui was amazed to hear him cooing at the cat as though he was talking to a baby.

Bolt also had 'inductions' with all the team leaders, including Geoff. Perhaps predictably, the kitten didn't get a very good report from the latter as the energetic kitten ran Geoff ragged. Back when Bolt was confined to base and the team leaders' door was constantly shut, Bolt had kept escaping to the corridor on Geoff's watch. Geoff could not figure out for the life of him how Bolt was doing it, and he kept having to chase after the kit-ten and bring him back – a game that Bolt enjoyed immensely! It turned out that the tiny kitten had been hiding behind a disused doorstop, and as soon as Geoff opened the door Bolt would dart out from his hiding place and make a run for it. He was so quick and so small, Geoff never spotted him. Bolt's Houdini skills were smashing even those of Felix!

Geoff had a few words for Felix now that the kitten had arrived. As their TPE colleagues bustled around Bolt, and Felix stared scornfully at all the fuss being made of him from afar, Geoff would call out to her. 'I told you, Felix: you should have stuck with me. Look at them all now. There's only me that cares about you, Felix.'

Of course, that wasn't true. Lots of people cared about Felix and were sensitive to her situation. Foremost among them was Jean Randall, whose return to work after more than a year off sick could not have come at a better time for the original station cat.

Felix was so very happy to see Jean back at work — especially now that Jean's arms were much improved. She was back at work on a phased return, as she was not yet strong enough to work full-time; she was fond of joking that she got Wednesdays off for good behaviour! In Felix's opinion, however, she was definitely strong enough for her most important duty: giving Felix some love. As the station cat stretched out on her radiator bed, Jean would indulge her with lots of long strokes and tummy-rubbing tickles. Whenever it was time for Jean to go, Felix would watch her all the way to the door, as though worried that if she took her eyes off her, she might vanish again. Jean made sure to spend more time with her as the autumn pressed on, wanting Felix to know that she hadn't been forgotten.

That could never happen. Angie Hunte still affection-ately called Felix her 'baby girl' and Angela Dunn was still her devoted lady-in-waiting. They still regularly pet-ted Felix and gave her cuddles and cared deeply for her. The thing about love is, it expands. It is infinite. The Angelas, and indeed all the team, still adored Felix — but now they also loved Bolt too.

And as the team spent more and more time with Bolt, he continued to endear himself to them. He draped him-self like a scarf round Angela's neck; he sat on Angie's shoulder like a parrot.

'Bolt, how am I going to get any work done?' Angie asked him, loving every minute.

Bolt's answer . . . was to get involved with the work! He

developed a penchant for 'helping' with paperwork, especially cashing up. Sad to say, however, the newest member of the team had a bit of a light-fingered touch. When the team leaders did their banking at night, they kept on finding, after they'd counted up all the cash, that they were consistently short – a five-pound note here, a twenty-pound note there. It turned out that the apprentice was nicking the notes and running off to play with them!

The cat burglar was fond, too, of stealing food. He was honest at least in the sense that he would never beg for his dinner if he had already been fed (unlike his boss, who still tried to persuade the person who'd fed her not ten minutes earlier that they were sorely mistaken). Then again, there was little need for Bolt to wheel out the amateur dramatics when he was such an effective pickpocket. The team kept discovering that things were going missing from the office. He nicked Jacqui's bag of nuts one night and, on another occasion, he stole Angie's chicken supper. They became smarter to stop him, not wanting Bolt to end up with the same weight problems that Felix was facing.

That possible eventuality was also easier to avert because Bolt's food was more tightly controlled than Felix's had ever been. It had been a free-for-all when Felix had first arrived at the station, with everyone mucking in – and therefore everyone giving her treats – but Bolt was very much Angie and Jacqui's boy and nobody fed him but the team leaders. Bolt, in fact, had a few tummy problems early on in his life that had required medicine, so Jacqui was strict in saying that he could not have any cat food other than the one that agreed with him, and no treats whatsoever.

Bolt didn't seem to miss them – and why would he, when he had such a marvellous playground to fool around in? His treats were the rolled-up balls of paper he could chase around the office for hours, or the multicoloured mouse with a bell on its tail that would tinkle as he hunted it down. (Bolt had lots of toys – some of them gifts from the senior pest controller's fans.) He had so much energy, he was always pouncing and rolling and leaping and striking at the innumerable objects he designated prey.

Observing him from a cool distance, Felix probably thought that his technique left a little to be desired. She could certainly have taught him a thing or two – had the cats been on speaking terms. For a start, he had no subtlety. Bolt would barrel down the corridor in a tangle of long limbs. He was easily distracted, switching prey the moment a new sound rang out or a sudden movement caught his eye. When he returned to his original target, he seemed to blame the object itself for his forgetfulness, as though it had conned him, and he would then attack it with renewed vigour. And while he undoubtedly had speed, he had no skill. Rather than quietly stalking his toys, he would run faster and faster towards them as he 'attacked' and the thundering of his paws would have had any real-life pest alert and away in an instant. Felix, slinking off after this poor display, almost rolling her eyes, tried to show him through her lazy grace how a grown-up *should* behave – but Bolt's attention had already been diverted.

Just as their size differences had been striking early on, as time passed and the kitten grew more active, the contrast in the two cats' movement was also noted. Felix was luxuriously slow-moving: a matronly lady dispassionately wandering through the world. Bolt, however, didn't seem to know who he was: a tiny tiger, a slithering snake, a jumping jack, a frog. He tried every trick in the book as he played, his battles with his toys often looking like ill-managed stage fights: a right hook here, a sliding tackle there. While Felix stared on from the sidelines, sensible and sedentary, Bolt skidded madly up and down the corridor, never once seeming to tire.

Of course, he did eventually. Then he would crash out – in his comfy brown bed, in the shower room, on a padded chair in the team leaders' room or even in the station manager's office. (Andy travelled regularly, as he also managed other stations on the network, so his office was often quiet and dark: the perfect place for a catnap.) When Bolt slept, he slept deeply, recharging his batteries. The team were amused to witness that he would stretch out in bed with the same confidence he always demonstrated while conscious, taking up more room than his little body seemed to warrant, dominating the space. As soon as he awoke, he'd be off again, getting into everything and generally proving himself to be rather a handful.

Oh, he was adorable – but it did make it hard for Angie Hunte to get her work done. One Sunday afternoon, about a month after Bolt had arrived at the station, she reached the end of her tether.

'Right, you, come on,' she said to the little kitten. She reached for her handbag – Bolt, for once, had not climbed into it when she wasn't looking – and pulled out her iPad, the diversionary tactic of all parents ever since the digital revolution. She quickly scrolled through her movies, pressed play on one and set up the iPad so that Bolt could see it.

On the screen, 101 black-and-white puppies ran across the room, barking and yapping wildly. 'Just watch this,' Angie told him patiently, 'and let me get on with my work.'

Of course she didn't. How could she – when Bolt's reaction to the film was so damn cute? It seemed he was a fan of *101 Dalmations*. His large ears pricked up straight away and he scooted forward till he was next to the screen. He even touched it with his paw!

It seemed Bolt was touching *everything* with his paws these days – and that included Felix. Perhaps he *had* been biding his time by cowering when he'd first met her. While he was still a fraction of her size, he'd got cocky enough to play a game with her, so now he started to test and tease her. If Felix was lying in the corridor of an afternoon, lazily fanning herself with her long fluffy tail, Bolt would become intent on getting at her. To him, that moving tail seemed the most glorious toy. Surely it was meant for him to hunt? He watched it as she flicked it uuuuuup and dooooown. Bolt was still learning how to use his tail and he stared at Felix's with absolute fascination. He thought she was teasing him. It wasn't long before the excited kitten started patting at her tail with a well-aimed paw, prodding and poking her whenever he was close.

Poor old Felix! The kitten had, ultimately, been introduced in the hope that, one day, he would help her have more peace and quiet. That would probably be the case, a few months or even a year down the road, but for now

Felix was swept up in all his games, whether she liked it or not.

At seven years old, Felix simply didn't have his energy. When he got too much for her, she would strike out at him with a gentle white-capped paw, but mostly she just gave him the filthiest looks. She raised her eyes to her colleagues too in world-weary appeal. 'Why won't he leave me alone?' At times she would hiss – but these days Bolt would bark right back. He had the sweetest little voice: a pathetically high, mousey squeak. Soon the squabbles of the station cats could be heard up and down the corridor.

Watching them, Angie and Jacqui knew it was time to change things up. Bolt had been at the station for a good month now. He'd settled in, he'd had his shots and he clearly had enough energy to power a rocket to the moon. Up until now, he'd been expending it on exploring the back offices – and on terrorising Felix. It was about time, they decided, that he channelled it in a more useful direction. On 7 October 2018, it was time for Bolt to start his training.

31. Training Time

'Right, mate,' said Jacqui to Bolt. 'Let's do it.'

Bolt blinked up at her with his khaki-green eyes. He was wearing a pale-blue harness studded with white polka dots that he'd happily let Jacqui slide over his ebony shoulders. He'd sniffed at it thoroughly as she strapped him in, his effervescent curiosity bubbling to the surface. This was a cat who feared nothing, a cat who would abseil using the lanyard of a photo ID if given half the chance. As Jacqui picked him up, he merrily enjoyed the journey, relaxed and calm.

But, as Bolt was about to discover, Jacqui was not carrying him along the corridor to save his long legs the effort. She was taking him outside. He had not been outside since his arrival at the station on 1 September.

She had specifically chosen a night shift for his first training session. Not only that but she'd picked a slot when no trains, not even freight services, were scheduled to run. The noise they made as they rushed through the station could be alarming; Jacqui wanted nothing to spook him this first time.

Earlier that evening, the big brass pole that secured the doors at the front of the station had been drawn across, so that no one but Jacqui, Dale, Felix and Bolt now roamed around inside it. Felix was already outside, off exploring somewhere. The crucial thing for Jacqui was that there were no other people about. Whatever happened next, Bolt could at least begin his training in privacy.

Taking a deep breath, Jacqui opened the door and stepped out with Bolt on to platform one. He shivered a little as the cool October air hit him, but he seemed happy enough in her hands, secure with his mother. However, the moment she put him down on the platform, the little kitten changed his mind.

'Shall we go for a walk, baby?' Jacqui asked him, making kissing noises to encourage him and tugging gently on the cat lead.

Well, Bolt did get to his feet – but only to walk straight back towards the door!

It must have been very scary for him. Even in the still of night, Huddersfield station is not silent. There is a constant thrum of electricity from the lights and the rails. Occasionally, from the ring road round the town, the roar of a boy racer on his motorbike will fire, while in the small hours the chronologically confused birds beyond platform eight often chirp and tweet. To Bolt's huge ears, used for weeks now only to listen to the muffled sounds inside, it *all* sounded strange. He padded a little on the cold concrete, disliking the sensation. Where was his warm lino that he so loved to slide along? He couldn't slide on this . . .

'Is it cold on your tootsies, mate?' Jacqui asked him, understanding. This was October in Yorkshire, after all; it was going to be cold. But it was *always* going to be cold – so Bolt had to get used to it. And the only way he could learn to do that was to experience it just as he was doing right now.

He didn't like it, though. That much was clear from the way he hugged the door which led back inside. Bless him, it must have been terrifying – what with all the strange sounds and smells, and that odd, discomfiting sensation of cool air all around him. Where were the radiators and oil heaters that he was used to in the office? Where was his air-conditioning? His wiry body trembled and he sat down, resisting Jacqui's attempts to persuade him to walk.

'Come on, baby,' she purred at him. 'Come on, baby boy.'

Bolt took a deep breath. Although he was still scared, he bravely got to his feet – and managed to take a few small steps, moving parallel to the door that he so longed to return through. He sniffed along its seam hopefully. Then, abruptly, as if inspired by the smells seeping through it, he promptly turned round, twisting himself up in his lead, and walked back the few short steps he had managed, clearly desperate to return inside. The brave, bolshie kitten who had so quickly made the back offices his own was scared stiff.

But Jacqui couldn't let him back inside just yet. He had been outside for less than a minute. She knew that outside was a world that Bolt could learn to love – he just had to give it a chance.

She watched him worriedly. If only someone could explain to the kitten that it would be OK, she thought. If only someone could show him that this world wasn't all bad – and that, actually, he might just like it. If only he could have a mentor, who could show him the way . . .

And then, so perfectly timed it was as if it was scripted,

a fluffy black-and-white cat padded slowly up the platform.

'See,' Jacqui said to Bolt. 'Felix is here now.'

She had come to see how her apprentice was getting along.

Felix the railway cat stalked along the platform with all the confidence that her seven years at the station had given her. She too had experienced training sessions like Bolt's when she had first arrived, as the team had helped her learn about the rhythms of the station and the world that would be her kingdom. Perhaps she remembered what it was like. At any rate, having spent the past few weeks avoiding Bolt as much as she could, she now *chose* to come closer to him, walking to within three feet of where the kitten still cowered against the door.

She seemed absolutely transfixed by him. And, oddly, she didn't seem cross to find that his domain was now expanding to include outside. She was curious. As Jacqui continued to encourage him – and Bolt continued to back against the door – Felix stood sentry, watching proceedings closely.

Then, a peculiar thing happened. Her steady, solid presence seemed to inspire Bolt. Suddenly, he gave himself a little shake and took a step towards her – and then another. He was not his usual, confident self, but from somewhere he found courage.

Bolt lowered his nose to the cold ground and sniffed. *That* was interesting . . . He did it again. As though finally intrigued – as though finally able to replace his fear with a small thirst for adventure – he tottered forward once more. He left the sanctuary of the door behind him and bravely ventured further afield, out on to the platform. Felix's emerald-green eyes watched him closely, missing absolutely nothing, as though she would be writing up a management report later and needed to note down every detail.

'Good boy!' Jacqui called, as the little kitten continued to prowl about.

Just then, the door opened and Dale stepped out.

'Look,' Jacqui told him in delight. 'Felix has come to escort him.'

And she had. As Bolt moved onwards, now heading towards Felix's favourite bike racks on platform one, she moved forward to see what he was up to. It could have been a territorial move, given Bolt had gravitated towards one of her favourite spots, but her observation did not have that quality. It was more that she was curious and wanted to keep a watchful eye on him. She mirrored Bolt as he stepped in and out of the racks, shadowing him, as though he was learning the steps for the first time and she was making sure he was getting them right. (He wasn't, necessarily; he hopped and skipped a little, pouncing on the shifting shadows, whereas Felix flowed through the metal bars like water, her body silken and smooth.)

As the two cats jointly picked their way through the forest of bike racks, it was inevitable that their paths would eventually cross. Indeed, so closely was Felix following Bolt's movements that, in the end, she wound up face to face with him. The two station cats stood together *nose to nose*, just like those pictures that Jacqui had sent to Angie way back when of her own cats welcoming Bolt.

And, after all this time, it *did* seem to be a welcome. Felix hadn't felt able to do that, nowhere near, when Bolt had first arrived, but out here on the platforms that October evening, during the camaraderie-rich night shift, it seemed she had finally turned a corner.

'Welcome to *our* world,' said her close attention. 'Watch how you go now, young 'un – you've got an awful lot to learn.'

Under the glow of the station lights, the two cats faced each other, noses sniffing hard. Their paws padded safely over the twisted shapes of the metal padlocks and chains that were usually used to secure bikes to the racks. It was here that they paused, a meeting of minds and moggies. And in those chains resting between them was a beautiful symbolism, as though this first training session was finally linking the two cats together – two pest controllers bonding through their shared experience.

Over the past seven years, Felix had loved her team and performed her duties to the best of her ability, but she had never had another cat with whom she could share all the adventures. Now, however, she stood nose to nose with Bolt under the arch of her favourite silver rack.

It curved above them like the future.

32. A Powerful Pair

Throughout that autumn, Bolt's training continued. Felix did not join him on every session, perhaps taking a paws-off management approach. Without Felix to follow, it took time for Bolt to gain in confidence during his early platform patrols. He seemed, at first, not especially to like the feel of the cold platform beneath his paws and always needed to be encouraged to step away from the grey-carpeted lobby. Yet Jacqui and Angie continued to take him out during the quiet night shifts, encouraging him to walk on his lead along the platform, and, slowly, he gained more skill. By mid-November he had got the feel of it and could be seen strolling along the platform in a sprightly manner, flicking his tail and happily exploring with his nose right down on the ground. At times he was so eager that Angie found herself having to tug back on the lead gently as Bolt raced ahead. As the weeks passed, his world widened. Moving on from platform one, Angie escorted him halfway along platform two. Then came the day when Bolt went on to the concourse for the first time.

He instantly seemed much happier there than he'd ever been on the platforms, perhaps taking some comfort from the more familiarly sheltered space. He especially loved the gateline, which boded well for his future shifts as part of the revenue protection team. Although if Bolt continued to express his affection for the gateline as he did on this first visit – by stopping dead on the grey rubber floor of the gates themselves – it would cause all manner of chaos in the middle of rush hour!

He seemed quite happy there. Not for him the luscious red carpets that Felix frequented; he was quite content with this rubbery grey one. He sat himself down and even took the time to have a bit of a wash, his little pink tongue flicking out firmly over his short black fur. He was too young to have gone to the groomers yet, but when the time came it was likely that he too would take the road trip to visit Louise on her exciting-smelling farm. After Felix's first feisty visit there, the senior pest controller had come to enjoy her time with Louise. The groomer joked that she was like a different cat! Even as soon as her second trip, the tiger had been tamed. Now, she closed her eyes when Louise combed through her fluffy fur, as though Louise was merely softly stroking her; her grumbling, if it came, was just a gentle underscore, emitting only if Louise had to tackle a particularly tough tangle. At the end of each session, they even had a cuddle.

Back on the concourse, Bolt's big ears pricked up and he wandered out from the gateline on to the cream marbled floor of the concourse. His tail, with which he was becoming increasingly familiar, wagged firmly from left to right, as though he was enjoying himself. With his more streamlined fur, Bolt's tail was more like a whip than Felix's. His energy slickly channelled through it now, as he showed Angie that this station cat business really wasn't half bad.

Now that Bolt was beginning to master his patrols, it

was time for stage two of his training: exposing him to the sounds of the services. It was Angie Hunte who took responsibility for this latest aspect of Bolt's apprentice-ship. She chose to ease him in gently. At four o'clock in the morning, a single night train was due to pull in at platform four. Angie escorted Bolt out on to platform one a short while beforehand. She hoped that as the train wasn't directly on their platform, and would be slowly drawing to a halt as it arrived, it would be the best way to introduce Bolt to the noises that would soon become second nature. This way, he'd get to hear them without the train being right on top of them.

Bolt was happily trotting along the platform when the first rumble of the railway tracks started to sound. He stopped dead and raised his head, his large ears twitching. As the noise got louder and louder, Bolt began to tremble. Angie pulled him back on his lead and he ran quickly to her. Immediately, she scooped him up and pressed him against her chest, trying to reassure him with the more familiar sound of her heartbeat. They walked up and down the platform together as the noise increased in intensity.

'It's all right, sweetheart,' Angie said soothingly. 'You're not going to be hurt. I've got you, Bolt. I've got you.'

But as the train arrived in full force with a monstrous roar of its engine, despite those comforting words, Bolt blinked up at her. He was shocked, startled and scared.

'This is a train, Bolt,' Angie explained to the appren-tice over the roar. 'These are noises you'll soon be hearing every day. You just need to get used to them.'

With a screeching squeal, the train applied its brakes, and this new sound made Bolt shiver all over again.

Afterwards, the terrifying train finally fell silent. The few passengers boarding the night service embarked, little knowing that across the way an apprentice railway cat was undergoing training.

Angie took Bolt back inside before the train departed. He was still shaking, and she didn't want to do too much too soon. There was time enough for all that. This little cadet could take as long as he needed to adjust to his railway life.

Despite his understandable early apprehension, Angie believed that Bolt was, overall, much more confident than Felix had been at the same age. If the door to outside was opened for him during a night shift now, he would choose to exit and sit outside on the grey carpet of the lobby, even if the door closed behind him. He was not yet confident enough to go any further than that lobby alone, but he was content to sit on the mat, nose twitching, as he slowly acclimatised himself to the big wide world. Angie didn't recall Felix doing that at *such* a young age. All in all, Angie had plenty of hopes that, with time and training, Bolt would soon be as sure-footed and safe on the railway as the original station cat.

As for that cat, as the autumn of 2018 unfolded, Felix was hitting yet more heights. Her special-edition Monopoly board came out to a big commercial fanfare and on 28 November Felix was highly commended at the Railstaff Awards in the Charitable category. She was continuing to raise thousands of pounds for charity with her 2019 calendar, a second book and even her own range of Christmas cards. Yet perhaps the biggest accomplishment came in the way that Felix had finally reached a truce with the tiny kitten who had invaded her world – but who was also, very slowly, coming to enrich it.

A few times now, Angela Dunn had come into the back-office corridor to find them both lying down in it within a mere foot of one another. Jacqui, observing this same closeness, also noticed that, as Felix lay there, she would expose her white tummy with its black splodge just below her heart. This belly exposure, in Jacqui's mind, proved that Felix now felt completely comfortable with the kitten. Despite her initial reticence and reluctance, she'd got used to him.

And even though Bolt, being Bolt, was unable to resist the temptation every now and then to pounce on the sleeping senior pest controller, Felix tolerated it pretty well. The two cats were so much better together than they had been. Truth be told, even when Felix's patience expired, and she gave Bolt a friendly swipe of her white-capped paw, it was by definition a play fight – and one that the original station cat, despite herself, rather seemed to enjoy. (Even if that was because it gave her a chance to remind him exactly who was boss.)

For Sara from the booking office, her heart was truly warmed by the way Felix had finally taken Bolt under her wing. The arrival of Bolt had been so lovely for Sara to witness. With her baby daughter due at the end of December, seeing the kitten had made Sara think more and more about her own impending motherhood. She and Dan had moved in together by now, into their own home, and they couldn't wait until Maisie arrived and the three of them became a family. It was rather nice for Sara to know that when she went on maternity leave, as she was very soon to do, this new station family would also be growing. And while she and Maisie were bonding, Felix and Bolt would be doing the same.

As Sara would soon find out, however, children grow up fast. As autumn drew to its close, Angie and Jacqui began to do double takes as they arrived at work after a few days off. What had happened to their little kitten? Who was this big boy, with his long, sleek form and an almost military bearing as he sat up straight on a TPE clipboard? Bolt grew bigger and more mature with every passing day. Jacqui could see it in his face; he looked more like a cat than a kitten, although he hadn't *quite* grown into his ears. His original polka-dot harness became too small for him as he healthily put on weight, so Jacqui upgraded him to a new neon-orange one. It glowed brightly against his black fur when he went out patrolling at night.

He also took up a new hobby – one inspired by watching Felix. She may have been rather hands-off on the platform training, apart from that very first session, but Bolt was picking up tips from his boss nonetheless. One evening, Felix sauntered into the team leaders' room (which was still where Bolt slept, but Felix was allowed to come and go as she pleased). As had been her practice for many a year, she wandered over to the wastepaper bin, where a plastic bin bag hung down over the sides. She started licking it, and then shredding it, which was one of Felix's favourite naughty habits. She liked to get right underneath the transparent bin liner, as though it was a veil across her face or as if she was behind a shower curtain, and then she'd scratch at it, rub her chin on it and bite into it savagely. She absolutely loved doing it; it was almost a Felix fetish.

After having demolished the liner, Felix walked away — and the little black kitten took that as his cue to have a go too. Bolt went to the liner, and up went his paws to scratch, scratch, scratch at the plastic. From his exuberant reaction, it seemed that this was a guilty pleasure — or a pastime, if you will — that the two pest controllers were set to share.

For the team, it was a promising sign. Would Bolt continue to copy Felix? Angie Hunte was intrigued about their future training sessions together, when both Bolt and Felix would be out on patrol; Bolt, eventually, without his harness. Felix being there would mean that Bolt's experience would be totally different from that of the original station cat. Felix had had to learn it all for herself — she had made the role her own — but Bolt had a boss. Would he copy her, as he had done with the shredding of the bin bag? Would she show him the ropes, albeit unknowingly, as a little black shadow followed in her footsteps? Or, with their truce holding firm, might they even become fellow explorers, with Felix generously revealing all her favourite hidey-holes? Not to mention what might happen when it came to pest control . . .

All that was for the future. There was still a way to go, but Angie Hunte was hopeful. She had a feeling that as Bolt grew older and began his own adventures on the railway, Felix's motherly instincts would kick in. And when that happened, she knew, nobody would be able to get near Bolt because Felix would always be there for him.

In truth, nobody knew what the future held for the two railway cats in the long term. Jacqui hoped that, as Felix took more of a backseat, as her increasingly lengthy daytime naps seemed to suggest she would, Bolt would come more front and centre, out on the platforms meeting people and being Mr Friendly. Jacqui didn't think they could have got a cat with a better temperament for the role that awaited him. Already he had stolen people's hearts, simply through the odd photograph posted on Felix's Facebook page. When he began to meet people in person, Jacqui knew he would charm them all the more.

As for Felix, while there was lots of life in the older cat yet, some of the team had started to ponder how her golden years might play out. If Felix got to the stage where she'd had enough, she deserved a peaceful retirement. Having seen first-hand how much she had enjoyed being a house cat, Jean Randall wondered if perhaps that might be Felix's destiny when she reached double figures, so that she could get away from it all and enjoy her lazy years with a sofa to lounge upon. But Jean also knew that the station was Felix's home; she'd had happy holidays in houses, but her world had always been the railway.

So, for now at least, the railway was where Felix would stay, continuing to touch hearts all around the world. Reflecting on the past few years, it was incredible how many people she had helped – and not just people like Gloria and Eva, who had relied on her special support at difficult personal times. Countless people had experienced audiences with the station cat that weren't necessarily big news, but which they would never forget. Such as the eighty-year-old lady whose daughter surprised her on her birthday with a visit to see Felix. The grey-haired lady sat in her wheelchair and Felix snuggled into her lap for a long old cuddle. The woman had seemed lost in the moment as her fingers softly stroked that world-famous fluffy fur.

'Thank you so much for this,' she said eventually, eyes shining with pleasure. 'This is the best birthday present I could ever have had.'

As the year drew to its close, Angie Hunte received the best present *she* could ever have. It happened one wintry afternoon as she was wandering around the back offices hunting for Bolt. Now given the run of the place – except for the ladies' locker room, which remained Felix's domain (plus, he was a boy, so was naturally forbidden entry) – he had developed a habit of disappearing, playing his own game of hide-and-seek that the team didn't even know they were involved in, until they looked around and realised he had vanished.

'Bolt!' called Angie now, as she checked his usual favourite places. But he wasn't behind the disused doorstop or snoozing in the shower room. 'Oh, Bolt!'

Angie's searches took her down the long corridor, until she came to a stop outside Andy Croughan's office. The door was ajar but the lights were off, as Andy was out and about. In his absence, a little cat had taken his chance to curl up on the comfy padded chairs facing the manager's desk, hoping for a sneaky catnap. Angie smiled to see him there, watching him through the glass of the window in the door.

Wanting to see more clearly, Angie pushed the door open wider. 'Oh my goodness,' she whispered, as the room came fully into view.

The sight that greeted her eyes was one that she had long dreamed of. For there wasn't just one cat curled up on the chairs. Facing Bolt, on her own chair, was Felix the railway cat. The two pest controllers were only inches away from each other, their faces turned towards their mirror moggy. Felix's tail was floating happily up and down, as though they were both stretched out on loungers in the sunshine and she was keeping them cool, fanning both herself and him with a massive fluffy palm leaf.

For once, Bolt wasn't watching that slowly flicking tail. He had eyes only for Felix's emerald-green ones. There was a calm, companionable spirit about the scene, as the two cats shared the close space they had carved out for one another. They gazed almost lovingly into each other's eyes. There was no pouncing or prodding, just a lovely silence as they sat side by side and cheerfully chilled out.

Huddersfield's pest controllers – both senior and junior – had, in the end, passed their probation with flying colours. Watching them, Angie could no longer imagine one without the other.

Carefully, so as not to disturb the animals, she slipped her phone out of her pocket and snapped a quick picture. It was funny, she thought, that they had chosen to present their partnership in the station manager's office. It was a coup of sorts, as the cats joined forces at last.

So, as she texted Andy Croughan the picture, she added a single, short caption. When he opened it up and saw the picture of the cats in his office – the two pussies all the more powerful for being a pair – he read Angie's words with an amused smile.

She had written, 'And you think you're the boss!'

But everyone already knew that was really Bolt and Felix.

Acknowledgements

As with Felix's first book, *Full Steam Ahead, Felix* would have been impossible to write without the fantastic contribution of the team at Huddersfield station. I'd like to thank Angela Dunn in particular, who gave up hours of her own time to escort me and Felix to the vet's and the groomer's, and who patiently answered every question under the sun about the ins and outs of Felix's life. Similarly, Angie Hunte, storyteller extraordinaire, made an invaluable contribution to this book. Ladies, as ever, it's been a pleasure.

Thanks are also due to all those at the station and at TPE who gave interviews, including Sara, Dan, Amanda, Chrissie, David, Jacqui, Reece, Liz, Geoff, Paul Ralphson, Carl Haigh, Geraldine Smith, Chris Bamford, Jack Kempf, Andrew McClements, Jean Randall, Dale Woodward, Dave Chin and not forgetting the station manager, Andy Croughan. Thanks too to Felix's vet and to her groomer, Louise, for allowing me to accompany Felix to her appointments.

As Felix's fame has spread, so too has that circle of people who have stories to share about her. Thank you to Adam Taylor, Peter, David, Alwen and the Friends of Huddersfield Station; to Jez Walsh and Bob Morse from the Men's Shed; to Amanda and Sarah from the Huddersfield branch of Waterstones; and to Christine Spicer, Rob Martin, Susie Beever, Julie Swift, John Cran, Pam Burgess,

Gloria Lewis and Helen and Eva Lear for all generously granting me interviews about their interactions with Felix.

For Felix's second book, many members of the public got in touch to share their own Felix stories, including but not limited to: Stuart Gelder, Elaine Carter, Daniel Goodrich, Gisela Kratochwil, Kathryn Haynes, Jennifer Adele Berry, Emma Gee, Rosemary Dayborn, Janis Phillips, Margaret Willerton, Alyson Meadowcroft, Tracey Kennedy, Barbara Blackie, Stephen Hack, Janet Goldsmith, Jan Norman, Judy Stock and John Rooney. It was a true pleasure hearing from you all about the difference Felix has made to your lives and the adventures she has had with you. Thank you to everyone who submitted stories, even though we did not have room to include or acknowledge them all.

Special thanks are due to Mark Allan for the help he kindly gave in sharing Facebook posts, photos and statistics, and for his own interview too.

I'd also like to thank Fi Crosby, Amy McWalters, Zennor Compton, Jennie Roman and all the team at Penguin for supporting Felix's second book of adventures.

For background research, I am indebted to the Manchester and Salford RSPCA, the *Huddersfield Examiner*, the British Transport Police, Vets4Pets.com, Cats.org.uk, Consciouscat.net, VCAHospitals.com, PetBucket.com, CureToday.com, Cuteness.com, the BBC News website and Felix's Facebook page. I also consulted *Huddersfield Through Time* by Paul Chrystal (Amberley Publishing, 2016) and *Huddersfield: Home Town Memories* by Melvyn Briggs and John Watson (The Derby Books Publishing Company Ltd, 2011).

Finally, I couldn't have written this book without the enduring support and encouragement of my husband, Duncan Moore, to whom I remain forever grateful.

Last but by no means least, thank you to Felix, the Huddersfield station cat, and to little Bolt, her brand-new apprentice – whose arrival towards the end of the writing of this book made for quite the literary challenge, but a rather lovely one at that!

He just wanted a decent book to read ...

Not too much to ask, is it? It was in 1935 when Allen Lane, Managing Director of Bodley Head Publishers, stood on a platform at Exeter railway station looking for something good to read on his journey back to London. His choice was limited to popular magazines and poor-quality paperbacks – the same choice faced every day by the vast majority of readers, few of whom could afford hardbacks. Lane's disappointment and subsequent anger at the range of books generally available led him to found a company – and change the world.

'We believed in the existence in this country of a vast reading public for intelligent books at a low price, and staked everything on it'
Sir Allen Lane, 1902–1970, founder of Penguin Books

The quality paperback had arrived – and not just in bookshops. Lane was adamant that his Penguins should appear in chain stores and tobacconists, and should cost no more than a packet of cigarettes.

Reading habits (and cigarette prices) have changed since 1935, but Penguin still believes in publishing the best books for everybody to enjoy. We still believe that good design costs no more than bad design, and we still believe that quality books published passionately and responsibly make the world a better place.

So wherever you see the little bird – whether it's on a piece of prize-winning literary fiction or a celebrity autobiography, political tour de force or historical masterpiece, a serial-killer thriller, reference book, world classic or a piece of pure escapism – you can bet that it represents the very best that the genre has to offer.

Whatever you like to read – trust Penguin.